W9-ARL-845

presents

The Pleasure
of Wine

presents

The Pleasure of Wine

The Learning Annex
with Ian Blackburn and
Allison Levine

WILEY

Wiley Publishing, Inc.

Copyright © 2004 by The Learning Annex
Published by Wiley Publishing, Inc., New York, NY

No part of this publication may be reproduced, stored in a retrieval system or transmitted in any form or by any means, electronic, mechanical, photocopying, recording, scanning or otherwise, except as permitted under Sections 107 or 108 of the 1976 United States Copyright Act, without either the prior written permission of the Publisher, or authorization through payment of the appropriate per-copy fee to the Copyright Clearance Center, 222 Rosewood Drive, Danvers, MA 01923, (978) 750-8400, fax (978) 646-8600. Requests to the Publisher for permission should be addressed to the Legal Department, Wiley Publishing, Inc., 10475 Crosspoint Blvd., Indianapolis, IN 46256, (317) 572-3447, fax (317) 572-4447, E-Mail: permcoordinator@wiley.com.

Trademarks: Wiley and the Wiley Publishing logo are trademarks or registered trademarks of Wiley Publishing, Inc., in the United States and other countries, and may not be used without written permission. All other trademarks are the property of their respective owners. Wiley Publishing, Inc., is not associated with any product or vendor mentioned in this book.

Limit of Liability/Disclaimer of Warranty: While the publisher and author have used their best efforts in preparing this book, they make no representations or warranties with respect to the accuracy or completeness of the contents of this book and specifically disclaim any implied warranties of merchantability or fitness for a particular purpose. No warranty may be created or extended by sales representatives or written sales materials. The advice and strategies contained herein may not be suitable for your situation. You should consult with a professional where appropriate. Neither the publisher nor author shall be liable for any loss of profit or any other commercial damages, including but not limited to special, incidental, consequential, or other damages.

For general information on our other products and services or to obtain technical support please contact our Customer Care Department within the U.S. at 800-762-2974, outside the U.S. at 317-572-3993 or fax 317-572-4002.

Wiley also publishes its books in a variety of electronic formats. Some content that appears in print may not be available in electronic books.

ISBN: 0-7645-4146-3

Cataloging-in-Publication Data available from the Library of Congress.

Manufactured in the United States of America

10 9 8 7 6 5 4 3 2 1

ABOUT IAN BLACKBURN

Growing up in a kitchen, and working at fine restaurants around notable Los Angeles chefs (like Jerry Comfort, Joachim Splichal, Jean-François Meteigner, Thomas Keller, and Ian's Mom Lori) showed Ian Blackburn what real passion for food and wine was all about. A graduate of California Polytechnic University with a Bachelors degree in Hotel and Restaurant Management, Ian is a perpetual student of wine—as all wine lovers are.

Frustrated by the elitist image of wine, and the lack of knowledge available to consumers, Ian founded Los Angeles' first wine education and event website, LearnAboutWine™ in 1995 (www.LearnAboutWine.com). Ian has conducted classes and seminars for over 10,000 students and maintains an active schedule of courses and events near his home in Southern California.

Ian holds local board positions with the American Institute of Food and Wine and Collins School of Hospitality Management Alumni of Cal Poly Pomona. He serves as Consulting Wine Educator for Cordon Bleu California School of Culinary Arts, the Learning Annex, and other major Southern California Institutions.

ABOUT ALLISON LEVINE

Allison Levine, a Certified Meeting Planner (CMP), is the Director of Marketing, Public Relations and Events for LearnAboutWine™ (www. LearnAboutWine.com). Allison developed her passion for food and wine while traveling, living and working abroad in Italy, France, Spain, and Australia. With a Master's Degree in International Communications and a career in Marketing Communications, Allison brought her vast experience to LearnAboutWine where she is responsible for building the brand and marketing strategy, as well as all public relations and event planning. Allison also holds a position on the local board of the American Institute of Wine and Food.

welcome to the learning annex

The Learning Annex is North America's largest provider of adult education, dedicated to enhancing the quality of people's lives through informative and inspirational seminars. We offer short, inexpensive courses that provide nuts-and-bolts information on a variety of topics, taught by respected leaders and luminaries in each field. The Learning Annex operates schools in numerous major cities across the United States and Canada, and through its monthly publication, it has emerged as a cultural barometer of what is of interest to the American people.

To learn more about the Learning Annex, visit us at www.learning annex.com

acknowledgments

The authors wish to thank The Writers' Lifeline, Inc.: Ken Atchity for his classic and mythic wine lore, Andréa McKeown, and especially Julie Mooney; also researchers John Robert Marlow, Jaqueline Radley, and Rosemary Serlucca. Also thanks to Roxanne Cerda, Cindy Kitchel, and Suzanne Snyder of John Wiley & Sons, and special thanks to Rigley Goldsborough; Jim White of www.ilovenapa.com; Brian Thomas, Secretary of the American Wine Society, Rochester NY Chapter; Gladys Horiuchi, Communication Manager for the Wine Institute; David Kegaries, Certified Wine Educator, Society of Wine Educators; and Margot and Rich Cirino, owners of NewYorkWineCork.com, for their time and expertise "beyond the call of duty."

table of contents

introduction

Welcome to *The Pleasure of Wine*. The purpose of this seminar is to help you maximize your enjoyment of wine, whether you're a first-time taster or a longtime wine lover. If you're new to wine, we welcome you to begin with Lesson 1, our introduction to wine, and work your way through the lessons sequentially. If you've had some experience with wine already, feel free to skip from lesson to lesson.

When you've completed this seminar, you'll be equipped with a basic understanding of wine: its production, its varieties and places of origin, proper storage and serving, and, most important, a working knowledge of the qualities and characteristics of a good wine. Wine is complicated; unfortunately, so are most wine books. Many wine books tell you everything you need to know except what you really need to know to appreciate wine: how wines smell and taste, what makes a good wine, how to find a good wine, and what to do with it once you've found it. We provide the information that's really useful in appreciating wine.

By increasing your knowledge of wine, you'll add new layers and greater sophistication to your experience: you'll not only get more pleasure out of drinking it, but you'll also be in a terrific position to enhance your guests' and companions' wine-drinking experiences. You'll enjoy a comfort level in choosing wines (whether in restaurants, for your home wine cellar, or as gifts), and you'll be armed with the necessary knowledge, skills, and equipment to make the most of the wines you serve to your guests.

Wine novices often sense a certain level of sophistication in wine. They fear that if they enter the world of serious wine, their ignorance will show. Many wines sold today are bland and noncommittal, because a substantial number of wine drinkers want inexpensive wines that go with everything. While there's nothing wrong with bland wines, you're missing a whole realm of exquisite pleasure if they are the only wines you ever try. Wines that are not made for mass appeal are a challenge, an acquired taste. You have to put some effort into appreciating them, and, like anything you invest yourself in, the experience is far more rewarding. If you're reading this book, you are probably attracted to this idea already and are seeking a more stimulating experience.

Be prepared for your taste in wine to evolve. The wine characteristics you like as a novice wine taster will almost certainly differ from the ones you'll prefer with a decade of wine experience under your belt.

No matter what level of experience you bring to this seminar, bear in mind that *nobody* knows all there is to know about wine. One of the things we learned in writing this book is just how much about wine even the experts don't agree on! Not one of us has tasted every *existing* wine, let alone the thousands of yet-untasted wines destined to come along each new year. The world of wine is vast, rich, and ever-changing. To be a wine lover is to be an adventurer: what exquisite pleasure it is to anticipate the experience that awaits in the next glass!

HOW TO USE THIS BOOK

This book is designed to be a "seminar in print," to allow readers to feel as much as possible as though they're attending one of our evening courses. We've divided the book into topics, titled "Lessons," each of which can be read within 5 to 10 minutes. We have designed this book to be completed in a single sit-down reading. Two sidebars will help give you additional, fun, and useful information:

- **A Note from the Instructor:** Insider tips from your instructors, Ian Blackburn and Allison Levine.

- **Student Experiences:** Words from seminar students—just like you—who are willing to share their experience with discovering the pleasure of wine.

lesson 1

what is wine?

What Makes Wine *Wine* • How Wine Is Made • Wine Types

Wine is an amazing journey through time, history, religion, climate, love, war, and fashion. It lends itself beautifully to any level of involvement, from sipping a simple glass of rosé on the back porch to traveling to the great wine centers of Europe and coming home laden with exotic wines. Wine is one of the most rewarding hobbies you can explore: There's always more to learn, more to experience—more to taste!

Unfortunately, the subject of wine intimidates many people. Some folks have grown shy of wine because they believe that there are "right" and "wrong" ways to enjoy it.

In addition to presenting you with good, basic wine information, our goal in this book is to encourage you to trust your judgment. If you find that you like red wine with fish instead of white, or you discover that you prefer your white wines at room temperature instead of chilled, or you decide to serve a dessert wine with your meal, we want you to feel free to do so. Remember, wine is fun!

WHAT MAKES WINE SPECIAL

Strictly speaking, wine is the fermented juice of any kind of fruit (like peaches, pears, or mulberries), grain (for instance, rice in sake), or plant (such as dandelion). In this book, we're going to talk only about wine made from grapes. But wine is much more than its physical components. It's an adventure, a challenge to the senses, a chance to immerse yourself in the pleasure of the moment. It's an ever-changing kaleidoscope of culture and craftsmanship, art and agriculture. In places where wine has been made for centuries, it is interwoven in the history, the land, and the lifestyles of the people who produce it.

Wine is also the world's most romanticized beverage. Poets and sages across time have praised its effects on the human spirit. Wine is almost synonymous with celebration and good living; its mere presence on the dinner table brings a festive atmosphere to a meal. Ask yourself, have you ever had a bad day drinking Champagne?

The Sensations of Drinking Wine

Drinking wine is an adventure that affects the senses in a complex variety of ways. Before the wine even touches your lips, you drink it in with your eyes. You appreciate the color and clarity of a newly poured glass of wine, whether it's a golden Sauternes, a ruby red Cabernet Sauvignon, or a Riesling so sheer and pale that it's almost transparent. Wine catches the light, reflects and glorifies the world around it, and tells the stories of its journey to your glass.

Wine impacts your sense of smell most profoundly. Any given wine contains hundreds of aromatic compounds that manifest themselves in unique combinations, allowing the "nose" of the wine to inspire its own language. No one could set a limit on the number of terms one could use to describe wine, but we can recognize a common structure in most wines and then identify subtle nuances, depending on hundreds of variables.

Wine's flavor is not just its sensation on the tongue, but the combined effect on the taste buds and nasal receptors. Have you ever tried to drink wine when you had a head cold? It's disappointing. Without its subtle aromas, wine's flavors become one-dimensional. Your mouth tastes only the basics: the wine's relative sweetness, acidity (sourness), and bitterness. But your nose processes its complex aromas.

Your sense of touch is part of the wine-drinking experience, too. Wine lovers talk of the "mouthfeel" of a wine: whether it's light, medium, or heavy in body and whether it's oily, sheer (like silk in your mouth), angular, chewy, or any number of other descriptors. You can enjoy wine with four of your five senses (or all five if you can appreciate the sounds of people drinking great wine or the satisfying *pock* of a cork slipping from a bottle—a sensory delight that heightens the celebratory mood).

A tremendous part of the pleasure of a good wine lies in immersing yourself in the sensual experience of exploring the multiple layers of the wine's personality. Wine challenges you to develop your senses.

Wine's Personality

No two wines are exactly alike. Tasting a special wine from a special place, made by gifted hands, is a completely different experience than gulping down a cola, because today's cola tastes pretty much like last year's, and cola from a plant in Des Moines is indistinguishable in flavor from cola made in Poughkeepsie (assuming that it's of the same brand)—at least that's what we've been told.

Even the same grape variety grown in the same place can look, smell, and taste different from year to year. In fact, a wine can taste different from day to day. That's the mystery, beauty, and romance of enjoying wine: appreciating these subtle differences!

We should make a distinction here between fine wines and those that are made for casual drinking. Everyday jug wines can be a pleasure to drink, and if you just want a wine that tastes good, you can find one without having to spend your inheritance on it. But when wine enthusiasts gather to taste and obsess over wine, they're talking about fine wine crafted with pride to present an extraordinary experience.

You're probably reading this book for the latter reason, because part of the beauty of jug wines is that they don't require much information to enjoy. Your enjoyment of fine wine, on the other hand, grows with knowledge and experience.

The Stories Wine Tells

The story of a wine's creation can be as intriguing as the wine itself. Sometimes the joy of drinking a particular wine lies in understanding its special significance. Was the wine made under difficult conditions? Is the wine so rare that only the very fortunate have even seen the label? Has the wine taken on mythical dimensions, like that of a rare coin? In addition to its sensuous pleasures, wine can offer the intellectual satisfaction of uncovering a great story.

Wine's Place in History and Culture

Wine has touched many of history's greatest events. Jesus Christ presented it as his blood at the Last Supper, a moment reenacted throughout the Christian world to this day. Napoleon celebrated his conquest with it; Thomas Jefferson wrote the Declaration of Independence while sipping it. The Spanish Armada sailed with wine; the czars of Russia included it in their celebrations. Baseball teams celebrate with it; couples toast with it. Wine bonds us and allows us to crystallize special moments. Wine allows us to reflect and release. It adds soul to a new memory.

For centuries, wine has been the drink of choice of poets, novelists, playwrights, artists, and composers. Great minds across the ages have sung its praises:

"[Wine] awakens and refreshes the lurking passions of the mind, as varnish does the colours which are sunk in a picture, and brings them out in all their natural glowings." —Alexander Pope

"The soft extractive note of an aged cork being withdrawn has the true sound of a man opening his heart." —William Samuel Benwell

"Wine is Sunlight, held together by water." —Galileo

"He will tether his donkey to a vine,
his colt to the choicest branch;
he will wash his garments in wine,
his robes in the blood of grapes." —Genesis 49:11

"What is the definition of a good wine? It should start and end with a smile." —William Sokolin

"Nobody ever wrote a great novel drinking water." —Ernest Hemingway

"I cook with wine; sometimes I even add it to the food."
—W. C. Fields

> **a note from the instructor**
>
> ## APHRODISIA RECIPE
>
> From *Aphrodisia* by Ken Atchity
>
> 1 bottle Pinot Noir, decanted in a crystal bowl
> 2 tablespoons honey
> 2 leaves of fresh mint
> 2 red or pink roses
> 1 teaspoon rose water
> Pour the Pinot Noir into a saucepan over the lowest possible flame. Add the honey, the mint (crushed gently in your fingers), and then the rose water. Leave it on the flame until the honey is liquefied, and then add a touch of cinnamon and a touch of cardamom. Turn off the flame, and sprinkle the petals of the two roses across the surface of the liquid. Pour into goblets, preferably gold ones (though crystal will do as a substitute), and serve.

Wine's Magical Effects on Food

Wine is made to go with food; it can turn a meal into a memorable event. And food returns the compliment: A fine wine only gets better when served with compatible food. Individually, great wine and great food can be wonderful soloists, but the combination of good food and wine is like a well-practiced symphony. Wine enhances your enjoyment of the food, and food enhances your enjoyment of the wine.

The combination of wine and food offers so many dazzling possibilities that it can't help but come down to a matter of personal taste. In this book, we're not going to focus much on the food and wine pairings that wine experts recommend; we'd rather encourage you to find out which combinations *you* like best. Lesson 14 contains much more information about the marriage of food and wine.

Wine's Sociability

Wine loves company. It eases the collective mood and encourages conversation. Its festive presence lends an air of elegance to social events. Wine inspires and invites lively commentary and brings a built-in topic of conversation to any gathering.

abcdefghijklmnopq rstuvwxyzabcdefgh ijklmnopqrstuvwxy a note from
the instructor

FOOD AND WINE PAIRINGS: BENDING THE RULES

Although volumes have been written about the "appropriate" wine for each food—such as red wines with meat and white wines with poultry and fish—today's wine-drinking wisdom simply states that you should pair wine and food according to what you like. After all, if you adhered strictly to convention, you'd never know the joy of Oregon Pinot Noir with grilled salmon.

When you pair food and wine, it works well to focus on the dominant ingredient, whether it's the sauce, the protein (meat, bean, or grain), or the spice. Using this rule, you'll be able to keep a much more open mind about food and wine pairing—and you'll take more chances (see Lesson 14 for more on this subject). While you're at it, open *two* bottles, a red and a white, and compare! Two wines with dinner are better than one anyway.

Remember, though, that your enjoyment of a wine is a separate experience from your *appreciation* of it. You can judge the qualities of a fine wine empirically, whether you happen to like the wine or not. On the other hand, you can find a great deal of joy in a simple bottle of wine that would never be judged world class.

THE MAKING OF WINE

At its highest level, making wine has become an art form. With continued evolution and increased understanding, winemaking and farming techniques allow producers to make better wines every year. But viticulturalists and winemakers find themselves under enormous pressure, because expectations run very high. Consumers have been conditioned to expect that a winemaker will create not only a wine product, but also an epic experience, a personality—a masterpiece.

Some of the greatest wines in the world, though, are products of great restraint. The winemaker did little to "make" the wine, allowing the wine to "make itself" and to fully reflect the vineyard from which it came. Tom Mackay of Sonoma Valley's St. Francis Winery says, "We can only make great wine when we have great grapes."

WINE IN TIMES PAST

Wine of centuries past was not the complex, "refined" drink that fine wine is today. Without slow fermentation in modern stainless-steel vats, controlled temperatures, and other technological developments, wine would still be as coarse as it probably was in ancient times.

Even without the modern fine-tuning, wine played a noteworthy role in the ancient world. Archaeological evidence reveals a thriving Greek wine industry at around 3000 BC, and recent findings suggest wine cultivation in Russia as early as 6000 BC. In the Roman Empire, wine was a symbol of the emperor's power. The ancient Greeks believed that wine was a gift from the god Dionysus. Since they knew nothing of the modern corks that keeps today's wine from oxidizing, Greek winemakers often topped off their wine vessels with olive oil to seal the wine from contact with the air. Winemakers coated wine vessels with pine pitch to retard evaporation, lending ancient wines a distinct piney aroma and flavor that are still prized in some Greek wines today.

Viticulture

Fine *viticulture,* or the growing of grapes for winemaking, seeks quality more than quantity. Fine winemakers would rather create a small amount of high-character wine that's a tribute to Mother Nature than produce a large yield.

Viticulturalists (grape-growers) and winemakers often work as a team. The vineyard manager may strive to create a crop that enables the winemaker to showcase the best qualities of the grape variety. Or the winemaker might try to craft a wine with certain attributes ideal to its type, like the tantalizing tannin of a fine Cabernet or the ripe stone-fruit flavors found in Chardonnay. In each case, they're working with a sensitive, often unpredictable set of variables at every step of the process, and the finished product is a testimony to their skill, their judgment, and a little good luck.

The elements of earth, wind, light, and water are Mother Nature's chess set. Her temperament is highly unpredictable: In certain years, she sets us up with high expectations only to punish us for our greed and disobedience, and in other years, we prepare for the worst and are pleasantly surprised. This combination of variables in a grapevine's environment is characterized and idealized by the French term *terroir* (tare-wah). Terroir can have subtle and not-so-subtle effects on a wine's character. A good wine can hint of certain things in its environment: For example, many German wines grown in slatey soils pick up mineral and wet stone flavors; rich red wines from the southern regions of Spain and Italy often carry the perfumes of the flowers that grow abundantly about the countryside. And in Napa Valley, a sweet dust can add a nice accent to the deep cherry flavors of the region's Cabernets and Merlots.

Most wine grapes prefer long, warm growing periods with plenty of sunshine during the day and cool temperatures at night. These conditions produce great complexity of fruit and acid. Grapes growing in otherwise marginal climates can thrive if they receive enough reflected sunlight from light soils and bodies of water. But too much direct, hot sunlight can cause the grapes to ripen prematurely. A light wind is generally a plus; it keeps the grapes from overheating (and maturing too quickly) and evaporates excess moisture. Too much wind, however, can shear off blossoms, leaves, and immature fruit and even stunt the vine's growth.

The optimal climatic conditions for a crop of wine grapes are a cold winter followed by a warm, wet spring and then a long, breezy, sunny summer—not too warm—with cool nights and moderate rain tapering

---

abcdefghijklmnopq rstuvwxyzabcdefgh ijklmnopqrstuvwxy

a note from
the instructor

A VICTIM OR A BENEFICIARY OF WEATHER'S WHIMS?

Wine grapes are highly sensitive to changes in their environment. A powerful wind at the wrong moment can rip tender buds from the vine and spoil the crop; too much rain in the fall can cause the grapes to rot; and too much heat can ripen the grapes too quickly, robbing them of the complexity that comes only with long, slow ripening.

Some wines, though, actually require growing conditions that you normally wouldn't think of as ideal. Sauternes, for example, can be made only from grapes that have been infected with the *botrytis cinerea* fungus. In a year with a dry autumn, the "noble rot," as winemakers call it, may not develop at all, and producers of fine Sauternes will release no botrytized wine for that year. (See Lesson 5 for more about this fungus.)

to a warm, dry autumn. A cold winter allows the vines to go dormant and rest, which strengthens them. A warm, wet spring can produce a large set of blossoms, and a long, sunny summer and fall give the grapes plenty of time to develop lots of character. But it's never predictable, and getting it just right is almost always a challenge. Most grape growers will tell you, "I'd rather be lucky than good anytime."

How Wine Grapes Grow

Grapes grow only from flowers that have "set" on the vine—a process easily halted by untimely storms, wind, or excessive early heat. If the flowers set successfully, they produce clusters of tiny green berries that gradually swell and change color, becoming grapes. All grapes start out green. White grape varieties turn various shades of gold or pink; red varieties flush red, purple, or black.

Once the berries begin to grow, vineyard workers often cut away some of the burgeoning bunches (called crop thinning) so that the vine can focus all its energy on the bunches that remain. Over time, the vine begins to crop thin naturally; in the sense that older vines make fewer grapes with more concentrated flavors. It's a common theory that old vines make better wines.

Vines also produce higher-quality grapes if they endure a certain amount of beneficial stress. Broad temperature fluctuations, brief periods of drought, and depleted soil can force a vine to work hard, dig its roots deeper, and focus its efforts on producing a small crop of intense berries.

Harvesting Wine Grapes

Grape-growers aim to harvest their grapes when the sugars and tannins have ripened and the decreasing acids and increasing sugars have reached a balance. In general, the longer grapes stay on the vine (viticulturalists refer to the total number of days on the vine as "hang time"), the more concentrated their sugars become, and the less acid remains. A good wine-grower knows that sweetness and acidity complement each other; a sweet wine needs the sharp edge that acidity brings to avoid becoming syrupy, and an acidic wine needs some sweetness to temper its sour disposition.

student experience

"My husband and I have visited several wineries and I always learn something at each one. One winery pointed out a field they had planted with lavender and other herbs with the plan of eventually plowing those crops under and growing grapes. Apparently the grapes pick up the subtle scents and flavors of the crops that linger in the soil, which impacts the flavor of the wine. I was fascinated to discover just how much the soil in which grapes are grown has an impact on their taste."
—Stephanie, business consultant

Tannin, the bitter compound found primarily in a grape's skin (which, in red wines, is critical for providing flavor, structure, texture, and longevity) also needs to ripen. A well-trained viticulturalist recognizes the taste of ripe tannin. Tannins are the all-important stagehands behind a fine red wine's performance; they give it the backstage support it needs to show off its complexities and nuances. The best reds for aging contain high levels of balanced, ripe tannin.

Harvest time can be dicey. In areas where autumn weather is unstable, the days leading up to harvest keep a viticulturalist on pins and needles. Do you harvest early and sacrifice some of the prized complexity of a more mature grape, or do you risk losing the crop to the season's first sleet storm? As the harvest approaches, more than at any other time in the growing season, a wine-grower's judgment can make the difference between an unforgettable vintage and a lackluster one.

When the harvest is called, skilled vineyard workers cut the grape bunches from the vines. Wineries that rely on mechanical harvesters generally produce wines of lesser taste and quality. Typically, the greater the care that is taken with well-grown grapes, the greater the quality of the finished product.

Traditionally, grapes were grown, crushed, fermented, aged, and bottled right on the winemaker's estate. The world's top wineries still make wine this way. But in large commercial enterprises, the grapes are often shipped to a distant location and sold to a number of winemakers for off-estate production. Today, most grapes *don't* come from the winery that makes them into wine. In fact, great vineyards are pretty rare and have tremendous demand placed on them, so the prices paid for the crops from these select vineyards are very high.

Vinification

Whereas viticulture is the art of growing grapes, *vinification* is the craft of turning them into wine. During vinification, the harvested grapes come into contact with yeast, and wine results. Along the way, the grapes go through a variety of techniques designed to optimize the expression of their fruit. The winemaker's philosophy and experience guide the grapes through destemming, crushing, one of a number of possible fermentation techniques, fining (or filtering), aging, and bottling. At every step, the winemaker chooses among variables: which, when, why, and for how long.

1. **Destemming:** Leaves, stems, and other nongrape matter are removed before the winemaking process begins. A destemming machine usually performs this work, and, like a mechanical harvester, it sometimes leaves a few stems and nongrape bits in the product. Destemming is especially important in fine white wines, which suffer more than heavier reds from remaining stems. Stems left in the wine can produce "green" or "stemmy" flavors.

2. **Crushing:** In a bygone era, crushing wine grapes required footwork: Winemakers literally stomped on the grapes with their bare feet. Today, in all but a few wineries, machines do the crushing—which makes curious wine lovers wonder what subtle flavors and aromas modern wine might be missing since the traditional foot method was abandoned.

3. **Adding yeast:** Yeast is the magical microscopic beast that transforms the juice of crushed grapes into the beverage of kings. Some traditional wineries still make do with yeast that forms naturally on the grapes in their environment; in a bygone era, winemakers used only this yeast. Today, most wineries add hybrid or synthetic yeast to kick-start the fermentation process.

   During fermentation, the yeast dines on the grapes' natural sugar, producing both alcohol and carbon dioxide as it feeds. The work of the yeast affects the sweetness of the wine and its alcohol content: If it's allowed to finish the job, the wine will be termed "dry" and will have reached its highest potential level of alcohol; if fermentation is halted early, the wine will be sweeter and lower in alcohol.

4. Fermentation: Ripe grape juice plus yeast equals heat, carbon dioxide, and wine (see the following illustration). Nearly all commercially produced wine ferments inside sterile, stainless-steel, temperature-controlled vats. Modern fermentation vats allow for greater quality control and a finer, subtler product. These vats also are equipped with machinery for "punching down" (not unlike what bakers do to rising bread dough: winemakers break up the cap of floating skins and pulp that rises to the surface and submerge it back into the liquid) and stirring the fermenting juice. In the past, wineries often accomplished this step by having a naked vintner plunge into the vat and wallow around. Today, many great wines of the world hand-stir the *must* (the vintner's term for the fermenting grape juice) as often as every few hours.

Ripe Grape Juice + Yeast = Heat, CO_2, and Wine

Ripe grape juice plus yeast equals heat, carbon dioxide, and wine.

- **Racking:** As fermentation proceeds, solids begin to settle out of the must. Winemakers periodically drain the liquid from these solids in a process called *racking*. Additional racking from tank to tank or barrel to barrel allows for further cleaning and removal of solids from the wine.

- **Fining:** When used in the context of winemaking, this term means "to make fine, or pure." It most likely came from the Latin *finire* ("to finish"). After fermentation, winemakers often filter and clarify the wine to remove excess particles and potentially harmful bacteria. They use a protein, often egg whites or a protein gel, to fine the particles away. Modern winemakers often use a step of cold stabilization and filtration in addition to, or instead of, fining the wine.

- **Barrel aging:** Many wines spend time aging in oak barrels. As wines barrel-age, they slowly evaporate and oxidize. Aging in oak barrels softens a wine and imparts some of the wood's flavor and tannin to it.

abcdefghijklmnopq
rstuvwxyzabcdefgh
ijklmnopqrstuvwxy

**a note from
the instructor**

TO OAK OR NOT TO OAK?

Many wine enthusiasts object to the heavy use of oak in a wine because it masks (or buries) the wine's subtle flavors. They argue that wine is supposed to taste like a fruit, not a tree. But plenty of wine lovers look forward to a wine's oaky qualities. If you're going for the complex nuances of a fine wine, overoaking is a problem; otherwise, it's a matter of individual taste.

How long a wine ages in its barrel depends on its type. Many styles of Chardonnay (including some Chablis) spend several months in oak. Cabernet Sauvignon and Merlot are typically aged for up to two years in barrels; Vintage Ports spend up to three years there. Beaujolais Nouveau, on the other hand, spends little or no time in barrels.

Winemakers often experiment: They may choose barrels made of American, French, or Slovakian oak, and they may have their barrels "toasted" or charred (lightly to heavily). All of these variables affect the flavor of the wine.

- **Bottle aging:** When wine is transferred from the barrel to the bottle, its days of gentle oxidation are over. As wine ages in the bottle, it develops nuances, or "bottle bouquet." The best condition for bottle aging is dark, cool, humid quietude.

When Is the Wine Ready to Drink?

Tradition and experience aside, determining when a wine is ready is a matter of taste—or, more accurately, of tast*ing*. As a rule, wines harvested in great years take longer to develop than wines from good or so-so years. A wine from an average vintage may reach its full potential in 4 or 5 years; a truly outstanding wine may take 10 to 20 years or more to reach its zenith. A fine old red that's beginning to go brown has probably already passed its prime, but the drinking experience still may be phenomenal.

TYPES OF WINE

Wines are categorized by the following characteristics:

- Color (red, white, or rosé)
- Intended use (aperitif, table, or dessert)
- Relative sweetness or dryness

In addition, sparkling wines are typically categorized separately from "still" (nonsparkling) wines. Most of these categories overlap: Sparkling and still wines can be red, white, or rosé; dry and sweet wines can be served with a meal or as desserts and aperitifs; and fortified wines, as described in this section, come in red, white, dry, and sweet styles.

White, Red, and Rosé

The color of a grape's skin generally determines the color of the wine it produces. Pale green or yellowish grapes make white wine. Grapes with dark or reddish skin generally make red wine. The time during which the fermenting juice is left in contact with the pulverized red skins largely determines the darkness of the wine, but exceptions do exist. When making a *blanc de noir* sparkling wine, for instance, a winemaker crushes red grapes (Pinot Noir or Pinot Meunier) but separates the fermenting juice from the skins after a few days so that the wine doesn't have a chance to pick up color.

Rosé wines, sometimes called blush wines, get their pink shade in one of two ways. Most often, red grapes are used, and their skins are left in contact with the fermenting juice long enough to add a desirable reddish tinge (as in "blush" or "white" Zinfandel). Other times, red and white grapes are fermented separately, and then their juices are blended to the desired flavor and shade of pink. You can find out more about white, red, and rosé wines in lessons 3, 4, and 5, respectively.

Table, Dessert, or Fortified

Table wine, as the name suggests, is to be enjoyed at the dining table with a meal. Dessert and aperitif wines like Tokay Aszu, Barsac, and Sauternes are meant for sipping before or after dinner, or to be savored on their own. Fortified wines are so named because they have been strengthened with extra alcohol, typically from distilled grape spirits.

---

*abcdefghijklmnopq
rstuvwxyzabcdefgh
ijklmnopqrstuvwxy*

a note from
the instructor

SWEET WINE TRIVIA

To make sweet "ice wine," winemakers leave the grapes on the vine until winter temperatures freeze them solid. The frozen grapes have an intense, concentrated sweetness. Many winemakers in New York, Canada, and Germany have made ice wine a specialty. In Germany, it's known as *Eiswein*.

In Australia, sweet wines are called "stickies." Many of Australia's stickies are made from Muscadelle and Muscat grapes and are fortified like Port or Sherry.

In the days before modern winemaking techniques and airtight containers, this fortification was necessary to keep wine from spoiling. The high alcohol content acted as a preservative and a barrier to oxidation. It also stabilized the wine enough for it to survive long, arduous journeys. Many of the first wines to be exported were fortified: Port, Sherry, and Madeira. Again, the distinction blurs a little when you realize that fortified wines make terrific after-dinner sippers and, if not too heavy, can even be enjoyed with a hearty meal. Lesson 5 contains more information about dessert, aperitif, and fortified wines.

Sweet or Dry

Whether red, white, rosé, sparkling, or fortified, nearly all wines are classified as sweet, dry, or something in between. Because the alcohol in wine comes from the sugar in the grapes, the level of sweetness is determined by how much sugar remains when the fermentation process is halted. In the driest wines, all the sugar has been converted into alcohol. In sweeter wines, fermentation is stopped earlier so that some sugar remains.

Some wine drinkers confuse sweetness with ripeness, but they aren't the same. A sweet wine has residual sugar that is left behind after fermentation has stopped; a *ripe* wine (wine made from fully ripened grapes) has plenty of natural sugars to begin with and tastes of sweet, mature fruit. A ripe wine, then, can be sweet or dry. An ultra-ripe wine may lack acidity, while many *sweet* wines owe their greatness to the high acidity that keeps them from becoming syrupy. When you say,

"Waiter, may I have a glass of dry white wine?" you're probably craving not a dry wine but a wine with crisp acidity. But "Waiter, may I have a glass of acidic wine?" just doesn't sound very appealing.

Champagne and Sparkling Wine

All wines could become sparkling wines if they were permitted to, because all wines produce carbon dioxide as they ferment. In Champagne, France, prior to the late 1700s, *not* having bubbles in wine was a challenge. Champagne as we now know it became popular only when the technique for producing it became popularized.

Not all sparkling wine is Champagne. Champagne, France, is a very special place where the soils are solid white from the high chalk content. When the grapes grown in Champagne's chalky soils are made into wine by using the special *méthod champenoise*, the result is the magical wine we drink for celebrations. While other sparkling wines are made by this labor-intensive, handcrafted method, only wines from the Champagne region of France can rightfully be called Champagne. You can read more about Champagne in lessons 5 and 7.

how to appreciate wine

How We Experience Wine • Evaluating Wine
The Wine-Tasting Process • Wine Characteristics
Attributes of Quality Wines • Talking about What You Taste

In this lesson, we take wine tasting to a deeper level, where knowledge and experience come together to enrich your appreciation of wine. We look at the human sensory organs with respect to the way they experience wine. Then we examine the various wine characteristics that those organs can recognize. We look at some of the differences between good wines and bad ones. Then we go through the steps of tasting wine like a pro and offer suggestions on how to discuss what you've tasted.

HOW YOUR SENSORY ORGANS EXPERIENCE WINE

Wine experts love to proclaim that 80 percent of a wine's apparent taste is really its smell—that wine is more of a treat for the nose than for the mouth. Not only are they correct, but they may even be understating things a little.

Your mouth hardly tastes at all. Everything you perceive as flavor is processed in an area behind the nasal cavity. Your mouth registers only four basic flavor sensations: sweetness, bitterness, acidity, and saltiness (salty flavors are not normally found in wine). Your tongue (and, to a lesser extent, other parts of your mouth) is covered with tiny taste buds capable of accessing these sensations. You can recognize all four flavors with any part of your tongue, but research suggests that the tip of the tongue tastes sweetness most acutely, the back is best for sensing bitterness (as in tannin), and the sides are most sensitive to sourness (acidity).

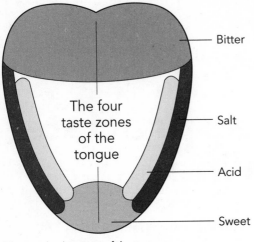

The four taste zones of the tongue

Bitter

Salt

Acid

Sweet

The tastebud regions of the tongue.

Your mouth's main job in wine tasting is to serve as a warming and aerating chamber, giving your sense of smell a greater surface to work with, and to register such physical sensations as body and texture. The nose's capacity to distinguish fine nuances of aroma, combined with sensitivity to a wine's *mouthfeel* (your perception of the wine's texture in your mouth), makes the human species ideally suited to enjoying wine.

TRADITIONAL WINE-TASTING STEPS

To get the most out of the wine-tasting experience, follow these steps:

1. Pour less than half a glassful to allow room for swirling the wine in the glass.

2. Swirl the wine gently in the glass to release its bouquet.

3. Examine the wine's color; hold up the glass against a white background. Examine both the hues of the liquid and, if it's a red wine, the tint that appears at its rim (where it meets the glass).

4. Stick your nose into the glass and inhale the wine's vapors for a few seconds (several short sniffs are more effective than one long snort) to capture its bouquet.

5. Take a sip of the wine with plenty of air, and hold it in your mouth for a few moments. Does the taste manifest itself right away, or does it take a moment to make itself known?

6. Notice both the variety of tastes that hit all at once and those that come along later.

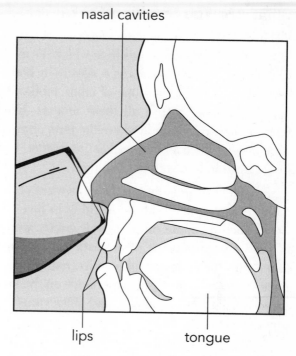

nasal cavities

lips   tongue

The nose and mouth work together to experience wine.

7. Note your perception of the wine in your mouth—whether it's astringent or smooth, oily or sheer.

8. Swallow, or spit if you're at a formal tasting: The lingering flavor and sensation are the wine's finish. Even if you spit out the wine, you won't miss the finish. The vapors that hang around after the liquid is gone will still give it to you.

What Are You Looking For?

A wine's color can be a clue to many things, including its age. White wines darken with age; reds become faded. White wines often evolve from straw and light gold to rich gold and amber; reds may start out reddish purple but take on hues of oxblood, garnet, or brick red. Sweet white wines are generally darker in color than dry ones. The rim of the wine, at its edge where it meets the glass, often manifests colors of its own. Young red wines often have a bluish or purplish tinge at the rim—a purple rim can also indicate that the wine was grown in a hot climate. A fine old red may develop an amber, russet, or orange rim.

What Are You Smelling For?

You are smelling for the wine's *bouquet*. A wine's bouquet is not just the aroma of the grape or grapes from which it's made. Wine develops a host of complex, subtle nuances as it ages in its bottle (earthiness, fruitiness, perfume, and a kaleidoscope of other subtle characteristics)—the bouquet is the sum total of all these aromas, like a bouquet of different types of flowers, which is where the term originated. A newly fermented wine doesn't have a bouquet, just an aroma. It has to mature in its bottle for a while to develop a bouquet.

Bouquet is paramount to the enjoyment of wine. This is probably the main reason so much of the world is in love with wine, as opposed to, say, fermented apple juice: A well-grown, well-crafted wine is capable of presenting *hundreds* of aromatic compounds. The unique bouquet that each wine ends up with results from several factors: its genetic heritage (variety, lineage), its experience on the vine (climate and soil conditions, hang time, vine age, and other variables), and the winemaking process itself.

What Are You Tasting For?

Good wines have three distinct layers of taste and aroma that manifest themselves while you hold the wine in your mouth. Each of these layers presents specific traits:

- **Primary:** This is the first impression—the most prominent aromas and flavors. It's also known as the *presentation.*

- **Secondary:** These aromas and flavors slowly dawn on your senses after you've held the wine in your mouth for a few moments and your senses have become accustomed to the primary flavors. This layer is where the subtle, complex flavor compounds take center stage—the part that wine lovers spend the most time obsessing over. That's why it's important to hold onto a mouthful of wine for a moment. If you swallow it right away, you'll miss the main event!

  This is also the time to evaluate the wine's body and texture— the effect of its physical presence in your mouth, or, as wine lovers call it, the mouthfeel.

■ **Tertiary:** After you swallow that mouthful of wine, you'll find
   that much of the sensation lingers—at least with a good wine.
   In many fine wines, the aftertaste, or "finish," carries a personality that's somewhat distinct from the first two phases. One of
   the great pleasures of drinking wine is to find one with a finish
   that lingers seemingly forever.

As you're tasting, you'll be able to evaluate the various characteristics of a wine. The following elements will reveal themselves to you as
you taste. These attributes are generally in the secondary experience,
except the finish, which is tertiary.

■ **Alcohol:** High-alcohol wines, like Chardonnays, tend to be
   rich, full, and shapely, but too much alcohol can numb the
   palate to the wine's subtler characteristics. If you can smell the
   alcohol, or if the wine feels hot in your mouth, it probably has
   too much alcohol. But alcohol content is a relative issue; a very
   sheer wine can have extremely low alcohol and still seem
   highly alcoholic. Wines need to balance flavor with alcohol
   content.

■ **Acidity:** Acidity creates the sour flavors in a wine. Wines may
   contain several different types of acidity (tartaric, malic, citric,
   and more), which can occur naturally during the growing season
   or can be created intentionally during fermentation. Acidity
   also allows you to experience a wine's "juiciness" because it
   causes your mouth to water. The right kinds of acid make for a
   lively wine; the wrong kinds can sour a wine. Try a German
   Riesling for an acidic wine.

■ **Tannin:** That bitter bite that you encounter, especially in heavy
   red wines, is tannin (see Lesson 1). Because of its natural
   astringency, tannin makes itself known with a skin-wrinkling,
   mouth-puckering sensation that can leave your whole mouth
   feeling coated. High-tannin wines like Barolo have a strong
   "presence" and also age the best. Tannic wines can be as harsh
   as espresso when they're young, but let them age quietly for a
   few years, and that sharp tannin mellows into an exquisite
   framework for the wine's mature flavors and aromas.

- **Sweetness or dryness:** A wine's sweetness is determined by the amount of natural sugars it's allowed to keep during fermentation. If all its sugars are converted into alcohol, the wine will be dry; to the extent that some sugars remain, it will taste sweet. Dry wines do tend to taste more complex, though; the sugar in all but the best sweet wines overwhelms subtler flavors. In a fine sweet wine, the sweetness is never allowed to become overwhelming because it's balanced by a healthy dose of acidity.

- **Fruitiness:** Fruity flavors and aromas are more common in young and white wines. Wines may be reminiscent of any number of fruits but are seldom described (at least not positively) as "grapey." A fine wine's fruitiness lingers long in the mouth.

- **Texture:** A wine's texture may be soft or hard, scratchy or smooth, silky, velvety, grainy, sharp edged, or any number of other possibilities.

- **Body:** Wines are described as light, medium, or full bodied according to how you perceive them when they're in your mouth.

- **Finish:** Finish is the length of time a wine's flavor lingers in your mouth and the quality of that final flavor.

Tasting Sparkling Wines

Tasting a sparkling wine is slightly different from tasting a still wine. The following are some pointers for tasting sparkling wines:

- **Don't swirl.** Although swirling is an important step in tasting a still wine, you don't want to do so with a sparkler. Swirling disperses the wine's bubbles too quickly. You actually don't need to swirl a sparkling wine the way you do a still wine because the rising bubbles release the aroma the way swirling would.

- **Look for small, active bubbles.** A good sparkling wine is full of tiny bubbles. The bubbles should rise in long phalanxes toward the surface. Once there, they should form a thick cream or mousse at the top. If the sparkling wine has aged for a long time, as with a fine Champagne, the bubbles won't move as rapidly.

- **Check the color.** Regardless of type, a sparkling wine should be crystal clear, not cloudy. Older white Champagnes take on a golden bronze hue; rosé and blanc de noirs should be rich seashell pink to salmon.

- **Expect subtler aromas.** Sparkling wines are typically made from younger grapes than those used to make still wines. You'll encounter predominantly light, spicy, fruity, and floral aromas. Champagne's secondary fermentation also provides aromas of its own. These aromas are usually creamy, nutty, or toasty.

- **Taste for secondary fermentation.** The creamy-toasty aromas that you discover should be even more evident in the wine's flavor.

HOW TO EVALUATE A WINE

How will you know whether the wine you're tasting is, objectively, any good? How does a high-quality wine manifest the elements we just discussed, as opposed to the way a so-so wine would? This list looks at some of the attributes of a truly *good* wine:

- **A good wine has a lot to say.** A simple, everyday wine is monochromatic: It has but a single flavor—a tasty one, maybe, but nothing to get excited about. A high-quality wine has a carnival of complex flavors and aromas. As you're tasting, notice whether the wine has a single flavor or many layers of flavor. Is the experience any different after the wine's been in your mouth for a minute—or after you swallow it? Good wine even tastes different in different parts of your mouth. You might experience the sunny citrus qualities of a Spanish Macabeo primarily on the sides and front of your mouth, and then get hit with a pronounced pineapple essence toward the back of your mouth as you begin to swallow.

- **A good wine is expressive.** It not only has a lot to say; it also says it with clarity and focus. Its aromas and flavors aren't muddied or masked. A so-so wine may sit dead in your mouth without revealing much flavor; a fabulous wine practically attacks you with its flavors. Where a lesser Cabernet Sauvignon might taste vaguely of some black fruit, a fine Cabernet tastes specifically like black *currants*.

- **A good wine is balanced.** All its components are integrated; none stands out. The wine isn't overwhelmed by its alcohol, tannin, acidity, or sweetness, and it has enough structure to support its flavors. If, for instance, you take a sip of a Riesling and your tongue constricts from the shock of acidity, you've just tasted a poorly integrated wine. But if you try another Riesling that has the sweetness and flavor to justify such high acidity, the other elements will keep that acidity from reaching out and taking your tongue hostage.

- **A good wine remembers where it came from.** A wine should taste of nature, earth, and life, not of technology. One of the magical things about wine is that it can tell you about the place it was grown: It tastes and smells of the soil that nourished it, of the perfume of wildflowers in the breeze that wafted past it when it was ripening on the vine. This is the way terroir is expressed in a wine. If a wine has been overly manipulated, it loses this sense of connection to its roots. Suppose you open up two different California Chardonnays. The first one tastes strongly of oak and little else. It may as well have been made from Thompson Seedless grapes grown in a city greenhouse. But the second Chardonnay carries a delicate flavor of sun-baked dust and a light whiff of sage because it was made carefully with a minimum of tinkering so that it can express the character of the place it came from.

- **A good varietal tastes like its grape.** A great varietal (from a single grape, not a blend of grape types) is true to its grape: It tastes like a typical example of its kind. A good Sauvignon Blanc has a sharp, green-herb essence; a poor one tastes almost identical to a cheap Chardonnay.

WHAT'S YOUR PLEASURE?

With practice, you'll be able to appreciate the qualities of almost any fine wine, but whether or not you like what you're drinking is a separate issue. Some people have a strong aversion to the feel and flavor of alcohol; if a wine is highly alcoholic, that's enough to kill the experience for them. Others simply hate the mouth-puckering sensation of a lot of tannin. Below, you'll find wine characteristics that can shape people's likes and dislikes, along with a few suggestions for wines that may work with those particular preferences.

IF YOU LIKE	TRY
Low alcohol	Gewürztraminer, Riesling
High alcohol	Chardonnay, Madeira
Low acid	Graves, Hermitage
High acid	Riesling
Low tannin	Zinfandel
Lots of tannin	Cabernet Sauvignon, Nebbiolo
Very dry	Chablis
Very sweet	Moscato, Sauternes
Very fruity	Beaujolais, Zinfandel
Berries	Tempranillo, Zinfandel
Citrus	Albariño, Macabeo
Earthiness	Graves, Médoc, Rioja
Flowers	Rheingau, Tempranillo
Nuts	Madeira, Port, Sherry
Spices	Gewürztraminer, Pinot Gris

DEVELOPING YOUR WINE-TASTING ABILITY

Your ability to appreciate wine will expand over time, with experience. The wines you like as a beginner will probably not be the same ones you gravitate to later on. One of the pleasures of wine is that it gives back when you invest in it: The more you develop your wine knowledge, the more pleasure wine will give you. In this section, we talk about some of the things you can do to develop your enjoyment of wine.

Keep Tasting Records

No one can remember all the nuances of a wine—particularly if you partake of several different kinds on a given evening. If you want to hang onto your wine-tasting experiences, consider keeping a written record. Train yourself to make notes about a wine and its characteristics after the first few sips. Some wine lovers even keep notes on their friends' reactions to certain wines so that they have a handy reference for what to serve them—and what to avoid serving—next time.

Keep notes on your wine purchases: the name of the wine, the producer, its place of origin and year, where you purchased it, and how

student experience

"When I first started drinking wine it was hard to make the distinction between the various sweetnesses and subtle flavors that more experienced wine drinkers around me could taste. What helped me the most was doing a wine tasting at a local winery at which they arranged the wines from driest to sweetest, letting me do side-by-side comparisons of various sweetnesses. Suddenly the differences became quite apparent and I was able to determine what my 'taste' in wine was."

—Michael, photographer

much you paid. If you're really into the idea of keeping a wine journal, you can do as many enthusiasts do: Soak the labels off your bottles of wine and paste them into your journal. Doing so will help jog your memory of the experience and make it easier to recognize the wine in the store if you decide to go back for another bottle. It also creates a nice conversation piece that you can share with your fellow wine lovers.

Organize Your Wine Tastings

You'll deepen your ability to appreciate wine if you organize the way you experience it according to a principle that enables you to compare and contrast. For instance, you may want to spend a month trying nothing but Rieslings, or drink nothing but wines from Australia for a few weeks. Or you may devote six months to reds and six to whites, or a month to sweet wines and another to high-acid wines. Try serving two or three different types of wine at dinner—the same bottles for two or three days in a row with different foods (see the section in Lesson 14 on storing opened wines). Doing so allows you to compare how each wine goes with a different dish.

HOW TO TALK ABOUT WINE

Wine lovers have developed their own language to describe the experiences they find inside their wineglasses. You'll enhance your experience if you arm yourself with the basic descriptors.

Don't, however, be afraid to come up with your own ways of describing wine, using words that make sense to you: Use colors, music, psychology, dog breeds—whatever turns you on. (But don't expect a sommelier to know what you're talking about if you say, "I'd like a Saint Bernard-bodied red with Pekinese acidity and a Labrador finish, please.")

a note from
the instructor

CULTIVATE AN APPRECIATION FOR VARIOUS KINDS OF WINE

Whatever you do, please don't become a wine snob. Don't get to the point where your appreciation of wine is getting *smaller* because of some notion you've developed of the way wine ought to be. And please don't use wine as a way to start an exclusive members-only club of people who are mysteriously in the know about a subject that should be available to all. Wine should bring people together, not drive a wedge between them. It should broaden your horizons, not shrink them. Avoid developing the following habits:

- ■ Don't become a one-type-only wine drinker.
- ■ Don't become too dependent on vintage charts.
- ■ Don't bludgeon people with your wine knowledge—or your enthusiasm.
- ■ Don't limit yourself to fine wines—if you can't enjoy a simple jug wine now and then, you're going to miss out on a lot of joy.

Here's what we hope you'll do instead:

- ■ Do continue to try new wines whenever you have the opportunity.
- ■ Do take risks: Buy wine from off years, obscure vineyards, strange places.
- ■ Do share your love and knowledge of wine when appropriate—that is, when someone's genuinely interested. But know when to shut up.
- ■ Do keep elitism out of your wine appreciation. Just because you've tasted a $400 Bordeaux doesn't mean that you have to swear off $4 white Zinfandels forever.

Common Wine Descriptors

You've probably heard a wine described as having blackberry notes, a tobacco essence, or a peppery finish. Does this mean that the wine contains blackberries, pepper, or tobacco? Not exactly. A wine's flavors come from a dazzling array of natural chemical compounds that develop at all stages of its life, from vine to bottle aging. Some of these compounds are similar in construction to other natural compounds. For instance, a wine with a pronounced blackberry essence may share some compounds with real blackberries, even though there's nothing in the wine besides fermented grape juice and maybe the ghosts of long-dead yeast cells. But wine lovers find it useful to compare a wine's aromas and flavors to the things it reminds them of.

Wine flavors and aromas are typically compared to the following:

- **Fruits:** Blackberries, raspberries, cherries, plums, apricots, apples, bananas, oranges—even kiwis
- **Other foods:** Toast, vanilla, roasted meat, nuts, pepper, spice
- **Plants:** Grass, herbs, tobacco, cedar, flowers
- **Earthy objects:** Damp earth, minerals, gunflint, leather, smoke
- **Animal smells:** Musk, manure, sweat, skunk, fox, horse blanket—even urine

Wine lovers use a similar strategy to describe the texture of wine as they experience it in their mouths. Wines can be described as silky, velvety, coarse, or flabby—even as having a "doughnut" if their flavor temporarily fades out while in the drinker's mouth.

Legs, Noses, and Bouquets

Virtually every wine has "legs"—the syruplike threads it leaves on the inside of the glass—which ultimately tell little about its quality. A wine's aroma, sometimes called its *nose* but more correctly called its *bouquet* (as mentioned earlier), is the key to its quality. A wine's subtlest and most exquisite aspects reside in its bouquet.

Describing Wine That's Gone Bad

Wine that's sincerely gone bad can be described as vinegary or cooked if it's oxidized; corked if it's musty from mildew in the cork; or like rotten eggs, sweat, sulfur, manure, acetone, or nail polish if it's spoiled.

lesson 3

white wines

White Wine's Characteristics • How White Wine Is Made
Popular White Wines • Unusual White Wines

This chapter takes a closer look at white wine—so called because the colors of both the grapes used and the wines that result are typically pale yellow, green, or amber instead of hues of red. In this chapter, you will examine the characteristics of white wine and some of the details of its creation, and then explore a number of white wine grapes, both popular and rare, and the types of wines they yield.

THE CHARACTER OF WHITE WINE

White wine, which is made from white grapes with the skins removed, is a lighter, younger, generally more refreshing drink than its red cousin. White wines are typically served as aperitifs, with light fare (like salads or pasta), or alone. Novice wine drinkers generally find light white wines friendlier, easier to get to know and like, than brooding reds. Because red wines tend to taste and feel heavier, many wine lovers prefer white wines in warmer weather—especially because they're served lightly chilled (see Lesson 12).

abcdefghijklmnopq
rstuvwxyzabcdefgh
ijklmnopqrstuvwxyz

a note from
the instructor

TWO WHITES FOR EVERY RED?

Caterers and restaurant managers frequently advise their clients to order two bottles of white wine for every bottle of red. They're probably right to do so more often than they're wrong, but in the end, it's a matter of personal taste. If you prefer red wine and you're aware that a substantial number of your guests feel the same way, order what you know they'll enjoy. You don't want to end up with several leftover cases of a wine that neither you nor anyone you know is likely to drink!

White wines vary from extremely sweet to bone dry. They may be light and sheer or sultry and full bodied, soft and mild or sharply acidic. They offer a dazzling variety of flavors, which, depending on the type of wine, may remind the drinker of citrus, honey, pepper, asparagus, wet stone, or any number of other taste sensations. Most are still, but many come in sparkling forms. They're typically lower in alcohol than reds.

Many white wines, including Chardonnay, Riesling, and Chenin Blanc, are found in a variety of styles, ranging from sweet to dry. Others, like the wines you'll see in the following chart, can be classified fairly reliably as sweet, off-dry, or dry.

SOME TYPICAL WHITE WINES AND THEIR CHARACTERISTIC STYLES

SWEET	OFF-DRY	DRY
Barsac	Gewürztraminer	Muscadet
Sauternes	Pinot Grigio	Orvieto
Tokay-Aszu	Viognier	Soave

This chart is by no means exhaustive; in your wine adventures, you're sure to find many more wines that tend to stay true to one level of sweetness or dryness. But in general, you'll run into a wide variety *within* a wine grape, particularly if you like Chardonnay. This versatile grape can make a fruity, sweetish wine (as many California Chardonnays are); a rich, full-bodied wine (the style found in many French white Burgundies); or a dry, sharp wine with steely, stony flavors (the kind the Chablis subregion of France's Burgundy wine region is famous for producing). Similarly, Sémillon, the grape that makes honey-sweet

Sauternes, is also used to make white Graves, an intense, dry wine with a gravel-like flavor. Chenin Blanc and Riesling grapes (as well as many lesser-known varieties) are made in such a wide range of styles that they cover the sweet-to-dry spectrum.

Most white wines are meant to be enjoyed while they're young. A handful of full-bodied whites, such as higher-quality Chenin Blancs, Chardonnays, and Sémillons, may evolve with a few years of aging, but the vast majority of whites should be drunk within four years of their vintage. The notable exceptions are fine white fortified wines (such as Sherry), some of which can age spectacularly for decades.

MAKING WHITE WINE

White wine grapes thrive in a variety of climates. They flourish in many areas that most red grapes find too chilly, such as Canada and Germany, yet they can also grow happily alongside reds in baking-hot regions like South Africa, parts of Australia, and the Mediterranean. Although it may be easier to drink a white wine than a red, white wines are more challenging to make. The grapes require more delicate handling during the harvest so that they're not bruised or crushed, and the process of making white wine involves extra steps, like the removal of the grapes' skins and the skimming off of the dead yeast cells after fermentation. Additionally, it's critical to keep white wines from contacting air while they're fermenting. They oxidize more rapidly than reds, and where a robust red can tolerate a small amount of air contact during the early winemaking stages, a fermenting white wine exposed to oxygen quickly loses flavor and color.

The procedure for making white wine differs significantly from that for making red. Winemakers press the white grapes and separate the skins and seeds from the juice before fermentation begins (in most wineries today, the separating is done by a machine). This step reduces the amount of tannin that remains in the must. Vineyard workers must be careful not to bruise delicate white grapes, because even a small amount of contact with the punctured grape skin can leach a noticeable amount of tannin into the fruit.

As white wine ferments, winemakers remove the spent yeast cells, called *lees,* from the wine. Some fine white wines state on their labels that the wine was aged *sur lie,* or "on its lees," which means that the wine and lees were left together for a period (generally less than a year) before the wine was racked off its lees. The prolonged contact with the spent yeast cells gives the wine a stronger character.

White wines may or may not spend some time in oak, depending on the style and the winemaker's preference. Some white wines (notably many popular Chardonnays) take on a heavy oak flavor that dominates the fruit. Other whites have classic flavors of their own, like sharp, grassy Sauvignon Blanc, which seldom sees oak at all.

POPULAR WHITE WINE GRAPES AND THE WINES MADE FROM THEM

In this section, we take a closer look at some of the most popular international white wine grapes and a few of the typical wines produced from them. The following table lists some of these white wine grapes, their origins, and where they are cultivated, as well as the respective wines that are made from these grapes, and some characteristics of these wines.

POPULAR WHITE WINE GRAPES

GRAPE	WINE	CHARACTERISTICS	ORIGIN	PRIMARILY GROWN IN
Chardonnay	Chardonnay, Chablis	High alcohol, medium-full body	France	Most wine-growing countries
Chenin Blanc	Chenin Blanc	Crisp, medium-full body	France	France, South Africa, U.S.
Gewürztraminer	Gewürztraminer	Crisp, peppery	Germany	Germany, cooler climates
Palomino	Sherry	Rich, nutty	Spain	Spain
Pinot Blanc	Pinot Blanc	Light body, mild to bland	France	France, Italy, California
Pinot Gris/Grigio	Pinot Gris/Grigio	Crisp, spicy, somewhat fruity	Italy	Italy, California, Oregon
Riesling	Riesling	Many styles, often highly acidic	Germany	Germany, cool climates
Sauvignon Blanc	Sauvignon Blanc	Crisp, grassy, medium body	France	France, U.S., New Zealand
Sémillon	Sémillon	Medium to full body, honeylike	France	France
Viognier	Viognier	Medium body, elegant	France	France, U.S.

All the wines mentioned here are produced and consumed in large quantities outside their country of origin. Many of these wines, like

Chardonnay and Sauvignon Blanc, have been around for a while, and their popularity holds strong year after year. Others, like Pinot Gris and Viognier, are relative newcomers to the international wine scene, and only time will tell whether they're short-lived trends or serious contenders.

The names you see as subheadings are all grape varieties. In most cases, the grape is used to make a varietal wine of the same name, but it may also be the sole or principal grape used to make other popular styles.

- **Chardonnay** (shar-don-nay): This popular, flavorful, easy-to-like grape is grown throughout the wine-producing world. It's known for its versatility and for the full-bodied presence of the wines it produces. Many styles of Chardonnay wine are aged in oak barrels, which impart a toasty vanilla aroma. A good buttery Chardonnay is a knockout with fresh buttered corn on the cob.

  The Chardonnay grape is used to make a number of popular styles of wine, including Pouilly Fuissé and Meursault. It's also the source of Chablis from the Chablis region of France. (Although you can buy a wine called Chablis that comes from California, in technical circles, nothing grown outside Chablis, France, is *true* Chablis.) Chablis carries a distinct flavor that many wine lovers describe as flinty or slatey. Chardonnay is also one of the primary grapes used in making Champagne.

- **Chenin Blanc** (she-neen blonk): This fruity, often sweet grape makes a wine of the same name that has a noticeable acidity and a thick, almost oily texture. It is grown extensively in South Africa, where it's called Steen, and in California. Chenin Blanc stands up well to spicy foods and pairs nicely with vegetables and chicken. Chenin Blanc is also the source grape of France's popular Vouvray.

- **Gewürztraminer** (geh-*voortz*-trah-mee-ner): The wine (of the same name) made from this German grape is dry, low in alcohol

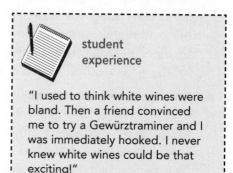

student experience

"I used to think white wines were bland. Then a friend convinced me to try a Gewürztraminer and I was immediately hooked. I never knew white wines could be that exciting!"

—Suzanne, musicologist

and acid, and deep golden in color, with a pronounced floral spiciness and an energetic character. Wine lovers have described its peppery, offbeat personality as quirky. Gewürztraminer makes a fine companion to food, despite its low acidity. It pairs well with Chinese and Japanese dishes, which are notoriously hard to match with wine. See Lesson 14 for more information on pairing wines with foods.

- **Muscat** (moos-cat): This ancient grape variety yields a wine bursting with ripe, fruity, floral aromas. Muscat is one of the only wines that can be pleasantly described as grapey. It's a bad sign when just about any other wine grape tastes like a grape, yet it's an intricate part of Muscat's fruity, perfumed character. Muscat (also known as Moscato) is blended with other grapes in a number of wine styles and is the star of Italy's sparkling Asti. Muscat is grown in most of Europe's wine-producing countries and in California.

- **Pinot Gris** (pee-noh gree): Called Pinot Grigio (pee-noh gree-joh) in Italy, this golden wine from the grape of the same name is crisp with hints of peach, orange, apple, and pepper. Pinot Gris/Grigio is grown extensively in France and Italy, as well as in California. In recent years, it has become popular in Oregon as well.

- **Riesling** (*reez*-ling): Known for high acidity and relatively low alcohol, Riesling is typically light bodied and fruity, often bearing a slight metallic taste, depending on where it was grown. It's often, but not always, made into a sweet wine. It can range from mildly acidic to a blast of tongue-rasping acidity that a friend of ours calls "lemonade wine." Riesling originated in Germany but is now grown around the world. Many wine experts claim that food couldn't have a better partner than Riesling—its acidity sharpens food's flavors and balances spice.

- **Sauvignon Blanc** (saw-veen-yon blonk): A powerful alternative to fruity whites, Sauvignon Blanc is assertive and edgy, with a sharp acidity and grassy, flinty flavors. Some rich Sauvignon Blancs have been described as having a slight cat urine aroma. New Zealand produces a unique, mouthwatering Sauvignon Blanc with hints of creamy asparagus. It's also found under the names Sancerre and Pouilly Fumé, and in California, it's sometimes called Fumé Blanc. It goes nicely with garlicky foods.

- **Sémillon** (*say*-mee-yon): With an almost oily texture, a honeylike flavor, and an aroma reminiscent of honey and stone fruits, low-acid Sémillon grapes are often used to make sweet dessert wines, like Sauternes, or very dry ones, like Graves.

- **Viognier** (vee-yon-yay): This unusual grape makes an elegant, exotic white wine with a musky, honeysucklelike flavor—it's often described as having a Froot Loop nose. Viognier has enjoyed a recent surge in popularity among wine drinkers in the United States. California wine growers are planting more of this French native in anticipation of the growing trend.

RARE, EXOTIC, AND LESSER-KNOWN WHITE GRAPES AND THEIR WINES

In this era of mass marketing, the vast majority of commercial wines are made from a short list of tried-and-true grapes. This section, however, explores a few of the more exotic white grape varieties and the wines that are made from them. The majority of the wines in this section are rare, primarily because they're seldom exported outside their native country or region. This is one of the reasons wine tourism has become so popular: A kaleidoscope of wine experience simply can't be had if you limit your wine adventures to the corner wine shop.

- **Assyrtiko** (as-seer-ti-*ko*): This rare Greek white grape makes a highly acidic wine. Assyrtiko wine, along with a handful of wines from other Greek grape varieties, are still made to carry the piney *retsina* flavoring reminiscent of the pine pitch the ancients used to preserve their wines.

- **Albariño** (al-ba-*reen*-yo): Grown primarily in Spain's Galician wine region, this grape (known as Alvarinho in Portugal) makes a sprightly, citrus-flavored wine of the same name.

- **Aligoté** (a-li-go-*tay*): The highly acidic wine made from this grape must be drunk young because it can't take aging. Aligoté is now grown in eastern Europe and portions of France, as well as in California.

a note from
the instructor

"CONTAINS SULFITES"

In the United States, it's mandatory that any food product to which sulfites have been added must declare this fact on its label. Wine contains some sulfites naturally; they're leftovers from the fermentation process. But wine-makers often add a small quantity of sulfites to protect the wine against oxidation and spoilage. White dessert wines have the most, dry whites have less, dry reds have the least. The sulfite content in wine is relatively low, especially when compared to that of many other foods. If the sulfites in orange juice, dried fruits, and packaged cookies and crackers don't bother you, you're not likely to notice them in your wine.

- **Furmint** (*foor*-mint): The grape used to make Hungary's world-famous dessert wine Tokay Aszu, Furmint also makes a fine white table wine.

- **Grüner Veltliner** (*groo*-ner *velt*-lee-ner): This lively Austrian grape, little known outside Austria, makes a musky, spicy wine.

- **Palomino** (pa-lo-*mee*-no): The principal grape of Spanish Sherry, Palomino oxidizes quickly, which makes it an ideal choice for making fortified wine.

- **Prosecco** (pro-*say*-ko): Prosecco hails from Veneto, Italy. The crisp, sparkling wine made from this grape has a nutlike perfume.

- **Rkatsiteli** (ar-*kat*-si-*tell*-ee): Also spelled Rkatsiteii, this cold-tolerant Russian grape makes a sharply acidic wine with spicy aromas similar to Gewürztraminer. It's now also being grown in New York's Finger Lakes region.

red wines

Red Wine's Character • The Making of Red Wine
Well-Known Red Wine Grapes • Unusual Red Wine Grapes

If you think of white wine as the preference for novices and casual drinkers, you could describe red wine as the drink of choice for more serious wine lovers. However, many red wine drinkers will tell you that you have to work at loving red wine—drinking it is a much more complex and challenging experience. Ask a red wine lover what's so great about red wine, and he'll probably tell you about the multiple layers of its aroma, the subtlety of its flavors, and the magical transformation that takes place when a red wine ages well. In this lesson, we take a look at the defining characteristics of red wine and at a few details of its creation, and then we explore some of the world's greatest, and lesser-known, red wine grapes.

THE CHARACTER OF RED WINE

Just about every wine drinker can enjoy a casual glass of white wine, but red wines really set our hearts ablaze. When you find wine lovers obsessing over a wine, nosing the glass and gushing over the complex aromas, secondary flavors, and finish, check the color of the stuff in their glasses—odds are it's red.

Wine lovers generally consider red wines to be richer, weightier, and more complex in taste than white wines. The tannins in red wine, which provide color and a distinct bitter note, create a support structure for the subtle, maturing flavors and make red wines age worthy. Many *reserve* wines (intended for aging) taste unbearably harsh when young, but give them a few contemplative years of bottle aging and you'll be amazed at their depth of flavor and subtle nuances.

Red wine is an acquired taste, which might explain why it's not nearly as popular as white—at least among casual wine drinkers. Many novice wine drinkers have trouble getting past the bitter bite of the tannins. If the tannic flavor in red wine bothers you, try eating cheese with your wine—the cheese helps moderate the effect of the tannin. Also, some red wines need to be aerated thoroughly, both to take the edge off the tannin and to allow the flavors to unfold, before you drink them.

How do you aerate? Contrary to popular wisdom, opening a wine bottle and letting it sit on a table does little good. All you're doing is letting the top inch breathe. If you have time, pour it into a decanter and swirl it around. Doing so will help, but keep in mind that all quality wines improve the most *in the glass*. Typically, a huge wine can take a couple of hours to exhibit a quantifiable adjustment, although some wines will start to change as soon as you get them into the glass. (See Lesson 13 for details on aerating and decanting wine.)

student experience

"When I first began to enjoy drinking wine on a regular basis, I was truly a white wine gal; I thought red wines were harsh. Then I was talked into sampling a Beaujolais Nouveau and its light fruity taste was like a window opening for me. Gradually I started trying more complex reds and now I'm totally content in both worlds."
—Rita, hospice nurse

HOW RED WINE IS MADE

As you learned in Lesson 3, the secret to making white wine is to remove the tannic grape skins early in the winemaking process. But with red wine, skin contact is the name of the game. Winemakers leave the skins on when they crush red wine grapes so that the wine ferments in direct contact with the skins. The rest of the process of making red wine is as described in Lesson 1, "What Is Wine?"

POPULAR RED WINE GRAPES AND THEIR WINES

In this section, we take a look at some of the world's most popular red wine grapes and the styles of wine that are made from them. As we did with white wine grapes in Lesson 3, we're including the international red grape varieties that are grown in numerous countries around the world.

The first three grapes you'll encounter here, Cabernet Sauvignon, Cabernet Franc, and Merlot, are (along with the lesser-known Malbec and Petit Verdot) the major grapes of France's Bordeaux region. They deserve special mention because of Bordeaux's longstanding reputation as the birthplace of the world's finest wine. The next two mainstay grapes—Gamay and Pinot Noir—although not from Bordeaux, are nonetheless natives of France that have become international favorites. Today, they're found in many of the world's most beloved wines.

- **Cabernet Sauvignon** (ca-ber-nay sow-veen-yon): The world-renowned elder statesman, flagship of the Bordeaux region, and reigning champion of French red wines. Wine from the Cabernet Sauvignon grape ages superbly, developing a full-bodied complexity loaded with such flavors as black currant, plum, cedar, and leather, all inside a solid wood frame derived from the barrel. California's Cabernet Sauvignon adds unique overtones of mint and chocolate to this delicious mix. This is *the* wine to have with roasted or grilled meats.

- **Cabernet Franc** (ca-ber-nay fronk): One of the five major Bordeaux grapes, along with Cabernet Sauvignon, Merlot, Petit Verdot, and Malbec. Cabernet Franc makes a rich, complex, fruity red wine. It's grown largely in France's Loire Valley and now in New York State, where it's often blended with other Bordeaux natives.

- **Merlot** (mare-low): The third grape in the Bordeaux trinity, Merlot is often described as a softer, fruitier, lighter-weight version of Cabernet Sauvignon, with many of the same characteristics and flavors. The Merlot grape, another Bordeaux native, is grown extensively in California and increasingly throughout the world. More laid-back and easygoing than Cabernet Sauvignon, Merlot works well with barbecue.

a note from
the instructor

MERITAGE: CALIFORNIA'S BLENDED BORDEAUX-STYLE WINES

The term *Meritage* refers to a class of Napa Valley wines that are a blend of five red Bordeaux grapes: Cabernet Sauvignon, Merlot, Cabernet Franc, Petit Verdot, and Malbec. (White Meritage, which is a blend of Sauvignon Blanc and Sémillon, also exists.) Napa Valley growers created Meritage wines because they wanted the freedom to blend their Bordeaux grapes as they saw fit, without having to worry about the California law that requires a wine to contain 75 percent or more of the grape that is named on the label. Examples of Meritage wines include Dominus, Insignia, and Opus One.

■ **Gamay** (ga-may): The grape used to make France's perennially popular Beaujolais. Light, cherrylike Gamay, grown largely in France, makes a fruity, outgoing wine and is often used in inexpensive jug wines.

■ **Pinot Noir** (pee-no-nwar): An earthy, silky, sensual wine, lighter bodied than its thicker-skinned brothers, Cabernet and Merlot. The Pinot Noir grape's cherry and plumlike flavors are accented with earthy tones of mushroom, cedar, and tobacco. Popular in the United States, France, New Zealand, and increasingly in many other countries, the Pinot Noir grape is, by its nature, the most difficult major grape to grow. Try Pinot Noir with roasted chicken, grilled salmon, or barbecued lamb.

■ **Syrah/Shiraz** (see-rah/shi-rahz): Recognized as one of the greatest grapes in the world, this Rhône Valley native is on the rise. Called Shiraz in Australia and South Africa, the Syrah grape is both rugged and graceful, its earthy, smoky, autumn-leaf aromas mingling with fruit and spice. Syrah is still the sole red grape of the northern Rhône and is now being grown extensively in the United States, South Africa, and Australia. Syrah is a first-rate wine to serve with barbecue.

■ **Zinfandel** (zin-fan-del): California's pride and joy, berrylike Zinfandel produces wines that range from dry to sweet; it's also

a note from
the instructor

SORTING OUT THE BEAUJOLAIS

Many novice wine lovers find themselves befuddled by the numerous types of Beaujolais wines they encounter on their wine store's shelves: everything from Beaujolais Nouveau and Beaujolais-Villages to Gamay Beaujolais. What do they all mean? We'll take them one at a time:

- **Beaujolais:** All genuine Beaujolais—in other words, that which comes from Beaujolais, France—is made from 100 percent Gamay grapes. Your basic Beaujolais (without any other designation) comes from the region's lesser-quality vineyards.

- **Beaujolais-Villages:** The next rung up in quality, this Beaujolais comes from a few dozen designated villages in central Beaujolais.

- **Beaujolais Cru:** The highest-quality Beaujolais, from a handful of specific villages. Grapes from these villages generally are not used to make Beaujolais Noveau.

- **Beaujolais Nouveau:** Beaujolais released to the public very early—sometimes when it's only a few weeks old. Beaujolais Nouveau, almost always made with grapes from the lesser Gamay growing areas, is a popular café-sipper in many parts of Europe. This wine is lively, refreshing, and piercingly fruity.

- **Gamay Beaujolais:** Gamay Beaujolais is not true Beaujolais at all—or Gamay, for that matter. It doesn't come from the Beaujolais region or the Gamay grape! Gamay Beaujolais is a relative of Pinot Noir grown in California.

- **Beaujolais Blanc:** There is such a thing as white Beaujolais; it's usually a blend of Chardonnay and Aligoté. But asking your local wine store for it is probably futile. It's made in relatively small quantities, and hardly any Beaujolais Blanc is imported to the United States.

All true Beaujolais, regardless of quality designation, are typically light, sweet, and fruity, designed to be enjoyed younger than most other red wines. Because of its refreshing quality, it's one of the easier red wines to get to know. It's also relatively affordable.

made into blush wine known as White Zinfandel. Zinfandel is one of the easier red wines for a novice wine drinker to like. It pairs nicely with the humblest of foods: tacos, pizza, and hot dogs. Look for this wine to become even more important in the future.

abcdefghijklmnopq
rstuvwxyzabcdefgh
ijklmnopqrstuvwxy

a note from
the instructor

RED ZINFANDEL: MYSTERY IN A BOTTLE?

Because Zinfandel styles vary so widely, how do you know what you're getting when you buy it? For example, if you're looking for a sweet Zinfandel for after-dinner sipping, how would you tell it apart from the dry ones? Unfortunately, telling which style of Zinfandel you're getting is nearly impossible without opening the bottle and tasting it. The labels seldom reveal this information. The only sure way out of this dilemma is to familiarize yourself with the Zinfandels that are available in your area. And if you don't trust your memory, keep lists of the sweet and dry ones! (See Lesson 12 for more information about buying wine.)

RARE, EXOTIC, AND LESSER-KNOWN RED WINE GRAPES

Now that we've looked at the classic red grape varieties, we'll introduce you to some of the less-famous red grape types and the wine styles produced from them. As we did with the white grapes in Lesson 3, we're introducing these grapes to give you a sense of the variety that's out there, although you're not likely to find all these wines in abundance at your local wine shop.

- **Barbera** (bar-behr-a): The most widely planted grape variety in Italy, Barbera makes a rich, medium-bodied wine full of blackberry and black plum flavors. It was once principally a cheap jug wine. It's now treated with more respect. Growers in Italy's Piedmont region may soon catapult Barbera to international greatness.

- **Concord** (con-cord): New York's most popular grape, and a principal grape in Manischewitz (kosher) wine. A native American variety, Concord makes a light, often super-sweet wine with a strong grape-candy flavor. It is also the grape used to make commercial grape juice and jelly.

- **Grenache** (gre-nash): Originally of Spanish origin (in Spain it's called Garnacha), the Grenache grape is capable of making elegant wine, particularly in concert with Syrah. Grenache produces a wine with a rich mouthfeel and berry flavors. It's one of the grapes used in Châteauneuf du Pape and one of the two grapes used in Spain's popular Rioja wine. (Tempranillo is the other.) Today, Grenache is grown extensively in the United States and Australia.

- **Nebbiolo** (ne-bee-oh-lo): Famed in Italy's Piedmont region for making well-aging Barbaresco and Barolo wines, Nebbiolo is difficult to grow. From a grape that makes a dark, almost black wine loaded with tannin, a well-aged Nebbiolo wine packs an espressolike wallop of flavor. Serve Nebbiolo-based wines with serious, savory meat dishes. Because they're meant for aging, Barbaresco and Barolo tend to be pricey—but lovers of fine old red wine swear that they're worth the wait.

- **Pinotage** (pee-no-taj): South Africa's unique cross between Pinot Noir and Cinsault grapes. The resulting wine, of the same name, has become extremely popular in South Africa—so much so that it can be compared to the popularity of Zinfandel in the States. South Africans enjoy Pinotage with barbecue. If your favorite wine shop carries South African wines, you'll probably find a selection of good Pinotages.

---

abcdefghijklmnopq
rstuvwxyzabcdefgh
ijklmnopqrstuvwxyz

**a note from
the instructor**

BEATING A RED WINE HEADACHE

Some wine drinkers complain of headaches after drinking red wine, and they're quick to blame the sulfites. (U.S. law requires that all wines carry a label that warns, "Contains sulfites.") But the sulfites are probably not the culprit: White wine contains more sulfites than red, and a single glass of orange juice packs a bigger wallop of sulfites than any wine.

None of these suggestions is foolproof, of course, but if you're plagued by headaches, they might make the difference between being able to enjoy an occasional glass and swearing off red wine forever:

- Drink lots of water before, during, and after your wine.
- Eat food with your wine.
- Limit yourself to a single 4-ounce glass of wine.
- Drink slowly—make the glass last half an hour.

- **Sangiovese** (san-jio-vay-say): The principal grape used in Chianti wine, Sangiovese is the workhorse of Italy's Tuscan wines. Chianti is widely available. In addition to Chianti, you may see a bottle of wine labeled simply "Sangiovese" at your favorite shop. California winemakers have played with this grape, but to date, none of them has produced a showstopper Sangiovese wine. Chianti and Sangiovese are nice companions for casual Italian foods with tomato-based sauces—especially pizza.

- **Tempranillo** (tem-pra-nee-yo): A forward, cherrylike Spanish grape that makes a wine of the same name, also popular in Argentina. Along with Grenache (or Garnacha), Tempranillo is the basis for Spain's popular Rioja wines. Tempranillo wines are fabulous companions for hearty meats.

lesson 5

special wines

Rosé and Blush Wine • Sparkling Wine and Champagne
Wine for Aperitifs and Desserts • Fortified Wine
Kosher Wine • "No Way" Wine

The wines you'll meet in this lesson are not your everyday red and white table wines, although most of them can be served with meals. Each of these types of wine is special enough to deserve its own category. These wines differ from ordinary table wines in some aspect of their production, as well as, in many cases, their intended use.

ROSÉS AND BLUSHES

Rosé and blush wines are pinkish in color, light in body, and typically sweet. Although rosés and blushes are made from red grapes (winemakers separate the skins early in the fermentation process) or occasionally from white wine mixed with a small quantity of red, they're usually treated more like white wines: They're chilled before being served and enjoyed when the occasion calls for a refreshing wine rather than a serious one.

Is there a difference between rosé and blush? Few wine experts make a distinction between the two, but when one is made, it's sometimes suggested that a blush is paler than a rosé. In general, the difference is more of an aesthetic one. Rosés have been around for ages; France, Spain, Portugal, and other serious wine-producing countries make plenty of them. But blushes came on the scene during the 1980s when the wine-drinking trend swung heavily toward white wines. On the heels of this fashion came wines like white Zinfandel—red wines trying to pass themselves off as whites.

What's the appeal of rosé and blush wines, besides the unusual color? Many of their fans might tell you that there's something romantic and bohemian about them. They're lighter and less serious than reds but more festive than whites. To a highly sophisticated palate, rosés and blushes may seem a bit boring, but pinkish wines like white Zinfandel remain relatively popular in America and elsewhere for casual wine drinking.

In spite of pink wine's casual reputation, winemakers in various countries produce a number of fine rosés (as shown in the table that follows). In France's Côtes-du-Rhône, the Loire Valley, and the southern Rhône, rosé wines are assertive and crisp, unlike their often-bland American counterparts. Champagne, France, makes a number of elegant rosé Champagnes, including a pale pink style that it calls *blanc de noirs,* or "white from black," made from red Champagne grapes. Spain exports a rosé version of its popular Rioja, and Austria makes a crisply acidic rosé known as Schilcher. But the more serious rosés aside, you can find Portugal's Mateus and Lancer's rosés in your local wine shop, still sold in the same distinctive bottles you may remember from the 1960s. They're still fairly cheap—just no longer as hip.

NOTEWORTHY ROSÉS AND BLUSHES

CATEGORY	EXAMPLES	CHARACTERISTICS
California Blushes	White Zinfandel, white Merlot, white Grenache	Semi-sweet, cherry, vanilla
California Rosés	Pinot Noir Rosé and others	Richer, spicier than blush
Rosé Champagnes	Blanc de Noirs and others	Pale to rich pink
French Rosés	Tavel, Anjou, Côtes-du-Rhône, Gigondas	Semi-sweet, fruity, spicy
Portuguese Rosés	Mateus, Lancers	Semi-sweet
Spanish Rosés	Rioja	Semi-dry, spicy
Austrian Rosés	Schilcher	Highly acidic

SPARKLING WINES

Sparkling wines are produced when winemakers trap the natural carbon dioxide that wine gives off during fermentation. (When making still wines, winemakers allow this gas to escape.) Sparkling wines are typically light, simple, and fun, but a few serious, complex, fine sparklers exist. Some sparkling wines, like German Sekt and Italian Asti, are so refreshing and versatile that they can be served at every course of a meal. Sparkling wines are best served well chilled (discussed at greater length in Lesson 14).

Varieties of Sparkling Wines

Nearly every winemaking country boasts a range of sparkling wines. The varieties are dazzling. Here are just a few of the most popular ones:

- **Asti Spumante:** Nowadays just called Asti, this fun, perfumy Italian sparkler is made from the Muscat grape.

- **Cava:** This light Spanish sparkling wine is usually made primarily from Tempranillo and a blend of other Spanish grapes.

- **Champagne:** The grande dame of sparkling wines, Champagne comes from the Champagne region of France and is produced by a centuries-old method in which a secondary fermentation is induced in the bottle, trapping the resultant carbon dioxide. This method is laborious—hence the high price tag. Many, but not all, Champagnes are blended from several grape varieties, particularly Chardonnay, Pinot Noir, and Pinot Meunier.

- **Sekt:** A popular German sparkling wine made from a number of grape varieites, Sekt is often crisply acidic. Most Sekt is cheap and simple, but a modest amount of fine Sekt is made on small estates.

Types of Champagnes

The world's most festive beverage comes in a seemingly endless variety of styles, from extremely sweet to bone dry; in red, white, and rosé; and in a dazzling array of bottle sizes.

- **Vintage:** Made exclusively from a single year's harvest—and only when it's been a fabulous year.

- **Nonvintage:** A blend of several years' harvests.

- **Blanc de blancs:** Literally, "white from whites," this light and elegant white Champagne is made exclusively from the Chardonnay grape.

- **Blanc de noirs:** Literally, "white from blacks," this pale, pinkish wine is made from the juice of red grapes minus the skins.

- **Rosé:** Made either by adding a small quantity of red Champagne to white or by removing the skins of red Champagne grapes shortly after fermentation begins. Rich pink in color.

---

 a note from
the instructor

"CARE FOR A NEBUCHADNEZZAR OF CHAMPAGNE?"

Diehard Champagne lovers are fortunate: They don't have to buy their favorite beverage by the standard-sized bottle. For a truly special occasion, they can opt for a Magnum (2 bottles' worth in 1) or, if they're really craving the bubbly stuff, a Methuselah (8 bottles) or even a Balthazar (16 bottles). For reasons lost to modern times, the largest Champagne bottles were named for ancient Hebrews (from Jeroboam to Nebuchadnezzar). The following are some of the bottle sizes in which Champagne is available, from smallest to largest. But don't run out and expect to find a Nebuchadnezzar on your wine store's shelves—the largest, most colorfully named sizes are rarely exported from France.

- Split   1½ glasses
- Magnum   2 bottles
- Jeroboam   4 bottles
- Methuselah   8 bottles
- Salmanazar   12 bottles
- Balthazar   16 bottles
- Nebuchadnezzar   20 bottles

Although most Champagne produced today is *brut*—that is, very dry—Champagne is available in styles ranging from those that contain almost no sugar to those sweet enough to stand up to the richest desserts. In the following table, you'll see a list of the common Champagne styles, with the amount of sugar they contain and how that amount of sugar translates into the sensation on your tongue. Once in a while, a producer adds a new term to this list, like LeClerc Briant's Brut Zero—drier than the Mojave.

DRY AND SWEET CHAMPAGNE CLASSIFICATIONS

CLASSIFICATION	SWEETNESS	AMOUNT OF SUGAR
Doux	Very sweet	55 grams of sugar per liter or greater
Demi-sec	Sweet	33 to 55 grams of sugar per liter
Sec	Semi-dry	17 to 35 grams of sugar per liter
Extra dry	Extra dry	12 to 20 grams of sugar per liter
Brut	Very dry	15 or fewer grams of sugar per liter
Extra brut	Extremely dry	0 to 6 grams of sugar per liter

FORTIFIED WINES

Fortified wines differ from mainstream reds and whites because of their typically higher alcoholic content, often extreme age, and higher price. Fortified wines (also known as liqueur, dessert, and aperitif wines) are those to which extra alcohol has been added during production. Ranging from dry to sweet and available in a dazzling array of styles, they often can age fabulously, even under conditions that would kill a tamer wine, such as extreme heat. Fortified wines are often served alone or with cheese, pâté, nuts, and the like. Port, Sherry, and Madeira are popular examples.

Major Fortified Wines

Rich, highly alcoholic, and sometimes fabulously old, major fortified wines such as Madeira, Port, and Sherry can be an intense pleasure to drink. Many wine lovers add the nutty, toffeelike essence of fortified wines to soups and other dishes. Others enjoy the air of exotic sophistication that these wines bring to the cocktail hour. In Spain (home of Sherry) and Portugal (Madeira and Port's native land), fortified wines are matters of national pride.

Madeira

From the Portuguese islands of the same name, Madeira wine is traditionally made from any of four white grapes: Bual, Malvasia, Sercial, and Verdelho (see the table that follows). It is highly alcoholic, due in part to the grape spirits that are added during fermentation. Although with most other wines, heat must be scrupulously avoided, Madeira is intentionally exposed to heat during its production—sometimes for as long as six months. The result is a rich, caramelized essence. High-quality Madeiras may be aged for decades.

STYLES OF MADEIRA

Style: Sercial (rare); Grape: Sercial	Dry, tart, acidic (aperitif)
Style: Verdelho; Grape: Verdelho	Medium dry, slightly nutty (aperitif)
Style: Bual (rare); Grape: Bual	Dark, medium sweet (after dinner)
Style: Malmsey; Grape: Malvasia	Dark, rich, sweet (after dinner)

Madeiras are found at a wide variety of quality levels, from those that have aged for less than 2 years all the way up to Vintage, which are Madeiras that have aged for more than 20 years. Unless a Madeira specifically states a vintage year on the bottle, it's likely to be a combination of several years' worth of grapes. Some Madeiras are still produced via the *solera* method (also used to make Sherry), in which rows of wine barrels are stacked from oldest (on the bottom) to youngest (on the top). As the oldest wine is drawn from the barrels on the bottom row, it is replaced with the second-oldest wine from the barrels in the row above, which is then replaced with the third-oldest wine from barrels in the row above it, and so forth. In this manner, multiple vintages are blended together.

Madeiras are fabulously long-lived. Occasionally, a devoted Madeira fan will run across a bottle on the market that hails from the late 1700s. Reportedly, Sotheby's auction house recently sold a bottle of Thomas Jefferson's own Madeira, which the buyer planned to drink.

Port

Port, Portugal's most famous wine, is available in many styles, nearly all of them sweet. If it's the genuine article from its native Portugal, the wine is called Porto. This sturdy, long-lived wine became popular back in the era of tall ships because it was one of the few wines that could survive a long, rugged voyage at sea. Some of the best recent years for Port are 2000, 1997, 1995, 1994, 1992, 1991, 1987, 1985, 1983, and 1980.

Ports may be red or white and are made from any of nearly 100 grapes, although only about a dozen are widely used. The following are some of the most popular styles of Port:

- **White Port:** Simple, cheap, and somewhat rare outside Portugal; usually sweet.

- **Ruby Port:** The simplest and cheapest red Port; sweet and tangy; fine for casual drinking.

- **Tawny Port:** Often a blend of Ruby and White Ports. Tawny Ports range in quality—the higher-end versions state how long they've aged (the finest may be more than 20 years old). **Young Tawny Port** is light colored and is a good aperitif; higher-quality **Aged Tawny Port,** aged 10 to 40 years, is a good aperitif and after-dinner drink.

- **Crusted Port:** A blend of vintages with lots of sediment, this type of Port is becoming rare.

- **Vintage Port:** The finest quality—and most expensive—style of Port. Vintage Port is made only in years when the quality of the grapes harvested is officially declared to be superior. It's usually aged for two years before bottling, and then requires a decade or more of bottle aging.

- **Vintage Character Port:** Good quality; blended with other Ports; some is barrel aged.

- **Late-Bottled Vintage Port:** Aged four to six years; not as good as Vintage.

- **Traditional Late-Bottled Vintage Port:** Becoming rare; aged four years; released ready to drink, but can age for many more years.

student experience

"Make sure your first taste of a fortified wine is a quality wine. My first experience with fortified wines was a cheap Sherry that a friend brought to a dinner party. It really turned me off the concept until another friend insisted I try a Port he picked up. It was fabulous and I've been a huge fan ever since. If you've had a bad wine experience in the past, have someone help you pick out a good example of that type and try it again; you might be surprised."

—Phoebe, bartender

- **Single Quinta Vintage Port:** Made entirely from a single estate *(quinta)* and year, usually aged two years and released ready to drink.

Port is usually served as an aperitif or after-dinner drink. White and Tawny Ports are typically served chilled; the rest may be served lightly chilled or at room temperature. Crusted Port, as the name implies, needs decanting, as may some of the other older styles. Most Ports will keep for a few weeks, or even a few months, after being opened.

Sherry

From Jerez, Spain, home of bullfighting and flamenco dancing, comes Sherry, a rich, nutty, strongly fortified wine. Most Sherries are made from the Palomino grape. Like many other fortified wines, Sherry owes its intense character to a process of careful, intentional oxidation. Like Madeira, Sherry is made by using the solera method of blending wine from sequential barrels, ranging from oldest to youngest.

Popular styles of Sherry include the following:

- **Fino:** A dry, pale style of Sherry that pairs well with seafood. Serve well chilled. Keeps for about a week once opened.

- **Amontillado:** Aged Fino Sherry that receives a second dose of fortification after it leaves the solera. Darker and richer than Fino, Amontillado ranges from sweet to semi-dry. Serve lightly chilled. Keeps for about a month once opened.

- **Manzanilla:** A light, dry Sherry with a crisp tang reminiscent of the sea. Serve well chilled. Keeps for about a week once opened.

- **Oloroso:** A richer, more aromatic Sherry than most other styles, Oloroso undergoes substantial oxidation during its production, which results in a dark color and a walnutlike essence. Most of today's Oloroso is sweet. Serve at room temperature or lightly chilled. Keeps for two or three months after being opened.

- **Pedro Ximénez:** A dark, thick, sweet style of Sherry produced from the grape of the same name, rather than the Palomino grape used to make most other Sherries. It's often served as a dessert wine. Serve lightly chilled. Keeps for two or three months after being opened.

- **Cream:** Oloroso Sherry mixed with Pedro Ximénez to create a rich, sweet wine. Serve at room temperature or lightly chilled. Keeps for two or three months after being opened.

A popular ingredient in cooking, Sherry is also served chilled as an aperitif. Its nutty aroma and flavor make it an ideal partner for nuts. It's fun to match the Sherry style to the type of nut its character suggests; for instance, serve Fino Sherry with almonds and pair Oloroso Sherry with walnuts.

Store Sherry as you would other wines: in a cool, dark place. Unlike many of its fortified brethren, Sherry generally doesn't keep long after being opened. A dry style of Sherry may fade after only a few days; others may keep for a month or more in the refrigerator.

Aperitif and Dessert Wines

Aperitif and dessert wines are typically very sweet. They're generally made from late-season grapes loaded with sugars or from grapes affected by the *botrytis cinerea* fungus, which dries the grapes and concentrates their sugars. These wines are served before or after a meal or by themselves. They may be served *with* dessert or *as* dessert. Sauternes, Barsac, and Tokay Aszu are among the most famous dessert wines.

Dessert wines are designed more for leisurely sipping than for quaffing. Nearly every wine-producing country makes a variety of these wines. When they're poorly made, dessert wines can be unpleasantly cloying and saccharine; when they're well crafted—particularly when they retain a certain amount of acidity to balance the sweetness—they can be elegant and complex.

The *botrytis* fungus, called "noble rot," bores into the grape and saps its moisture. The juices that remain inside the desiccated grape are super-concentrated: They have all the complexity of—and a much higher sugar content than—fresh grapes. Wines made from botrytized grapes are expensive because even the most skilled wine-grower can't predict when, where, or whether the fungus will attack, and because a lot of intensive labor goes into making this type of wine. But at least once in your wine-drinking career, split the cost with friends and try a fine Sauternes, Barsac, or Tokay Aszu.

a note from
the instructor

THE REAL THING IS FROM FRANCE

Your local wine shop may sell a dessert wine called Sauterne, with or without the final S, but beware—this may *not* be the genuine article from the Sauternes district in France. Many sweet dessert wines produced in the United States (with or without botrytized grapes) have borrowed the name of France's famous dessert wine. We've heard that some of these American wines are downright drinkable, so if you're curious, by all means try them. But if you want to experience the real thing, fuzzy gray French grapes and all, make sure that your bottle of Sauternes has both an S at the end of the name and is from France.

Sauternes and Barsac

Sauternes and Barsac are prized French dessert wines often made from Sémillon and Sauvignon Blanc grapes, which are traditionally harvested by hand and must be infected with the *botrytis cinerea* fungus. Made from the same two grapes by the same procedure, Sauternes and Barsac are named for the Bordeaux subregions in which they're grown. Sauternes tends to be richer than Barsac, which is made from grapes grown in chalkier soils.

The best Sauternes and Barsac are exquisitely complex and sweet and have a long, lingering finish. Honey and apricots are two of the more common flavor descriptors. These wines can age for 10 to 20 years. The best recent years for these wines are 2000, 1995, 1990, 1989, 1988, 1986, 1985, 1983, and 1981.

Store your Sauternes and Barsac in a cool, quiet place. Serve them lightly chilled, alone or with dessert or strong cheese. Their sweetness is so powerful that they need to be paired with rich desserts (but not terribly sweet ones—see Chapter 14 for pairing wines and foods) like crèmes and custards or sharply flavored foods like blue cheese and foie gras.

Tokay Aszu

Hungary's most famous wine, Tokay Aszu, is often acclaimed as the world's best dessert wine. Like Sauternes and Barsac, Tokay Aszu is made from botrytized grapes, but instead of being made of Sémillon or Sauvignon Blanc, Tokay Aszu is traditionally made from the native Hungarian grape Furmint. Its crisp acidity keeps its sweetness from becoming too overpowering and enables it to pair well with blue cheeses and rich, creamy desserts.

KOSHER WINES

Kosher wines have come a long way. In times past, they suffered a bad reputation for their overwhelming sweetness. Much U.S.-made kosher wine has the added disadvantage of coming from native *vitis labrusca* grapes, which taste about as much like European varieties as cough syrup tastes like cherries jubilee. The most popular brand, Manischewitz, is made from Concord grapes, the same grape used to make grape juice and jelly.

Today's kosher wines have improved substantially. In fact, some kosher wines are now considered world class. This category is likely to expand in the future.

---

abcdefghijklmnopq
rstuvwxyzabcdefgh
ijklmnopqrstuvwxy

a note from
the instructor

KOSHER, KOSHER FOR PASSOVER, AND MEVUSHAL

These three categories affect the process by which a kosher wine is made, according to the purpose for which it's intended:

■ **Kosher:** These wines are made according to methods that satisfy rabbinical requirements for religious Jews. They're produced under strict rabbinical supervision.

■ **Kosher for Passover:** In addition to the preceding kosher restrictions, these wines must not have come into contact with bread, dough, or leavening at any time during their production, or from the moment they leave the winemaker's hands to the time they arrive at the table. (Religious Jews must abstain from these substances during Passover.)

■ **Mevushal:** *Mevushal* is the process of rendering a kosher wine acceptable to be served to Jews by non-Jews during religious observations. Mevushal wines were once boiled, a process that destroyed nearly everything that made them worth drinking. Today's mevushal wines are pasteurized by a modern method that preserves their finer qualities.

JUNK AND JUG WINE

There's nothing wrong with drinking junk and jug wines if you happen to like them, but be forewarned that when you're sojourning among serious wine drinkers, two types of wine are definitely verboten: the so-called junk wines like Thunderbird and Night Train and the bland mass-market jug wines sold by mega-producers.

The purpose of screw-cap cheapies like Night Train, MD 20/20, Boone's Farm, and Thunderbird is pretty obvious: They're a low-budget way to get drunk fast. They're a whopping commercial success because they fulfill their purpose pretty well. Flavor is irrelevant. 'Nuff said.

Jug wines are a different story. They're made to provide a casual experience—not necessarily a drunken one, but a fun one. For simplicity's sake, we'll include in this category all casual wines, from $8 gallons of Chardonnay to wine coolers and bottled wine cocktails. Flavor does matter to a degree: Jug wines do need to taste nice. But they don't have to taste complex, outstanding, or challenging. In fact, for a really laid-back dinner, who would want them to?

The vast majority of wine from every wine-producing country falls into this category. Most of it stays in its own country. California makes gallons and gallons of inexpensive, great-quality jug wine. Most of it doesn't bother with pretense, but a small amount of everyday wine tries to portray itself as something higher class. Beware: Some grape varieties, like French Colombard, may sound sophisticated but are grown primarily for the jug wine market. Sometimes the better-respected grapes, like Gamay, are used to make lesser-quality wines. You can't go wrong if you arm yourself with knowledge; know what you're drinking and you'll never be caught serving the wine equivalent of fish sticks at a Lobster Thermador moment.

Again, there's nothing wrong with drinking these wines if you enjoy them—and we hope you never become a wine snob incapable of having fun with simple, easy wines. But among serious wine enthusiasts, you're better off letting loose with a sonorous, ripping belch than mentioning one of these "lowbrow" wines. Just remember that old maxim about there being a time for everything. When you're in the company of fine-wine lovers, break out your most cultivated tastes and sophisticated knowledge. When you're picnicking with your best friends, drop the pretense and knock back whatever you like.

north america's wine regions

The United States • Canada • Mexico

North America's fine wines have come a long way in the past few decades. California's trailblazing wine industry is legendary throughout the world and is a model for wine producers in other countries. Oregon, Washington, and New York have firmly established themselves in the wine world, and other states are following suit. Canada, too, has made notable contributions—and Mexico is new on the radar. In this lesson, we take a closer look at the wines of North America.

THE UNITED STATES

Although Americans don't drink nearly as much wine as Europeans do, the United States is the fourth-largest wine producer in the world—despite the fact that the lion's share of the U.S. wine industry, and particularly its fine-wine industry, is only a few decades old. Every U.S. state produces wine, but California leads the pack.

Increasing numbers of U.S. citizens have developed a taste for wine in recent decades because the California wine industry has made good

wines so abundant. Consumption also has risen since the announce-
ment in the 1980s of wine's health benefits. Moreover, since the 1970s,
there's been a growing trend toward quality in American wine. Today,
California, New York, the Pacific Northwest, and now Texas and Virginia
offer high-quality wines.

The U.S. wine industry is the epitome of New World thinking. It's
modern, high-tech, experimental, and commercially focused. Its goals are
not to make a wine taste like a perfect example of its variety or to make
a wine that tastes of its terroir, but simply to make a wine that tastes
good. American wines are more approachable and less intimidating
than European wines, although European wine loyalists might call many
of them bland and monochromatic. Furthermore, U.S. wine labels actually make sense and the prices of U.S. wine have remained reasonable.

Many American wines are made from crosses between the classic
European *vitis vinifera* vines and the native *vitis labrusca.* These hybrid
grapes are much more resistant to the vine-destroying *phylloxera* mite,
which has been a problem for U.S. winegrowers for centuries. America
had been trying to get a wine industry started since the seventeenth
century, but this tiny pest kept foiling it. The colonists' attempts to cultivate the European vines they brought from their homes on the other
side of the Atlantic failed.

Wines made from the abundant native *vitis labrusca* grapes alone left
much to be desired: They didn't taste much like wine from European
grapes, and many wine lovers found them downright nasty. It wasn't
until the advent of hybrids and grafting in the mid-nineteenth century
that American wines got a foothold. Then two world wars, Prohibition,
and the Great Depression kept the fledgling industry straggling, until in
the 1960s and 1970s a group of visionary investors opened a series of
bold new wineries in California. The rest is winemaking history.

American Wine Classification

Classification of U.S. wines began in 1978 with the establishment
of American Viticultural Areas (AVAs). Like France's AOC (Appellation d'Origine Contrôlée; see Lesson 7), each AVA is defined by its
geographical features. But AVAs don't carry the same restrictions on
grape types and quantities grown as their French counterparts. American winemakers may plant any variety of grape they want. Today, the
United States has more than 140 registered AVAs.

If an AVA is identified on the wine label, at least 85 percent of the grape must be from that AVA. If an AVA is not named, the grapes are not required to have come from any particular AVA. Similarly, if a label identifies a vintage, 95 percent of the wine must be from that year; and if it identifies a key grape used, at least 75 percent of the wine must be this variety. Although not all American wines are blends, winemakers may blend as they see fit—the only restriction to blending is on what types of labels their wines can wear.

California

California winemakers are the pioneers of a new age of wine. The investors and speculators who moved here in the 1960s and 1970s to establish wineries shunned tradition and took a more adventurous— and more commercial—approach to their industry. Their bold methods (for instance, defining a wine predominantly by style and blend rather than by terroir or variety, and producing wine on a massive scale) proved so successful that they were soon attracting winemakers from Europe, who enjoyed the freedom to experiment that had been denied them in their homelands.

Californians make really good jug wines: friendly, likable, casual sippers that harmonize with the hang-loose California spirit. Gallo, the wine giant (which alone outproduces some winemaking countries), and a few others were the major players in establishing the California jug wine business. But from the beginning, and increasingly as fine-wine consumption rises worldwide, California has produced (and produces) some downright elegant wines. Its Cabernet Sauvignons, Merlots, and Chardonnays are distinctive, and its fruity contribution, Zinfandel, is a perennial favorite.

California Wine Regions

California has proven to be the ideal staging point for this U.S. wine-making revolution. It boasts an enormous variety of soils and climates, many similar to Europe's, but they impart their own special qualities to the wine. Its diverse wine-growing regions range from the baking-hot Central Valley to Mendocino's cool coastal climate.

Following is a brief description of California's major wine-growing regions, although wineries can be found all over California.

NORTH: A few hours to the north of San Francisco—even farther north than Napa Valley, Sonoma County, and Carneros—these three wine regions are spread across the northernmost third of the state, with Mendocino the farthest west, Lake County in the middle, and the Sierra Foothills the farthest east.

- **Mendocino:** Mendocino's rugged coastal vineyards produce Chardonnay, Gewürztraminer, Petite Sirah, Sauvignon Blanc, Zinfandel, and a few rare Mediterranean varieties like Arneis and Fiano.

- **Lake County:** This county contains a huge body of water known as Clear Lake. Lake County vineyards produce fine Pinot Noirs, plus Chardonnay, Gewürztraminer, Sauvignon Blanc, and Zinfandel. Wine producer Kendall-Jackson makes its home here.

- **The Sierra Foothills** (El Dorado and Amador counties): This mountainous region features areas of volcanic soil. At the higher elevations, the grapes remain small but their flavors are highly concentrated. The Sierra Foothills area produces Cabernet Sauvignon, Syrah, and Zinfandel.

Major producers in these northern wine regions include Boeger, Guenoc, Hidden Cellars, Kendall-Jackson, Lava Cap, Lolonis, Montevino, Navarro Vineyards, Renwood, Roederer Estate (which makes a fine sparkling wine called L'Ermitage), and Steele.

---

abcdefghijklmnopq *rstuvwxyzabcdefgh* *ijklmnopqrstuvwxyz* **a note from the instructor**

ROBERT MONDAVI: CALIFORNIA'S VARIETAL WINE PIONEER

In 1979, a bold new wine phenomenon came to California: Opus One, the joint venture between Baron Phillipe de Rothschild (of Bordeaux's famous Mouton-Rothschild) and wine pioneer Robert Mondavi. Mondavi experimented with a range of winemaking techniques—everything from barrel types to filtration methods—but he's probably best known for his work with *varietals*, or wines made from a particular kind of grape. Working with several classic French vine varieties, he developed innovative new styles of each wine. The result: California-grown wines with their own distinct personalities.

NORTH COAST: These three popular wine regions are clustered due north of San Francisco.

- **Napa Valley:** Although it produces only 4 percent of California's wine, the name Napa Valley has become synonymous with elegant wines. This mountainous area features numerous soil types, some of which are volcanic. Its climate is moderate.

  Napa Valley produces fine Cabernet Sauvignon, Chardonnay, Merlot, and Zinfandel. It's also home to California's unique Meritage wines: blends of Cabernet Sauvignon, Merlot, Cabernet Franc, Malbec, Petit Verdot, Gros Verdot, and Carmenére. White Meritage blends Sauvignon Blanc, Sauvignon Vert, and Sémillon.

- **Sonoma County:** Sonoma's wines are frequently compared to Napa Valley's, but the culture among Sonoma's winemaking community is more laid back. Sonoma vineyards and wineries, which lie to the southwest of Napa Valley, produce magnificent Cabernet Sauvignons, Pinot Noirs, and Rieslings, plus a dazzling variety of other wines—all in a breathtaking setting. Sonoma is home to the giant wine franchise of Ernest and Julio Gallo.

- **Carneros:** Smaller than its famous neighbor, the Napa Valley, Carneros is a cool region suffused with ocean air. Carneros's climate allows for the slow ripening that creates complex, elegant wines. Its landscape is a series of low, undulating hills. Carneros is noted for its Pinot Noir and Chardonnay.

student experience

"One great piece of advice I got when I first became interested in wine was to choose one region in one country to learn about (I chose Napa Valley in the U.S.).

"Whenever I went to wine stores or restaurants, I tried Napa Valley wines and slowly figured out what I liked and didn't like. When I found a wine I liked, I looked up the vineyard on the Web and read about it.

"Later, as I began exploring wines from other countries, I had something to compare them to and was much more confident when ordering a new wine at a restaurant."

—Brendhan, software engineer

Major producers on the north coast include Arrowood Vineyards, Beaulieu Vineyards, Beringer Vineyards, Carneros Creek, Etude, Peter Michael Winery, Mumm, Opus One, Joseph Phelps Vineyards, Ridge, Rochioli Vineyards, Saintsbury, Shafer Vineyards, Silver Oak Cellars, Stags' Leap Wine Cellars, Stony Hill Vineyard, and Trefethen Vineyards.

NORTHERN CENTRAL COAST AND LIVERMORE VALLEY: The following two subregions lie to the south of San Francisco in the central third of the state. The Livermore Valley rests to the south of Oakland; the regions of the northern central coast encompass the land around Monterey, Carmel, and Salinas. Unfortunately, much of this region, particularly around San Francisco, is losing out to the demand for housing. Its Pinot Noirs are fabulous, its Zinfandels are rich, and its sparkling wines are of high quality.

- **Livermore Valley:** Similar in geography and climate to southern France, the Livermore Valley is hot in the daytime, cold at night, and frequently windy. These conditions make for rustic, Rhône-like wines (see Lesson 7 for details on this French region). Chardonnay, Cabernet Sauvignon, Zinfandel, and Petite Sirah are grown here.

- **Santa Clara Valley, Santa Cruz Mountains, Monterey County, Mount Harlan, Carmel Valley, Chalone:** These areas are largely coastal and mountainous and feature a number of microclimates. Some areas offer a low yield because of difficult terrain; others, like Monterey County, share space with major agricultural production. Much of the area offers the cool climate that Pinot Noir and Chardonnay like; other portions are bathed in the brilliant warmth that Cabernet Sauvignon, Merlot, and Zinfandel prefer. Chalone, Mount Harlan, and Carmel Valley contain limestone soils like those in Burgundy, France and produce fine Pinot Noirs and Chardonnays.

Some of the northern central coast's and Livermore Valley's major producers are Bonny Doon Vineyard, Calera, Durney Vineyards, Cedar Mountain, Chalone Vineyard, Chouinard, Concannon Vineyard, Mer Soleil, Mirassou, Morgan, Murrieta's Well, Ridge, and Wente Vineyards.

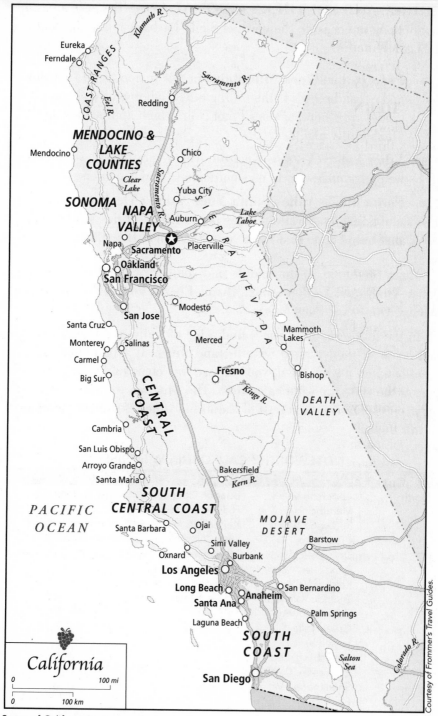

Eureka
Ferndale
COAST RANGES
Klamath R.
Sacramento R.
Eel R.
Redding
MENDOCINO &
LAKE
COUNTIES
Mendocino
Chico
Clear
Lake
Sacramento R.
SONOMA
NAPA
VALLEY
Yuba City
Auburn
Lake
Tahoe
Napa
Sacramento
Placerville
Oakland
San Francisco
SIERRA
Modesto
San Jose
Santa Cruz
NEVADA
Monterey
Salinas
Merced
Mammoth
Lakes
Carmel
Big Sur
CENTRAL
COAST
Fresno
Bishop
Kings R.
DEATH
VALLEY
Cambria
San Luis Obispo
Arroyo Grande
Santa Maria
Bakersfield
Kern R.
SOUTH
CENTRAL COAST
PACIFIC
OCEAN
Santa Barbara
Ojai
MOJAVE
DESERT
Barstow
Simi Valley
Oxnard
Burbank
Los Angeles
San Bernardino
Long Beach
Anaheim
Santa Ana
Palm Springs
Laguna Beach
SOUTH
COAST
Salton
Sea
Colorado R.
California
0   100 mi
0   100 km
San Diego

Courtesy of Frommer's Travel Guides.

Some of California's wine-producing regions.

MIDDLE AND SOUTHERN CENTRAL COAST: These areas are found along the coast to the north of Santa Barbara and to the south of the Carmel Valley.

- **Paso Robles/York Mountain:** In this region, gentle sunshine and ocean breezes bathe rolling hills. Cabernet, Syrah, and Zinfandel grow here, as does Pinot Noir, which appreciates the area's chilly nights.

- **Edna Valley/Arroyo Grande:** This region's cool, wet breezes help give character to its Chardonnays and Viogniers.

- **Santa Maria Valley/Santa Ynez Valley:** The Santa Maria and Santa Ynez valleys enjoy ocean fog and brisk sea breezes that help create fine Pinot Noir, Sauvignon Blanc, and Syrah.

Major producers in the middle and southern central coast include Alban Vineyards, Au Bon Climat, Byron, Eberle, Foxen, Peachy Canyon Winery, Qupe, and Zaca Mesa.

In the following table you'll find a list of California regions, AVAs, and a few of their typical wineries and wines. If a particular AVA is mentioned on a wine label, you can use this chart to determine which part of the state the wine came from. The wineries you'll find here are only representative; hundreds of California wineries are not mentioned in this table.

NOTEWORTHY CALIFORNIA WINERIES

REGIONS	AVAS	WINERIES	WINES
North	Anderson Valley, Mendocino, Redwood Valley, Clear Lake, Dry Creek Valley, Alexander Valley, Knights Valley, Guenoc Valley, Solano County, Green Valley, Suisun Valley, Clarksburg, Lodi, El Dorado, California Shenandoah Valley, Fiddletown	Boeger, Guenoc, Hidden Cellars, Kendall-Jackson, Lava Cap, Lolonis, Montevino, Navarro Vineyards, Renwood, Roederer Estate, Steele	Chardonnay, Gewürztraminer, Petite Sirah, Sauvignon Blanc, Syrah, Zinfandel

REGIONS	AVAS	WINERIES	WINES
North Coast	Napa Valley, Sonoma, Carneros	Acacia, Arrowood Vineyards, Beaulieu Vineyard, Beringer Vineyards, Carneros Creek, Domaine Carneros, Etude, Iron Horse, Littorai, Mason, Peter Michael Winery, Mumm Cuvée Napa, Joseph Phelps, Pride Mountain Vineyards, Ridge, Rochioli Vineyards, Saintsbury, Schramsburg Vineyards, Shafer, Silver Oak, Stags' Leap Winery, Stony Hill, Trefethen	Chardonnay, Merlot, Cabernet Sauvignon, Zinfandel, Meritage
Northern Central Coast	Livermore Valley, Santa Clara Valley, Santa Cruz Mountains, Mount Harlan, Carmel Valley, Chalone, Santa Lucia Highlands, Arroyo Seco, San Lucas	Bonny Doon Vineyard, Calera, Durney Vineyards, Cedar Mountain, Chalone Vineyard, Chouinard, Concannon Vineyard, Mer Soleil, Mirassou, Morgan, Murrieta's Well, Ridge, Wente Vineyards	Chardonnay, Cabernet Sauvignon, Zinfandel, Petite Sirah, Pinot Noir
Middle and Southern Central Coast	Paso Robles, York Mountain, Edna Valley, Arroyo Grande, Santa Maria Valley, Santa Ynez Valley	Alban Vineyards, Au Bon Climat, Byron, Eberle, Foxen, Peachy Canyon Winery, Qupe, Zaca Mesa	Chardonnay, Pinot Noir, Viognier, Sauvignon Blanc

*Note: Not all the wineries mentioned carry all the wines listed for that particular region.

California Wine Characteristics

Although California boasts an ever-growing number of wine specialties, its unique Cabernet Sauvignon is what put it on the wine-lover's map. Thirty years ago, California Cabernet was somewhat harsh; over decades of development, however, it has taken on a lush, velvety quality, with overtones of mint (and some say chocolate) found nowhere else in the world. Most California Cabernets will age well for five to eight years. The state's Pinot Noir, particularly from Carneros, is the best made outside of France.

New York

With deep, well-drained soil and reflective waters that vines love, plus a cool climate that creates grapes of character, New York produces quality Riesling and Chardonnay, as well as wines from native varieties like Concord, Cayuga, and Catawba. Most people still think of jelly, juice, and table grapes when they think of New York, because that was the direction the industry headed during Prohibition. In fact, Welch's, the enormous jelly and juice producer, still makes its home here. Today, New York is growing an increasing number of French and German wine grape varieties—and much of the wine that results is world class.

New York Wine Regions

Although the climate throughout the state lends itself well to cold-weather white and German varieties, New York also grows its fair share of reds, including Cabernet Franc, Cabernet Sauvignon, Merlot, and Pinot Noir. The following major regions are further subdivided into AVAs:

- **Hudson River Valley:** One of the earliest areas of American settlement, this large historic region first began growing wine in 1677. It is currently planting a vast array of varieties, both popular and rare, many grown experimentally.

- **Finger Lakes:** One of the largest, fastest-growing wine-producing areas in the state, the Finger Lakes district produces a number of fine Rieslings and sparkling wines (such as blanc de blancs), as well as wines from popular hybrids.

- **Lake Erie:** This is ground zero for the nonwine grape industry, producing 95 percent of its grapes for jelly and juice. Many of the wines from the region, including a number of kosher wines, are made from Concord grapes.

- **Long Island:** The newest New York wine area, the North Fork of Long Island is home to a great deal of Bordeaux-inspired winemaking. The area is doing particularly well with Merlot and is coming along nicely with Cabernet Sauvignon, Sémillon, Riesling, and Chardonnay.

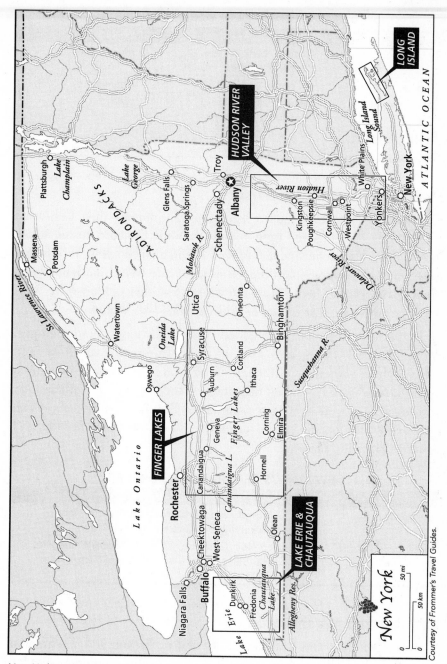

New York's wine-producing regions.

Courtesy of Frommer's Travel Guides.

NOTEWORTHY NEW YORK WINERIES

AVAS	WINERIES	WINES
Long Island	Gristina, Lenz Winery, Palmer Vineyards	Merlot, blends
Hudson River	Millbrook	Chardonnay
Lake Erie	Merritt Estate Winery, Woodbury Vineyards	Hybrids
Finger Lakes	Bully Hill Vineyards, Standing Stone Vineyards	Riesling, Gewürztraminer

New York Wine Characteristics

Surprisingly, New York makes a brisker Chardonnay than California does and its Rieslings are light and clear. Many Concord kosher wines like Kedem, Manischewitz, and Mogen David also call New York home. New York's refreshing sparkling wines are made from Chardonnay and Pinot Blanc grapes. Some of its ice wines (like that produced by Wagner Vineyards) are made from hybrid varieties like Vignoles.

In the following chart, you'll find New York's most popular grapes. We've divided them into two groups: European varieties and native/hybrid varieties. Although other states produce wines from hybrids, New York has taken this practice further than any other state. The result is a wine that tastes similar to European varieties yet can better resist the deadly phylloxera mite. New York wines from hybrid varieties are often blended.

NEW YORK'S LEADING WINE GRAPES

VARIETIES	GRAPES
European	Cabernet Franc, Cabernet Sauvignon, Merlot, Chardonnay, Gewürztraminer, Riesling
Native and hybrid	Baco Noir, Catawba, Cayuga, Concord, Niagara, Seyval Blanc, Vidal Blanc, Vignoles (also known as Ravat)

Oregon and Washington

With less sunlight and heat than other states, Oregon and Washington may seem like unlikely wine regions. Yet they produce unique, complex wines in years when the weather cooperates, and conditions in parts of these states are wonderful for finicky Pinot Noir.

Oregon

Although Oregon produces elegant Cabernet Sauvignon and Merlot, Pinot Noir is its specialty. Oregon's Pinot Noirs are low in acid and high in tannin (you can age them for three to five years). Native Oregonians love to drink it with local grilled salmon, which proves that there's an exception to the white-wine-with-fish rule. The best recent years for Oregon Pinot Noir are 1998 to 2002.

Oregon's other most famous wine is the hip, spicy, dry white wine Pinot Gris, whose focused fruit makes it a perfect complement to food. Oregonians enjoy it with salmon, trout, sturgeon, barbecued prawns, crab cakes, and fish stew, among other regional favorites. David Lett of Eyrie Vineyards brought both Pinot Noir and Pinot Gris to Oregon in the 1960s. Today, Oregon's production of Pinot Gris is greater than that of Chardonnay or Sauvignon Blanc. Oregon Pinot Gris ranges in price from less than $10 to more than $30 per bottle.

Oregon's AVAs include Columbia Valley, Rogue Valley, Umpqua Valley, and Willamette Valley. A few of Oregon's noteworthy wineries are Adelsheim, Amity, Bethel Heights, Cameron, Domaine Drouhin, Elk Cove, King Estate, Ponzi, and Yamhill Valley.

Washington

Warmer and drier than Oregon, the state of Washington produces wonderfully structured Merlot and Cabernet Sauvignon. Its red wines carry distinctive blackberry, raspberry, boysenberry, and cherry flavors. The Yakima Valley has its own specialty, a light, fruity, low-acid red called Lemberger, named for the rare German Limberger (or Blaufrankisch) grape from which it's made. Washington's Lemberger *can* be found outside the state—although it takes some diligent hunting to locate it.

Washington's wine regions are Puget Sound, Columbia Valley, Yakima Valley, and Walla Walla. The following table shows representative wines and wineries.

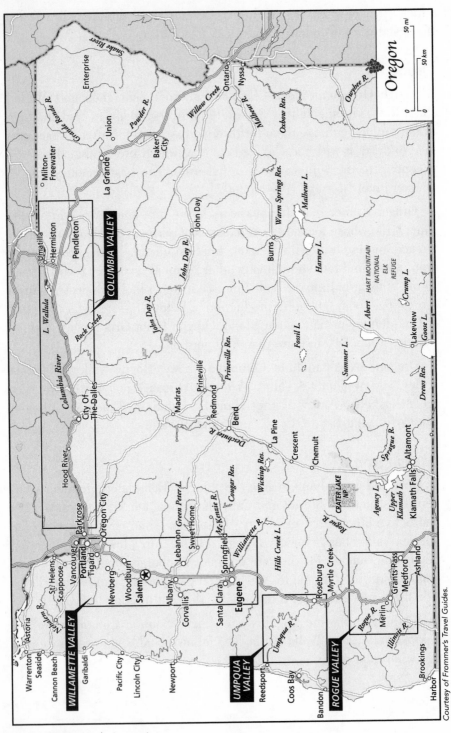

Oregon's wine-producing regions.

Courtesy of Frommer's Travel Guides.

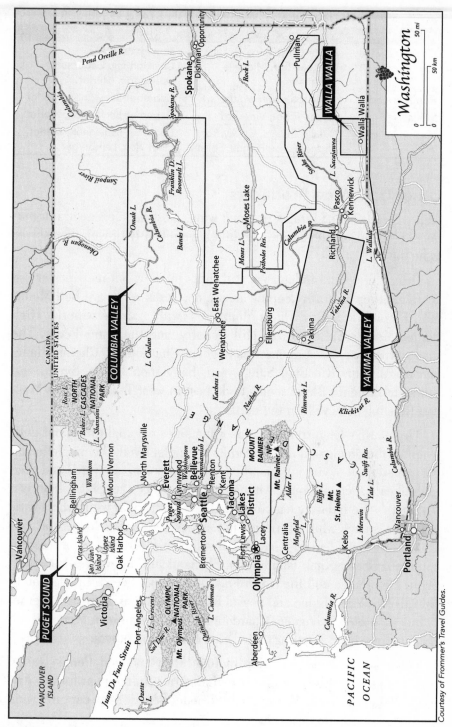

Washington's wine-producing regions.

Courtesy of Frommer's Travel Guides.

SOME NOTEWORTHY WASHINGTON STATE WINERIES

AVAS	WINERIES	WINES
Columbia Valley	Arbor Crest Wine Cellars, Chateau Ste. Michelle, Snoqualmie	Sauvignon Blanc, Chardonnay, Cabernet Sauvignon, Merlot
Puget Sound	Quilceda Creek Vintners	Cabernet Sauvignon, Merlot
Walla Walla	Canoe Ridge Vineyard	Cabernet Sauvignon, Merlot
Yakima Valley	DeLille Cellars, Covey Run Vintners, The Hogue Cellars	Cabernet Sauvignon, Merlot, Pinot Noir, Lemberger

Other U.S. Wine Producers

Although all 50 U.S. states produce wine, most have escaped international recognition. Texas and Virginia have recently proven themselves to be the exceptions.

Texas's fine-wine industry is still in its infancy, but its wines are so good that they're worth keeping an eye on. Texas AVAs are Bell Mountain, Escondido Valley, Davis Mountains (with a single winery), High Plains, Mesilla Valley, Texas Hill Country, and the Trans-Pecos. The state currently grows Cabernet Sauvignon, Chardonnay, Chenin Blanc, Merlot, Muscat, Riesling, Sangiovese, Sauvignon Blanc, Syrah, and Zinfandel. Chenin Blanc seems to do best in west Texas, as does Muscat; Riesling does well in the north.

Virginia has been trying to grow wine since colonial times, but until recently, the phylloxera mite foiled its attempts. Even Thomas Jefferson got in on the act of viniculture—he visited European vineyards and tried to duplicate them at home, without success. Since the 1970s, however, Virginia's wine industry has finally achieved a toehold with hybrid varieties and French whites. Virginia has six AVAs: Monticello (central Virginia), Northern Neck (George Washington's birthplace in eastern Virginia), Rocky Knob (southwest), Shenandoah Valley (west), Eastern Shore (northeast), and the North Fork of Roanoke (west). In addition to hybrids like Vidal Blanc and Seyval Blanc, Virginia is growing Cabernet Franc, Cabernet Sauvignon, Chardonnay, Gewürztraminer, Merlot, Pinot Grigio, Pinot Noir, Riesling, Sauvignon Blanc, and others.

Other states worth watching include Maryland and Pennsylvania, which are also cultivating fine-wine industries. In the near future, Arizona, Missouri, New Mexico, and Rhode Island may capture wine enthusiasts' attention as well.

CANADA

One of the up-and-coming wine-producing nations is Canada, known for its ice wine, made from frozen grapes (usually Riesling or Vidal Blanc) harvested in winter. It also produces Gamay as well as other French varieties. The Okanagan Valley of British Columbia and the Niagara Peninsula of Ontario are Canada's two primary wine regions, producing 80 percent or more of Canada's wine. Both areas are close to lakes, which moderate the climate. The majority of Canada's wines are white, since it offers few areas with a long-enough warm season to allow red varieties to ripen.

Canada's wine classification follows the French AOC model, with the Vintner's Quality Alliance (VQA) certifying wine regions by a precise set of standards. The VQA recognizes two quality levels: Provincial Designation (PD) and Designated Viticultural Area (DVA). Canada's DVAs are similar to U.S. AVAs; Its PDs are the equivalent of calling a given wine from California a California wine as opposed to a Sonoma wine.

Ontario currently has three DVAs: Niagara Peninsula, Pelee Island, and Lake Erie North Shore. British Columbia has four: Okanagan Valley, Similkameen Valley, Fraser Valley, and Vancouver Island. The following table shows the DVAs, wineries, and wines of Ontario and British Columbia.

CANADIAN DVAS, WINERIES, AND WINES

DVAS	WINERIES	WINES
Ontario: Niagara Peninsula, Pelee Island, Lake Erie North Shore	Cave Springs Cellars, Henry of Pelham Estate, Inniskillin', Pillitteri Estates Winery, Thirty Bench Vineyard and Winery, Vineland Estates Winery	Cabernet Franc, Chardonnay, Merlot, Riesling, hybrids, ice wine
British Columbia: Okanagan Valley, Similkameen Valley, Fraser Valley, Vancouver Island	Blue Mountain Vineyards, Burrowing Owl Vineyards, Hawthorne Mountain Vineyards, Quails' Gate Estate Winery, Sumac Ridge Estate, Tinhorn Creek Vineyards	Chardonnay, Gewürztraminer, Riesling, hybrids, ice wine

MEXICO

Though still in its infancy, Mexico's fine-wine industry is one to keep an eye on. Much of Mexico is too hot and dry for fine grape cultivation, but the country is full of tiny pockets of cooler, high-altitude micro-climates that are ideally suited to viticulture. Although small quantities of wine are produced in Querétaro, Sonora, and Zacatecas, the Baja Peninsula is the primary source (90 percent or more) of Mexico's fine table wine.

The four largest of Baja's dozen or so vineyards are La Cetto, Monte Xanic, Pedro Domecq, and Santo Tomas. Santo Tomas is by far the oldest of the four, having been planted with Mission grapes in the 1800s. Pedro Domecq, which got started in the brandy industry in the 1950s, now exports about half of the wine it produces, with 40 percent of its exports sold in Europe. Baja is also home to a handful of garage (small-scale) winemakers, many of whom produce fine wines in limited quantities.

Since the 1990s, Baja winemakers have been setting their sights on the international wine market. They've been moving toward growing varietal grapes (notably Cabernet Sauvignon) and toward the use of modern techniques and equipment.

Mexican wine is typically smooth, dry, and low in acid. Such high-tannin international favorites as Cabernet Sauvignon, Malbec, Merlot, Nebbiolo, and Syrah do well here, as do Grenache and Zinfandel. Mexico also grows several white varieties: Chardonnay, Chenin Blanc, Riesling, Sauvignon Blanc, Sémillon, and Viognier.

In the future, Mexican winemakers could do well to focus on aromatic reds and whites: Barbera, Sangiovese, Viognier, and the like. They face fierce competition over standard French varieties. As of now, few wine shops stock Mexican wines; the only sure way to find them is to go online (see Lesson 12)—or to Mexico.

france's wine regions

French Wine's Individuality • Wine Regions of Northern France • Wine Regions of Southern France • Wine Regions of Coastal France

France's dazzling array of wines comes from its patchwork of diverse soils and climates, ranging from chilly slopes and chalky soils to sunny regions carpeted with wildflowers. French wine is also deeply influenced by the cultures of its various regions. In this lesson, we take a closer look at France's fine wines and tour its legendary wine regions.

WHAT'S DISTINCTIVE ABOUT FRENCH WINE

Wine is a major part of French culture. The French have taken wine seriously since ancient times, and it shows in the wines they produce.

France produces more wine than any other country except Italy; it makes more *fine* wine than any other country in the world. France, more than any other country, rates its vineyards and their products strictly. In thousands of carefully regulated vineyards and wineries, it produces hundreds of wines, many of them the definitive examples of their types. France's complex, multitiered *château* system of classifying and ranking wines is also emulated throughout the world.

About two-thirds of French wine is red; 90 percent of it comes from 36 types of grape. All French grapes are descendants of varieties planted by the Romans in ancient times.

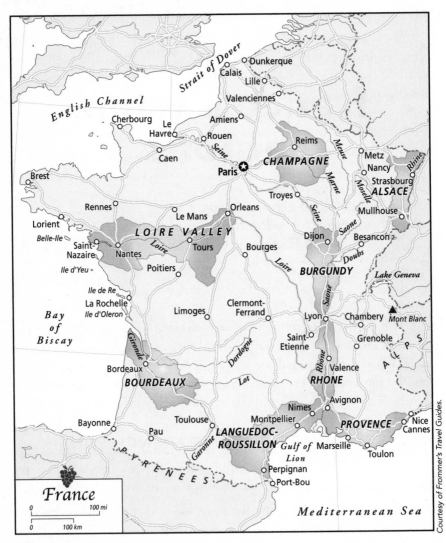

France's major wine regions.

France has many different ideal climates for producing wine—in fact, it has *all* of them, from northern regions that produce lively, high-acid wines to sun-drenched zones in the south that are home to many rustic, fragrant wines. France invented the concept of *terroir*, the idea that a wine's character comes from the harmony of its environment and its climate.

FRENCH WINE CLASSIFICATIONS

All French wines are classified according to quality, although the way these classifications are assigned varies significantly from region to region. Each wine's classification appears on its label. (Where on the label this information is placed varies somewhat from producer to producer.) The classification of any given wine doesn't *ensure* its quality, but rather states that a wine *should* have a certain level of quality. All four levels contain great and not-so-great wines.

In the following table, you'll find a list of France's wine classifications and what they mean.

FRANCE'S WINE QUALITY CLASSIFICATIONS

CLASSIFICATION	DESCRIPTION OF RANK	COMMENTS
Appellation d'Origine Con- trollée (AOC)	The top rank	Nearly every aspect of winemaking is strictly regulated for these wines.
Vins Délimités de Qualité Supérieure (VDQS)	Superior quality	The laws that govern production of these wines are strict, although not as strict as for AOC wines.
Vins de Pays	Literally "country wines"	Their quality is controlled, although not to the extent of the top two levels. Some wines in this classification are pretty good. Most are affordable.
Vins de Table	The lowest rank	These wines may come from any part of France. Usually, they're blends. They're not assigned a vintage.

The cornerstone of the French classification system is the *Appellation d'Origine Controllée* (AOC), which translates to "regulated place name." On an AOC bottle of Sauternes, for example, the designation appears on the label as *Appellation Sauternes Controllée.* AOCs are strictly governed; only specific regions qualify, and these regions may grow only certain grapes, with a maximum yield. Obligatory winemaking standards and numerous other demands must be satisfied along the way.

If a wine doesn't quite merit an AOC rating, it may drop to the next level, *Vins Délimités de Qualité Supérieure* (VDQS). These wines still must meet exacting standards, but the laws are not quite as strict.

Below AOC and VDQS is the classification known as *Vins de Pays*— literally "country wine." The quality of Vins de Pays is controlled, but not as strictly as AOC or VDQS wines. Don't think that these wines are of poor quality, though: The fun thing about French wine is that national standards are so high that even a "lowly" Vin de Pays can be a wonderful find. The phrase *Vin de Pays* is always followed by a place name on the label, as in *Vin de Pays des Côtes du Tarn.*

Below Vins de Pays come *Vins de Table,* which, unlike the three higher quality rankings, are not assigned a vintage or a place of origin. Vins de Table are usually blends of grapes from many sources, and the laws controlling them are more relaxed. The Vins de Table classification generally appears on the label in roughly the same place as the other designations do—usually somewhere below the line that identifies the type of wine.

If the regulations stopped there, the system would all be too simple. On top of the AOC, VDQS, Vins de Pays, and Vins de Table designations, many French regions maintain classifications of their own. Bordeaux's system of *crus* ("growths," meaning "wine estates"), for instance, was established in 1855. That system ranked four elite crus (today there are five), continuing downward for several levels until it came to the *crus bourgeois.* Bordeaux ranks wines by quality—not necessarily the quality they *have,* but the quality they *ought* to have. Since the 1855 designation, few estates have changed their crus despite variations in quality and changes in ownership.

WINE REGIONS OF NORTHERN FRANCE: CHAMPAGNE, ALSACE, AND BURGUNDY

The vineyards of northern France endure cool, rainy temperatures that can create delicate wines but also can wreak havoc on a year's harvest. Chardonnay and Pinot Noir grow abundantly here. Chablis, Meursault, and many other wines named for their hometowns also hail from northern France, as do Champagnes and Burgundys.

Champagne

The Champagne region of France lies northeast of Paris. Reims, the ancient city famous for the coronation of kings, is found here. This region is home to the most celebrated beverage in the world: Other sparkling wines might be known as "Champagne," but the real thing is grown and made only here.

Champagne's climate is cool and damp, the kind of weather that often creates deep character in wine. Its legendary soils are full of chalk, minerals, and fossils, which are largely responsible for the wine's distinctive flavors.

Champagne is usually made from a blend of three grapes: Chardonnay, Pinot Noir, and Pinot Meunier. The traditional *méthode champenoise* of making Champagne from these grapes requires enormous effort. After cask fermentation, Champagnes are bottled and allowed to undergo a secondary fermentation. Because this fermentation takes place in the bottle, the carbon dioxide produced from the process has nowhere to go but back into the wine, hence the bubbles. Champagne bottles are inverted at an angle during the aging process so that the spent yeast cells collect in the bottlenecks. These cells are removed before the final corking. The result is an effervescent miracle, richer and characteristically creamier than any other sparkling wine on Earth.

In Champagne, the term *cru* refers to the 312 villages that produce grapes for Champagne. *Grand Cru* ("great growth") and *Premier Cru* ("first growth") are quality designations indicating higher-ranking villages.

The term *prestige cuvée* usually refers to a given producer's premium Champagne. Cuvée Champagnes typically are made with only the first pressings of a batch of grapes. Below prestige cuvée is vintage, and below that, nonvintage: the simplest, cheapest, and least-aged Champagne a producer sells.

The following table lists Champagne's popular houses and their products. When more than one Champagne is listed for a house, we rank them in order from highest to lowest quality. Recent good years for Champagne are 1985, 1986, 1988, 1989, 1990, 1995, and 1996.

abcdefghijklmnopq
rstuvwxyzabcdefgh
ijklmnopqrstuvwxy
a note from
the instructor

MÉTHODE CHARMANT

If we described the *méthode champenoise* as the Champagne of sparkling winemaking techniques, then by comparison, the *méthode charmant* would seem more like a $5 Chardonnay. Whereas the *méthode champenoise* is a laborious, expensive process and a matter of regional pride, the *méthode charmant* is a cheap, quick way to making sparkling wines.

In the *méthode charmant*, wines are fermented in a sealed tank, retaining the carbon dioxide that would normally be released from still wine. The result is a sparkling wine that may be fun to drink but is definitely not Champagne. Where Champagnes are painstakingly refermented in their bottles with the help of additional yeasts and sugars, sparkling wines are bottled as is. The difference, say some diehard Champagne lovers, is that *méthode charmant* wines taste like effervescent still wines, where true *méthode champenoise* Champagne tastes like no other beverage on Earth.

POPULAR AND NOTEWORTHY CHAMPAGNES

HOUSE	CHAMPAGNE(S) PRODUCED	STYLE(S)
Bollinger	Prestige cuvée, special cuvée, nonvintage	Brut
Krug	Clos de Mesnil, prestige cuvée, nonvintage	Brut
Moët & Chandon	Dom Perignon, White Star	Extra brut, demi-sec
Mumm	Cordon Rouge	Brut
Perrier-Jouët	Prestige cuvée	Brut
Taittinger	Prestige cuvée, vintage	Brut
Veuve Clicquot Ponsardin	Prestige cuvée, vintage, nonvintage	Brut

Alsace

A couple of hundred miles east-southeast of Paris, the region of Alsace lies on France's easternmost border, just across the Rhine River from Germany. Alsace has been passed back and forth between Germany and France so many times that its culture at first appears to be a blend of both countries. But upon further examination, it becomes clear that Alsatian culture is a phenomenon all its own.

You can almost taste the staunch regional pride in the wines of Alsace. The wines from its two main winemaking regions, Bas-Rhin and

Haut-Rhin ("Lower Rhine" and "Upper Rhine"), combine French and German influences. Alsatian wines come in distinctive tall bottles called *flûtes* and carry labels that denote both their place of origin (typical of French wines) *and* their grape (as German wines do). The place is stated simply as "Alsace."

Although located nearly as far north as Champagne, Alsace is not as cool and damp as that region, thanks to the mediating effect of the local Vosges Mountains. Alsatian soil is varied, ranging from chalk to sandstone, which permits subtle nuances in flavor from vineyard to vineyard.

Both French and German grape varieties grow in Alsace. Alsatian winemakers craft their wines to express both their grape (as German winemakers do) and their terroir (as do the French). For this reason, the grape is usually a single variety. Nearly all Alsatian wines are dry and white; many have a sharp acidity. The following table lists some of the distinctive characteristics and flavors of Alsatian wines.

IMPORTANT ALSATIAN WINES

WINE	CHARACTERISTIC(S)	FLAVOR(S)
Crémant d'Alsace	Sparkling, blended varieties	High acid
Pinot Gris	Dry and sweet styles, full bodied	Peach, spice
Gewurztraminer	Dry and sweet styles	Mineral, spice, fruit
Pinot Noir	Delicate	Earthy
Muscat	Dry, medium to full body	Citrus, floral
Riesling	Dry, powerful	Mineral, citrus

Alsatian Gewurztraminers (no umlaut on the *u* in France), Muscats, Pinot Blancs, Pinot Gris, and Rieslings differ markedly from their German counterparts. Whereas German wines tend to be sheer and precise, the Alsatian versions are rich and powerful. Alsatian Pinot Gris is much fuller bodied than Italy's Pinot Grigio. Until recently, Alsatian Pinot Gris was sometimes called Tokay-Pinot Gris, although it has no connection to Hungary's Tokay Aszu beyond the speculation that it may have originated in Hungary. Alsatian Rieslings are full of flavor and may be aged for a decade. Alsatian Pinot Noir (the only red grape grown in Alsace) is capable of great elegance.

Burgundy

Near France's eastern border with Switzerland, predominantly clustered along the western side of the Saôme River, lie the wine regions of

Burgundy. At the far northern extreme of this region lies Chablis. Dijon lies to Burgundy's northeast, Lyon to its extreme south. Burgundy's major wine regions are Chablis, Côte d'Or, Côte de Nuits, Côte de Beaune, Côte Chalonnaise, Mâconnais, and Beaujolais.

Burgundy is known predominantly for its red wine. Its grape crops depend largely on the amount of sunshine and rainfall they receive each growing season. Much of Burgundy's soil is stony and full of lime and prehistoric fossils, which contribute to the character of the wine. In Burgundy, small wine establishments are the norm. Thousands of communally owned vineyards produce an astonishing array of wines in minuscule quantities. Burgundian winemakers attempt to showcase how the minute differences in terroir affect the wine's character.

Because of this focus, and because much of Burgundy's red wine comes from the thin-skinned, difficult-to-grow Pinot Noir grape, the quality of Burgundy's red wines can fluctuate unpredictably. But many wine lovers claim that unpredictability is part of Burgundy's charm and delight in the adventure of searching out high quality wines among lesser-known ones. Because the Burgundy region produces only a quarter of what Bordeaux does, most of it in small batches, this search can amount to a real challenge.

In Burgundy, the terms *Grand Cru* ("great growth") and *Premier Cru* ("first growth") are applied to the region's top-rate wine-growing villages. Burgundy boasts a few dozen Grand Cru villages and several hundred Premier Cru villages. If a Burgundy hails from a Grand Cru or a Premier Cru village, the label states this fact prominently—and proudly.

---

abcdefghijklmnopq | **a note from**
rstuvwxyzabcdefgh | **the instructor**
ijklmnopqrstuvwxy |

CHABLIS AND BURGUNDY FROM CALIFORNIA?

Your local wine store probably carries wines called Chablis and Burgundy that have never been anywhere near France. Many of California's large commercial wineries sell gallon jugs of wines with these names. Technically, these wines are not true Chablis and Burgundy, but wines created to mimic the styles of the wines from these French regions. As with Champagne, only wines grown and made in Chablis and Burgundy are *true* Chablis and Burgundy.

SOME OF BURGUNDY'S WINE DISTRICTS

REGION	TYPICAL WINE(S)	PRODUCERS
Beaujolais	Beaujolais	Georges Deboeuf, Kermit Lynch, Moulin-à-Vent
Chablis	Chablis	Domaine Laroche, Guy Robin, Louis Michel
Côte Challonnaise	Mercurey, Montagny	Antonin Rodet, Louis Latour, Michel Juillot
Côte de Beaune	Pommard, Volnay	Chevalier-Montrachet, Corton-Charlemagne, Le Montrachet
Côte de Nuits	Marsanny	Clos de Vougeot, Le Chambertin, Le Musigny
Mâconnais	Mâcon, Poully Fuissé, St.-Véran	Domaine Corsin, Georges Deboeuf, Louis Jadot

Classic Burgundy reds and whites are lush, sensuous, and aromatic. Chablis is famous for its crisp, steely Chardonnay. Beaujolais, atypical of the rest of Burgundy, is known for a certain type of fun, fruity red wine made primarily from the light Gamay grape. Beaujolais winemakers apply a technique called *carbonic maceration,* in which the uncrushed bunches of grapes are placed in a special tank filled with carbon dioxide, which allows them to ferment while still whole to preserve more of the wine's fruitiness.

Beaujolais Nouveau, a popular offering in cafés around the world, is a special first-release type of Beaujolais designed to be enjoyed very young—sometimes when it's as little as seven weeks old. Amid much hoopla, each year's Beaujolais Nouveau is released, by law, no sooner than the third Thursday of November. Because of its light, fruity character, some say that it's a great way to help white wine drinkers transition into an appreciation of red wine.

Burgundy also makes a wonderful sparkling wine known as *Crémant de Bourgogne* that often forms the basis for exciting cocktails. It's produced in numerous parts of Burgundy.

WINE REGIONS OF SOUTHERN FRANCE: PROVENCE, THE RHÔNE, AND LANGUEDOC-ROUSSILLON

The wines from these warm regions have a sunny, Mediterranean quality, but excess heat sometimes ripens them too quickly to allow for fullness and complexity. Viognier, Muscat, and Syrah grapes are found in abundance here.

Provence

Provence is located on France's sunny Mediterranean coast. The seaside cities of St.-Tropez and Toulon are on its borders. Provence's landscape is full of wild herbs, reflected light, and sea-swept air, a magical combination for producing fragrant, flavorful wines. Probably better known for its cuisine than for its wines, Provence makes a wide variety of wines designed to stand up to its garlicky fish dishes.

Provence's four most prominent wine regions are Bandol, Cassis, Côteaux d'Aix-en-Provence, and Côtes de Provence. Bandol produces spicy rosés and wild, rough reds. Cassis (not to be confused with the black currant liqueur of the same name) makes dry white wines that go well with fish. Côteaux d'Aix-en-Provence produces rich, hearty reds, and Côtes de Provence makes flavorful rosés.

PROVENCE'S WINE DISTRICTS

REGION	TYPICAL WINE	PRODUCER(S)
Bandol	Tavel	Chateau de Pibarnon, Domaine Tempier
Cassis	Cassis	Clos Sainte-Magdeleine
Côteaux d'Aix-en-Provence	Côteaux d'Aix-en-Provence	Chateau Domaine de Trevallon, Mas de la Dame Vignelaure
Côtes de Provence	Rosé	Domaine Richaeume

The Rhône

Along the Rhône River lie the 12 subregions of the Rhône wine region. The Rhône is divided into southern and northern portions; some of the northern subregions include Côte Rôtie, Château-Grillet, Condrieu, St.-Joseph, Crosez-Hermitage, Hermitage, and Cornas; some of the southern are Gigondas, Vacqueyras, Châteauneuf-du-Pape, and Tavel. The two halves of the Rhône are not continuous—an area with few vineyards separates them. The cities of Lyon and Valence lie near the northern subregions; Nimes and Avignon flank the south.

Northern and southern Rhône wines are distinctly different in character: Northern Rhône wines exude smoky, gamey, peppery qualities, while those from the south are fruitier and exhibit more Mediterranean influences. The north's vineyards are made up largely of steep, slatey slopes lined with gnarled old vines; the south's are surrounded by a distinctly Mediterranean landscape and cooled by breezes off the Alps. Syrah is the northern Rhône's predominant red varietal, while its white wines are generally made from Viognier, Marsanne, or Roussanne grapes. Grenache is favored in the southern Rhône, along with many other grapes, including Syrah, Cinsaut, and Mouvédre. The south is also known for its fine rosés.

In the following table, you'll find some Rhône regions with wines of the same name and some of the region's/wines' notable producers.

> **student experience**
>
> "Getting into French wines was what got me into wine journaling. The array of French wines available is simply so staggering that I couldn't remember what I'd tried and what I hadn't. On the first few pages I jotted down a cheat sheet of the national and regional quality designations to use while shopping and I chose a small leather-bound notebook that wouldn't look tacky when I pulled it out in restaurants."
> —Becky, librarian

POPULAR RHÔNE WINES AND THEIR PRODUCERS

REGION/WINE	PRODUCERS
Châteauneuf-du-Pape	Château Beaucastel, Clos des Papes, Les Cailloux
Cornas	Jean-Luc Colombo
Côte Rôtie	E. Guigal, Michel Ogier
Gigondas	Domaine du Cayron, Domaine les Palliéres
Vacqueyras	Domaine le Sang des Cailloux

One of the Rhône's most famous wines is the colorfully named Châteauneuf-du-Pape. This wine, produced in both red and white varieties, is blended from Grenache, Syrah, Cinsaut, Grenache Blanc, and Roussane grapes, and is full of earthy, meaty flavors.

Another famous wine from the Rhône is Côte Rôtie, the name of which means "roasted slope." Like Châteauneuf-du-Pape, exemplary Côte Rôtie is bursting with earthiness, as well as a sharp, peppery spice.

Languedoc-Roussillon

To the southwest of Provence, near the southern crescent of France's Mediterranean coast, lie the subregions of Languedoc-Roussillon, including Faugères, St.-Chinian, Frontignan, Minervois, Corbières, Rivesaultes, and Banyuls. Vineyards grow grapes in soils that range from chalky to pebblelike. Languedoc-Roussillon is an ancient wine-growing region; its viticulture dates back to Roman times.

French wine drinkers habitually associate Languedoc-Roussillon with good, simple Vins de Pays. This region, with a climate similar to that of Provence and wines that carry a distinct herbal earthiness, has only recently begun to garner a reputation for serious wine, even though it produces more wine than any other region in France. As a result, Languedoc-Roussillon wines remain an exceptional value. Until recently, this region produced much of its wine from lesser-known grape varieties like Syrah, Mourvèdre, Grenache, and Carignan. It's now moving toward more international varieties and developing an international mindset to match. Many Australian winemakers are moving into this region, bringing innovative techniques and technology with them. Languedoc-Roussillon is attempting to develop a reputation as "the California of France."

In the following table are a few classic Languedoc-Roussillon wines/regions, a description of each wine's character, and typical producers.

TYPICAL LANGUEDOC-ROUSSILLON WINES

WINE/REGION	CHARACTERISTICS	TYPICAL PRODUCERS
Corbières	Dry, spicy; red, white, and rosé	Domaine de Grand Crès
Faugères	Dry, spicy; red	Gilbert Alquiers & Fils
Minervois	Smooth, fruity	Le Caves des Vignerons de St.-Jean-de-Minervois

a note from
the instructor

THE VDNS OF LANGUEDOC-ROUSSILLON

Languedoc-Roussillon is home to a famous regional specialty: Vins Doux Naturels, or VDNs. These wines are naturally super-sweet because of the extended length of time their grapes hang on the vine. The grapes aren't harvested until they're full of concentrated sweetness. Languedoc-Roussillon's VDNs are typically made from the white Muscat grape, like Muscat de Frontignan, or the red Grenache grape, as in Banyuls. They're often fortified with the addition of grape spirits.

Languedoc-Roussillon wines are often described as reflecting the sweet, herbal, wildflower-strewn landscape in which they grow. Corbières and Faugères wines, which are typically made in a dry style, are spicy, rustic, and refreshing. Minervois is the same, but with a smoother texture. Frontignan and Banyuls are known for sweet, often fortified Vins Doux Naturels—see the sidebar "The VDNs of Languedoc-Roussillon" for details.

WINE REGIONS OF COASTAL FRANCE: THE LOIRE VALLEY AND BORDEAUX

Bordeaux and the Loire Valley are two of the most famous winemaking regions in the world, home to such areas as Graves (so named because of the gravelly soil that produces an exquisite mineral-tasting wine of the same name), the Médoc, Sauternes, and Pomerol. The humid coast can keep vineyards cool but also may produce a variety of harsh conditions. Sauvignon Blanc, Sémillon, Cabernet Sauvignon, and Merlot grapes call this region home. The humidity that favors the *botrytis* fungus makes this region ideal for producing sweet Barsac and Sauternes.

The Loire Valley

Dotted with castles and ancient landscapes, the Loire Valley lies in northwest France, southwest of Paris. The cities of Nantes and Tours are in this vicinity. The Loire is home to three major wine regions: Muscadet (west), Anjou-Saumur (middle), and Touraine (east). Within Anjou-Saumur are five main subregions: Savennières, Quartes de Chaume, Côteaux du L'Aubance, Côteaux de Layon, and Bonnezeaux. Touraine also contains five main subregions: St.-Nicholas-de-Bourgueil, Bourgueil, Vouvray, Chinon, and Montlouis.

An old winemaking region with a wide range of terroir, the Loire Valley is characterized by diversity. Although all the subregions share a cool climate, some receive more sunlight or more humidity than others; in many parts of the Loire Valley, the quality of the year's harvest depends heavily on the season's weather patterns.

The Loire produces elegant white wines, setting the European standard for Chenin Blanc and Sauvignon Blanc. Savennières, a stony, acidic wine made from Chenin Blanc, and Muscadet, a dry white wine that's the perfect companion for seafood, both hail from this region, as does Vouvray, another wine from the Chenin Blanc grape, which ranges from sweet to dry. The Loire's tangy Sancerre and flinty Pouilly-Fumé are made from Sauvignon Blanc. A few noteworthy rosés hail from this region as well, some of which are made from blends of the local Grolleau grape. The Loire is also known for a crisp, sweet sparkling wine called Saumur.

In the following table, you'll find a list of the Loire's major wine regions. For each region, we list a few wines and typical producers.

LOIRE VALLEY WINE REGIONS: THEIR WINES AND PRODUCERS

REGION	WINE(S)	PRODUCERS
Western	Muscadet	Guindon, Batard, Domaine de l'Ecu
Eastern	Sancerre, Pouilly-Fumé	Didier Dagueneau, Domaine Henri Bourgeois
Middle	Savennières, Bourgeuil, Chinon	Château d'Epiré, Clos de la Coulee de Serrant

Bordeaux

The world-famous wine region of Bordeaux is located in France's southwest corner. In the vicinity are the towns of Bordeaux, Montbazillac, and Bergerac.

More wine lovers associate Bordeaux with fine wine than they do any other region on Earth. Bordeaux is ground zero for the world's most complex, aged, elegant wines. In fact, Bordeaux produces 10 percent of France's wine but a whopping 26 percent of its AOC-class wines.

Eighty-five percent of Bordeaux's wines are dry reds. The archetypal Bordeaux is a rich, deep red full of dark fruit flavors like black currants and plums, with overtones of cedar and tobacco.

It takes time for a fine Bordeaux to rise to greatness. Many take 20 years or more to age to perfection—and some of the greatest Bordeaux ever produced have been known to age beautifully for a century. Premier Cru ("first growth") Bordeaux sell for hundreds of dollars a bottle, but fortunately, many good ones from lower-quality ranks can be had for as little as $20. Tuck these wines away in a quiet corner of your basement for five years—they'll be worth the wait.

In Bordeaux, the word *cru* (literally, "growth") is synonymous with *château*, particularly in the context of rank. Each château is ranked according to the quality of the grapes it grows so that each vineyard is either a Premier Cru, Deuxièmes, or a Cru Bourgeois. In the following table, you'll find the names of important Bordeaux châteaux ranked by cru.

IMPORTANT BORDEAUX CHÂTEAUX

RANK	REPRESENTATIVE CHÂTEAUX
Premier Crus (First Growth)	Château Haut-Brion, Château Lafite-Rothschild, Château Latour, Château Margaux, Château Mouton-Rothschild
Deuxiémes Crus (Second Growth)	Château Cheval Blanc, Château Lafleur, Château L'Angélus
Cru Bourgeois (Lesser Quality)	Château le Breuil, Château MauCaillou, Château Poujeaux

Bordeaux's wine regions flank the Gironde and Dordogne rivers. Most of Bordeaux's regions are close enough to the ocean to enjoy moderate seasons. The soils range from gravel to chalk to clay. The Médoc lies at the mouth of the Gironde River, closest to the Atlantic Ocean. To the south of the Médoc, along the Gironde's southwestern bank, is the Haut-Médoc, with its subregions Listrac, Margaux, Moulis, Pauillac, St.-Estephe and St.-Julien. Still farther south, just below the town of Bordeaux itself, are the regions of Pessac-Léognan, Graves, Barsac, and Sauternes. Across the river from these are a number of smaller subregions, including Côtes de Blayes, Côtes de Bourg, Côtes de Castillon, Côtes de Francs, Fronsac, Canon-Fronsac, and Entre-Deux-Mers. In the center of this cluster are Pomerol and St.-Emilion.

Bordeaux's red grapes are Cabernet Franc (earthy, with black currant notes), Cabernet Sauvignon (dark, tannic, and cedary), Malbec (heavy and tannic), Merlot (with mint and plum flavors), and Petit Verdot (acidic, with plum flavors). Most Bordeaux red wines are a blend of two or more of these varieties.

---

a note from
the instructor

BORDEAUX PETIT CHÂTEAUX

Famous names aside, Bordeaux is home to a number of small-time growers that produce fine wines in extremely small quantities. These wines often rival the quality of those made by the big-name châteaux but don't have the same name recognition and, for that reason, can't command the kinds of prices the famous producers do. Bordeaux's "petite châteaux" have become very popular in recent decades because they frequently offer fabulous wines at affordable prices.

Bordeaux also produces magnificent white wines. Bordeaux's main white grapes are Sauvignon Blanc and Sémillon, although Muscadelle and Ugni Blanc (a simple white grape used for blending) are used as well. Sémillon is the primary grape for Sauternes and Barsac. Graves, home to Château Haut-Brion, is made in both red and white styles, with white Graves typically being a blend of white Bordeaux grapes.

In the following table, you'll find the names of a few typical producers for Bordeaux's major wine regions. (*Note:* The name of the wine is generally either the same as the region or is specific to the producer.)

BORDEAUX REGIONS AND PRODUCERS

REGION	TYPICAL PRODUCERS/ESTATES
Côtes de Blaye/Bourg/Castillon/Francs	Château de Francs, Château Les Jonqueyres, Château Puygeraud, Château Roc des Cambes
Entre-Deux-Mers	Château Bonnet, Château Peyrebon
Fronsac/Canon-Fronsac	Château Dalem
Graves	Château Haut-Brion, Château Pape-Clément
Médoc/Haut-Médoc	Château Ducru-Beaucaillou, Château Margaux, Château Talbot
Pomerol	Château Lafleur, Château le Bon Pasteur
St.-Emilion	Château Ausone, Château Magdelaine, Cheval Blanc
Sauternes/Barsac	Château Climens, Château Guiraud, Château d'Yquem

You'll probably recognize the names of some of these great Bordeaux *appellations* (places of origin) from discussions earlier in this book. For instance, you'll likely remember Sauternes and Barsac as sweet, botrytised dessert wines. Graves (discussed earlier in this lesson) hails from this area. There's also Pauillac, home of three out of five of the Premier Cru châteaux (Lafite-Rothschild, Latour, and Mouton-Rothschild). Pauillac wines are widely acclaimed as some of the most elegant in the world. They're generally blends of the top red Bordeaux grapes, predominantly Cabernet Sauvignon and Merlot. Pomerol is famous as the home of the elusive Château Pétrus, a wine so rare that only a privileged and determined few have tasted it. Pomerol wines are characteristically smooth and soft. Margaux (home to Premier Cru Châteaux Margaux) produces wines that are capable of being delicate yet powerful.

italy's wine regions

The Character of Italian Wine • Northwestern Italy's Wine Regions • Northeastern Italy's Wine Regions • Central Italy's Wine Regions • Southern Italy's Wine Regions

To Italians, wine is synonymous with a passion for living. Italian wine is astonishingly diverse, widely available, and generally reasonably priced. From the rugged mountains of the northwest come wines as delicate as Asti and as hearty as Barolo. In the northeast, Italian wines take on an international flair, where Austrian, German, and French winemaking traditions mingle. Central Italy, the heart of Italian culture, is home to such quintessentially Italian wines as Chianti. Southern Italy offers a cornucopia of casual wine, as well as several high-quality specialties. In this lesson, we take a closer look at the wines and wine regions of Italy.

WHAT'S DISTINCTIVE ABOUT ITALIAN WINE

Wine is a daily part of life in Italy; Italians wouldn't think of eating a meal without it. Every area has its own special cuisine and wines that match it. Italians excel at pairing specific wines with particular dishes.

Major Italian wine regions.

If anything, wine is so abundant in Italy that it's taken for granted. Italians have a reputation for maintaining a blue-jeans attitude toward their wines. If France is synonymous with quality wine, Italy brings to mind casual, fun wine. Statistically speaking, that's true: The vast majority of the wines that come from Italy's 900,000 or more registered vineyards are everyday wines for local consumption. Yet Italy is also home to some of the world's finest wines.

With hundreds of microclimates, thousands of grape varieties, a vast array of styles, and a mind-boggling mélange of cultural influences, the diversity of Italian wine is astonishing. If you love discovering new wines, you could happily drink your way from town to town in Italy for the rest of your days and never taste them all.

But until recently, Italian winemakers placed little emphasis on creating an international market for their fine wines. Italian varieties are still seldom grown outside Italy, so many wine novices have never heard of such classic Italian grapes as Aglianico, Barbera, and Nebbiolo.

student experience

"Italian wines hold a certain bit of excitement for me. They have so many good wines hiding under what, technically speaking, are lower classifications. My friends and I sometimes get together and each bring a bottle of Italian wine under $10; each time we find at least one true winner!"
—Bernie, food critic

ITALIAN WINE CLASSIFICATIONS

Italy recognizes three legal classifications for its wines. The highest rank, the *Denominazione di Origine Controllata e Guarantita* (DOCG), holds similar standards to France's AOC. Only certain types of wines qualify for DOCG status: They must come from a long history of traditional winemaking and must bear a DOC designation for at least three years before they're eligible.

In the following table, you'll find a sampling of wines and their producers from various Italian regions that qualify for DOCG status.

SOME OF ITALY'S BEST KNOWN DOCG WINES

WINE	WINE TYPE	PRODUCERS
Asti	Sparkling white	Braida, Gancia, Martini & Rossi
Barbaresco	Red	Giacosa, Paitin, Vietti
Barolo	Red	Altare, Bricco, Gaja, Vajra
Brunello di Montalcino	Red	Argiano, Casse Basse, La Fortuna
Chianti Classico	Red	Antonori, Castellare, Ruffino
Moscato d'Asti	White	Icardi, Marchesi di Gresi
Vino Nobile de Montepulciano	Red	Avignonesi, Poderi Boscarelli

A few of these wines, like Chianti, have been famous on the international scene for decades. Others, like Barbera, are only beginning to make their international debut. You probably know Asti best by its former name, Asti Spumante. Asti is a famous sparkling wine from the town of Asti, but Moscato d'Asti is a still, delicate, slightly fizzy white wine, very popular among the Piedmontese. Brunello di Montalcino, made from a special clone of Sangiovese, is one of Italy's pricier wines. Its thick texture and powerful structure permits it to age for as long as 100 years.

Below DOCG is DOC, the *Denominazione di Origine Controllata*. This classification is open to a broader category of wines but still specifies maximum yields, alcohol content, and geographic origin.

The *Indicazione di Geografica Tipica* (IGT) is more or less equivalent to France's Vin de Pays. It's the lowest tier of quality, based on geographic location.

Anything that doesn't make the quality ranks is called *Vino di Tavola:* basic, ordinary table wine. But since Italian winemakers often scoff at classifications, some of Italy's most extraordinary wines hide under this humble label.

ITALY'S NORTHWESTERN WINE REGIONS: PIEDMONT, LIGURIA, LOMBARDY, AND VALLE D'AOSTA

Italy's northwest is a rugged, mountainous area, a tricky place to make wine. As a result, the wines tend to be pricey. The heavy harvest fogs, or *nebbia,* give their name to the massively tannic Nebbiolo grapes that age into such magnificent wines as Barolo and Barbaresco. But light, sparkling Asti, Barolo's alter ego, also hails from here, as do youthful Dolcetto and hearty Barbera.

- **Piedmont:** This Alpine region is Italy's premier wine region, the home of the most serious Italian winemaking. Piedmont has been called the Burgundy of Italy because of its tiny vineyards, its many producers, and the Piedmont winemakers' philosophy of letting a single variety express itself through its environment.

Piedmont can be subdivided into smaller areas, the most important of which are Alba and Asti. Alba's soils are primarily clay and limestone, which enrich its abundant Nebbiolo vines. Asti, to the north of Alba, shares these limestone-rich soils, but the dominant grape here is Moscato.

The wines of Piedmont are mostly red. Piedmont's major red grapes are Barbera (the most widely planted), Dolcetto, and Nebbiolo; its white grapes are Arneis, Cortese, and Moscato. Piedmont produces Italy's popular Barolo and Barbaresco wines, as well as local specialties like Dolcetto and Gattinara (the latter is a hard-edged red wine made from the highly tannic Nebbiolo grape). The sweet, spiced wine Vermouth, popular in cocktails, also calls Piedmont home.

Piedmont's nearest city, Turin, is home to the famous Shroud of Turin. Piedmont is also home to another famous delicacy: white truffles.

- **Liguria:** Known as the Italian Riviera, Liguria is primarily white wine country. Christopher Columbus's hometown of Genoa is in this region. Liguria is home to Cinqueterre, a bland but nevertheless popular white wine named for five local villages. It grows on mind-bogglingly steep slopes.

- **Lombardy:** This region is best known for its dry sparkling wine, Franciacorta. Much of Lombardy's remaining wine production is devoted to casual wines from Barbera and other grapes. The city of Milan is located in this region.

- **Valle d'Aosta:** This small Alpine region is located due north of Piedmont, near Italy's Swiss and French borders. This area's mixture of Italian and French cultural influences are evident in its wines. Many of its vines grow on terraces. Even in this mountainous area, reds can flourish because Valle d'Aosta's valley floors receive sufficient warm sunlight to ripen the grapes. Valle d'Aosta is home to the rare white wine Blanc de Morgex, as well as French varietals like Gamay, Pinot Noir, and Syrah.

a note from
the instructor

DOLCETTO AND BARBERA: TWO PIEDMONT FAVORITES

Two of the most popular wines among native Piedmontese are Dolcetto and Barbera. Dolcetto is a spicy, lightweight red wine with hints of semi-sweet chocolate. It's easy to drink because its tannin and acidity are low. Dolcetto is sometimes called Italy's Beaujolais because it inspires the same kind of fun, easy drinking. Barbera, from the Nebbiolo grape, is juicy but somewhat coarser. It's noticeably more tannic than Dolcetto but doesn't contain nearly as much tannin as Barolo or Barbaresco. In recent years, Barbera has risen dramatically in quality.

In the following table, you'll find a few of the typical wines and producers for two of northwestern Italy's major wine regions:

GRAPES, WINES, AND PRODUCERS FROM TWO OF NORTHWESTERN ITALY'S WINE REGIONS

REGION	GRAPES	WINES	PRODUCERS
Piedmont	Nebbiolo, Barbera, Moscato	Barbaresco, Barbera D'Alba, Barolo, Dolcetto D'Alba, Gattinara, Gavi, Moscato D'Asti	Gaja, Icardi, Prunnoto, Vietti
Lombardy	Chardonnay, Pinot Grigio	Franciacorta, Lugana, Valtellina	Bella Vista, Berlucci, Cavalleri

Lombardy's dry, sparkling Franciacorta, made from Chardonnay or Pinot Grigio, is an elegant drink. Barolo, with its impressive load of tannin from the Nebbiolo grape, is capable of great depth and structure and can age well for 10 to 20 years.

ITALY'S NORTHEASTERN WINE REGIONS: TRENTINO-ALTO ADIGE, FRIULI-VENEZIA GIULIA, AND VENETO

Italy's northeastern regions enjoy a distinct international influence because of their proximity to France, Germany, and Austria. Many of the regions' wines are grown and crafted in the French, German, or Austrian traditions, but they also cultivate their own specialties, such as Refosco, a tarry, red wine.

- **Trentino-Alto Adige:** Nestled together in the Alps, these two DOCs are so close to one another that they're generally mentioned as a single region. The cities of Bolzano and Verona are nearby. Mountainous, panoramic Alto Adige is known for intense, focused wines with a strong Germanic influence. Surprisingly, this area produces more red wines than whites. Its typical grapes include Schiava and Lagrein Kretzer. Alto Adige's neighbor, Trentino, is home to numerous Italian, French, and German varietals, as well as Champagne-style sparkling wines.

- **Friuli-Venezia Giulia:** This area is near the Slovenian border. The city of Venice lies approximately 75 miles to its south. Friuli-Venezia Giulia is home to some of Italy's most energetic white wines. This area has historically been influenced by the cultures of Austria and Hungary, which explains the predominance of noticeably fruity white wines—a rare quality in Italian wines.

  The sloping Alpine foothills of this region provide warm days and cool nights for growing a variety of reds and whites. Friuli grows white Pinot Bianco (Pinot Blanc), Picolit, Pinot Grigio, and Tocai Friuliano grapes, as well as the white French standards Chardonnay and Sauvignon Blanc. Its primary reds are Refosco and Schioppetino, plus Cabernet Franc, Cabernet Sauvignon, and Merlot.

  Friulian winemakers often blend Italian grapes with such French classics as Sauvignon Blanc, Chardonnay, or Pinot Grigio. Pinot Bianco, insipid when grown elsewhere, has a distinctive lemony flavor here. This region is also home to nutty Tocai, sweet Picolit, and sharply spicy Schioppettino (not to be confused with Italian winemaker Mario Schiopetto, who produces fine Merlot, Tocai, and Pinot Bianco).

- **Veneto:** This cool region produces a huge quantity of wine, much of it DOC quality. Everyday wines like Soave, Valpolicella, and Bardolino are made here, as is the highly alcoholic Amarone della Valpolicella. The famous city of Venice is in this region. Veneto's primary white grapes are Chardonnay, Pinot Bianco, and Pinot Grigio; its primary reds are Cabernet Sauvignon and Merlot. Veneto is also home to the popular lightly sparkling wine Prosecco, which Venetians enjoy during afternoon coffee breaks.

In the following table, you'll find a list of the typical wines, grapes, and producers for northeastern Italy's important wine regions.

NORTHEASTERN ITALY'S WINE REGIONS AND A SAMPLING OF ITS GRAPES, WINES, AND PRODUCERS

REGION	GRAPES	WINES	PRODUCERS
Trentino-Alto Adige	Lagrein	Lagrein Kretter, Rosé	Foradori, Terlano, Zeni
Friuli-Venezia Giulia	Picolit, Refosco, Tocai	Picolit, Refosco, Tocai	Enofriuila, Jermann, Zamo & Zamo
Veneto	Corvino, Molinara, Trebbiano	Bardolino, Prosecco, Soave, Valpolicella	Allegrini, Anselmi, Zardetto, Zenato

Friuli's popular Tocai is not related to Hungary's Tokay, despite the similarity of their names. Tocai is a spicy white wine with a slightly stony flavor. Picolit, Friuli's rare, expensive dessert wine, has an almost herbal essence. Refosco, a thick, berrylike red wine, is a good match for food because of its relatively high acidity.

ITALY'S CENTRAL WINE REGIONS: ABRUZZO, EMILIA-ROMAGNA, LAZIO, TUSCANY, UMBRIA

The cradle of the Roman Empire, this area is replete with ancient history. These regions are considered the heart of Italian culture, and are home to such well-loved Italian wines as Chianti and Lambrusco.

- **Abruzzo:** This region lies on Italy's eastern coast, near the Adriatic Sea. The city of Pescara is nearby. Montepulciano, Nebbiolo, and Sangiovese grapes grow here in abundance. Abruzzo (also widely known as "the Abruzzi") produces the famous red Montepulciano d'Abruzzo and the white Trebbiano d'Abruzzo (which, incidentally, is *not* made from the Trebbiano grape).

  Abruzzo's reds have a characteristically heavy mouthfeel. Montepulciano D'Abruzzo, with its thick texture and robust flavors, is a very substantial wine for the price. Ancient tradition lingers in this region: Wines by Abruzzo producer Emidio Pepe are still made by crushing the grapes by foot.

- **Emilia-Romagna:** Bordering the Adriatic Sea, with the city of Bologna at its midsection, this area is home to light, fizzy Lambrusco—a very mild red wine that is sometimes dulled down for the tourist trade (and is therefore known as "the Bolognese Coca-Cola"), although DOC regions make a zesty and sparkling style. The area's light reds steal most of the limelight; its whites are relatively anonymous.

- **Lazio:** This central west coast region is also known as Latium. The city of Rome lies in its center. In contrast to Emilia Romagna, nearly all this region's wines are white. Many Lazio whites have crisp apple and pepper flavors.

- **Tuscany:** This famous region lies on Italy's west coast just to the north of Lazio. The historic cities of Florence, Siena, and Pisa are located in this area. It's the home of internationally famous Chianti, as well as Brunello di Montalcino (an up-and-coming but expensive wine with powerful tannin) and Rosso di Montalcino (a cheaper, younger-drinking Tuscan red).

  Tuscany is divided into a number of subregions, including Chianti Classico, home to much of the world's finest Chianti. The primary red grape of Tuscany is Sangiovese. Tuscan whites include Chardonnay, Malvasia, Sauvignon Blanc, Trebbiano, and Vernaccia.

  A line of fancy, pricey, heavily marketed Tuscan reds, known as "Super Tuscans" emerged in the '70s and '80s. The Super Tuscans blend Sangiovese with Cabernet Sauvignon and Merlot to create a sophisticated, structured red wine. They're often aged in oak. Super Tuscans are relatively high in tannin and acidity, so they're suitable for aging. Some of the popular Super-Tuscan products are Cepparello, Flaccianello, Masseto, and Sassicaia.

- **Umbria:** This area in the center of Italy is filled with peaceful landscapes and rolling hills. Umbria's wines are primarily white, of which the most famous, Orvieto, carries a distinct smoky flavor, in sweet or dry styles. White Orvietos (made primarily from the Trebbiano grape) are crisp, elegant, and slightly peachy. Umbria also produces a far lesser known red Orvieto.

In the following table, you'll find the typical grapes, wines, and producers for Italy's central wine regions.

CENTRAL ITALY'S IMPORTANT WINE REGIONS, GRAPES, WINES, AND PRODUCERS

REGION	GRAPES	WINES	PRODUCERS
Abruzzo	Montepulciano	Montepulciano D'Abruzzo	Umani Rochi, Valentini, Zaccagnini
Emilia-Romagna	Lambrusco, Albana	Lambrusco, Romagna, Sangiovese di Romagna	Cavicchioli, La Tosa
Lazio	Trebbiano, Malvasia	Aprilia, Ceveteri, Frascati	Colli di Catone
Tuscany	Sangiovese	Brunello di Montalcino, Vino Nobile di Montalcino, Chianti	Fontodi, Ruffino, San Felice
Umbria	Trebbiano	Orvieto, Sagrantino di Montefalco	Adanti, Lungarotti

Tuscany's Chianti needs little introduction—it's a perennial favorite with spaghetti or pizza. Chianti isn't widely known for its elegance, but the best Chiantis are robust and full of character. Look for high-quality Chianti Classico, from the Chianti Classico DOC.

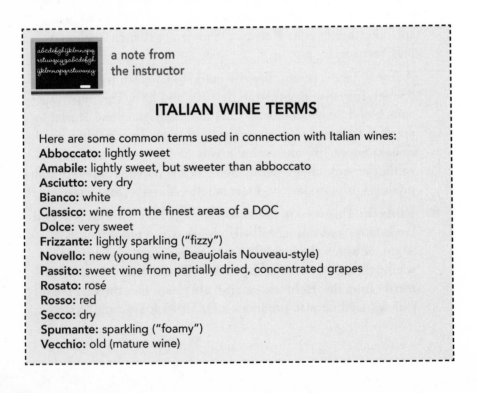

a note from the instructor

ITALIAN WINE TERMS

Here are some common terms used in connection with Italian wines:

Abboccato: lightly sweet
Amabile: lightly sweet, but sweeter than abboccato
Asciutto: very dry
Bianco: white
Classico: wine from the finest areas of a DOC
Dolce: very sweet
Frizzante: lightly sparkling ("fizzy")
Novello: new (young wine, Beaujolais Nouveau-style)
Passito: sweet wine from partially dried, concentrated grapes
Rosato: rosé
Rosso: red
Secco: dry
Spumante: sparkling ("foamy")
Vecchio: old (mature wine)

As with Chianti, the best Orvietos bear the title "Classico," indicating that they come from the heart of the Orvieto DOC. Some Orvietos take on a noticeably peachy essence.

ITALY'S SOUTHERN WINE REGIONS: PUGLIA, BASILICATA, CALABRIA, CAMPANIA, AND SICILY

Southern Italy is one of the country's most prolific wine-growing areas, yet relatively few of its wines have achieved international fame. Marsala is made here, as is the Isle of Capri's Lacryma Christi (known as much for its poetic name as for its taste).

- **Puglia:** This warm southeastern area in the "heel" of Italy's "boot" has the largest total wine production in Italy, but most of it is local-consumption jug wine. The few fine wines Puglia makes are intense and concentrated. Puglia's most famous wine is the hearty Salice Salento, from the bitter, black Negromaro grape. It's also known for another red wine, Primitivo, which is similar to Zinfandel.

- **Basilicata:** This relatively chilly, mountainous region (in the instep of the boot) is home to the dramatically named red Aglianico del Vulture. Basilicata wines are almondy and slightly dusty.

- **Calabria:** Quiet and mountainous Calabria, located in the toe of the Italian boot, is most famous for its Ciro, the wine presented to Olympic champions. Some of Calabria's sweet wines contain hints of orange.

- **Campania:** An ancient Roman wine-growing area north of Basilicata and south of Lazio (and home to the city of Naples), Campania is the birthplace of Greco di Tufo, a licorice-flavored white wine which ages well, and Taurasi, a red, plummy, tannic wine.

- **Sicily:** This historic island has been growing wine for more than 4,000 years. Sicily produces huge quantities of simple wine (more white than red), but is now starting to work toward higher quality. It's most famous for Marsala, a highly acidic fortified wine with brown sugar flavors. Sicily is also home to Corvo (red and white), and Moscato di Pantelleria, a light, sweet white wine with an applelike essence. The white Catarratto Bianco is Sicily's dominant grape.

---

abcdefghijklmnopq rstuvwxyzabcdefgh ijklmnopqrstuvwxy	a note from the instructor

SICILIAN MARSALA: NOT JUST FOR COOKING

For many of us, Marsala is not a table wine, but a cooking ingredient. We're more accustomed to putting it in our stews and meat dishes (like zabaglione or Veal Marsala) than we are to putting it in our wine glasses. But since the late 1700s until recent times, Marsala was considered a premiere fortified wine and a first-rate cold weather sipper—right up there with Port and Sherry. Since a turnaround in quality some time in the 1980s, Marsala has been making a comeback.

Marsala takes its name from the ancient port city on its home island of Sicily. Marsala is made from Grillo and Catarratto Bianco grapes, and like other fortified wines, it can handle a great deal of aging. A fine Marsala must age at least one year before being released to the public; the highest grades must age for ten. Marsala comes in dry, sweet, and very sweet styles, and may be *oro* (gold), *ambra* (amber), or *rubino* (ruby) in color. Enjoy Sicilian Marsala lightly chilled as a dessert or aperitif.

The following table offers a few of the typical grapes, wines and producers for southern Italy's primary wine regions.

A SAMPLING OF GRAPES, WINES, AND PRODUCERS FROM SOME OF SOUTHERN ITALY'S WINE REGIONS

REGION	GRAPES	WINES	PRODUCERS
Puglia	Negromaro	Primitivo, Salice Salentino	Brindisi, Copertino, Leverano
Basilicata	Anglianico	Aglianico del Vulture	Fratelli d'Angelo, Paternoster
Sicily	Grillo, Catarratta Bianco, Zibibbo	Marsala, Moscato di Pantellerina	Florio, Marco de Bartoli

The nearly black red wine Taurasi, from Campania, is made from the Anglianico grape. Its sharp, tarry bitterness is reminiscent of unsweetend cocoa. More famous than Taurasi is another wine made from the same grape, Anglianico del Vulture. This robust red wine gets its colorful name from the extinct Mount Vulture volcano.

lesson 9

other european wine producers

Spain • Portugal • Germany • Austria • Hungary • Greece

Although they aren't currently the international wine giants that France and Italy are, the European countries we discuss in this lesson are nonetheless significant contributors to the world of wine. Not long ago, Germany was considered the only country besides France where a wine lover could go to find plentiful fine wine. Austria's fine wines remain little known outside its borders but are of such high quality that they're worthy of more attention. Hungary and Greece have produced wine since ancient times, and Spain's and Portugal's fortified wine industries lubricated the tall-ship era of exploration.

SPAIN

Spain has more vines under cultivation than any other country in the world—even more than wine-saturated Italy. Yet it produces less wine, ranking third behind Italy and France, because its soils are poor and its climate is harsh. But somehow, for grapevines as for people, a little suffering seems to add a certain strength of character.

Spanish wines are typically aged longer than any other wines in the world, which has given them a reputation for being dark, musty, and heavy. Some Spanish wines deserve this reputation, but the majority of the country's wines today are lively and fruity. Spain is famous for vibrant wines like Rioja (made from Tempranillo, Grenache, and other grapes), sparkling Cava, and rich, fortified Sherry.

Spain is also working steadily toward competing in the international wine market. Spanish winemakers are bringing in modern technology, planting more of the popular French grape varieties (notably Cabernet Sauvignon, Chardonnay, and Pinot Noir), and adapting wine styles to international tastes. Today's Spanish reds are typically light and floral, and its whites are crisp, with hints of peach and pineapple. Spain is currently one of the hottest movers and shakers in the wine world.

Spanish Wine Classifications

Spain's wine classifications are roughly based on France's AOC system. *Denominacion de Origen Calificada* (DOCa) is the highest rank, reserved for wine regions of top quality. Currently, only the Rioja region holds a DOCa. More than 40 regions qualify for the second rank, *Denominacion de Origen* (DO). Below this classification comes *Vino de la Tierra* (VdlT), roughly the equivalent of France's Vin de Pays. *Vino Commercial* (VC) is a small step down from Vino de la Tierra; 28 areas are VC certified. And in last place is *Vino de Mesa* (VdM)—literally, "table wine." Table wine's quality is checked, but these wines are assigned no vintage or region. This doesn't mean that the wines are bad, though. As with Vin de Pays and Vino di Tavola, hidden treasures often lurk within this humble classification.

Spanish Wine Regions

Spain's wine regions range from the cool, Mediterranean climates on its coasts, where French grape varieties thrive alongside national favorites, to its baking-hot interior portions, where only the hardiest grapes grow.

- **Northwest:** This area, known as Galicia, lies along Spain's border with northern Portugal. Wines of northwestern Spain are characterized as highly aromatic—and very expensive. Important DOs in this region are Rias Baixas and Ribera del Duero;

also the prestigious, centuries-old winery Bodegas Vega Sicilia is located here. The region's cooler temperatures and sufficient rainfall allow for the growing of grapes with well-developed character. The lemony-white Albariño, which makes zesty, high-alcohol wines of the same name, is the region's principal grape.

- **North Central:** From the northern coast at the Bay of Biscay to the Duero River, this area is home to the regions of Rioja and Castilla y León and enjoys a mixture of cool maritime and warm Mediterranean climates. Rioja is Spain's only officially designated DOCa, the country's highest rank of quality. Rioja wine has a long and honorable tradition dating back at least five centuries—it was one of the first products to bear a trademark. Crianza is the youngest and simplest Rioja; Rioja Reserva and Gran Reserva are aged longer and tend to be of higher quality. The Rioja region also grows a sprightly, acidic white grape with a pineapple/grapefruit flavor, Viura (also called Macabeo), which is used to make white Rioja.

- **Northeast:** The region of Catalonia and the areas to the south of Barcelona are rich in reds and rosés. This area, on Spain's northeastern border with France, is the trailblazer for the modernization of Spain's wine industry. Catalonia's climate is Mediterranean: mild to warm, with moderate rainfall. Tempranillo and Garnacha (Grenache) grapes, along with a few international varieties (Cabernet Sauvignon, Chardonnay, Merlot, and others), grow in the lush foothills and river valleys. Priorato and Penedés DOs lie in this area.

- **Central:** The vast region of La Mancha in the hot interior of Spain has modernized rapidly and is now producing a number of inexpensive, fruity young wines with international appeal. The city of Madrid is in this area, as are two noteworthy DOs: La Mancha and Valdepeñas. Because of the temperatures, most of the wine produced here is red. Wine production in this dry plateau region focuses on cherrylike Tempranillo grapes. The dominant white grape is the drought-resistant Airén. Wines from central Spain are often blends of red and white grapes.

- **East:** On Spain's Mediterranean coast, between the regions of Valencia and Murcia, lie about a dozen DOs, including

Valencia. This area produces primarily simple, everyday wines, most of which are red.

■ **South:** Southern Spain, from Andalusia to the southern Mediterranean and Atlantic coasts (near the city of Seville), is too roasting hot for delicate wines—the grapes bake away to early ripeness before they can develop much complexity. Instead, this region historically has been devoted to producing fortified wines that can withstand the brutal temperatures. Southern DOs of note are Jerez, Condado de Huelva, and Montilla-Moriles. Condand de Huelva produces Sherry-style wines. Montilla-Moriles produces strongly alcoholic *oloroso*-style wines (see Lesson 5 for a description of the oloroso style) from the Pedro Ximénes grape, as well as wines from the white Airén.

Spain's and Portugal's wine-growing regions.

In the following table, you'll find some of Spain's important *bodegas,* or wineries, along with the typical wines produced.

SOME NOTEWORTHY SPANISH WINES AND BODEGAS

REGION	WINE(S)	BODEGAS
Northwest	Albariño	Bodegas Alanis, Granja Fillaboa, Santiago Ruis
North Central	Rioja	Campo Viejo, Cune, Montecillo, Muga, Navajas, Pesquera, Vega Secilia
Northeast	Cava, French varieties Cava, Albariño, Sangre de Toro	Cavas Hill, Cordoniu, Masia Barril, Torres, Beau Leon, Segura Viudas
South	Sherry	Barbadillo, Garvey, Hidalgo, Osbourne, Valdespino

Light, sparkling Cava is the wine of celebration in much of Spain. Made by the *méthode traditionale,* also called *méthode champenoise* (see Lesson 7 on France for details), Cava was originally called *champaña.* It tastes vastly different from Champagne, however, as it is made from Spanish grapes. A famous producer of Cava is Freixenet—look for its famous black Cordon Negro bottle. Sangre de Toro ("bull's blood") is a simple but powerful red wine with earthy flavors.

Of course, the most famous Spanish wine contribution over the last several centuries is Sherry, the fortified white wine that hails from southern Spain. The light, crumbly clay soil of this region helps reflect sunlight onto the grapes to speed ripening. Sherry, made primarily from the Palomino grape, is available in a variety of styles, from the light *fino* to the hearty *oloroso.* Although Sherries are produced in other parts of the world (like California and Australia), Spain continues to be the major international supplier of this popular fortified wine. For a closer look at Sherry, review the section on fortified wines in Lesson 5.

From Montilla-Moriles in the south, comes a Sherrylike wine known as Montilla. Montillas are made in styles similar to Sherry, by a similar method, although they're not fortified as Sherry is. As a result, they're often enjoyed as a lighter alternative to Sherry.

PORTUGAL

In this hot, humid, hilly country steeped in tradition, modern winemaking is taking hold, yet wine is still frequently made the old-fashioned way: hand picked, foot crushed, and lovingly tended.

Portugal is the home of two historic, world-famous fortified wines: Port and Madeira. Most Port makers hand-craft their wines by using the same methods their medieval ancestors used. They add grape spirits to the must to halt fermentation, leaving the residual sugars that account for Port's sweetness. Then they age it according to its style. Madeira is made by using a similar process but is left to age in hot attics, sometimes for unbelievably long stretches of time. This long period of aging is what gives Madeira its characteristic lush, caramelized flavor. For more information about Port and Madeira, review Lesson 5.

Portuguese Wine Classifications

Portugal's *Denominaçao de Origem Controllada* (DOC) is based on France's AOC system. Eighteen Portuguese wine regions qualify for this highest rank. Next in line are roughly three dozen IPRs, or *Indição de Proveniência Regulamentada*, about the same level of control as France's VDQS. Below these levels are *Vinho Regional* (VR), the Portuguese equivalent of France's Vin de Pays, and *Vinho de Mesa*. Wines from this lowest classification are not required to state a vintage or a place of origin on the label.

Portuguese Wine Regions

The mainland of Portugal has two distinct winemaking regions marked by extremes of climate. Its eastern region, facing the ocean, is so humid that the vines must be trained up tall trellises to help them get air. Its western border with Spain is a blast furnace of dry heat. Last but not least is the island of Madeira off Portugal's southwestern coast, home to the fortified wine of the same name. The following are a few of Portugal's important DOCs:

- **East:** Within Portugal's hot, dry interior lie the winemaking regions of Douro, Dão, and Alentejo. In the north, Douro, set along the river of the same name, is the primary source of grapes for Port. Dão is near the center of the country. The Alentejo region is found in the south, north-northeast of Lisbon, near the Spanish border.

- **West:** At Portugal's Atlantic coast are the wine regions of Vinho Verde (in the large Minho region), Bairrada, and Setúbal.

These areas enjoy cooler temperatures because of their proximity to the ocean, but they often suffer from the dampness. Vinho Verde produces much of Portugal's Vinho Verde, or "green wine," in crisp white and tangy red varieties (white Vinho Verde is made from Alvarinho and other grapes; red Vinho Verde comes from Trajadura and others). Setúbal, south of Lisbon, produces a fortified wine from white Moscatel grapes (not to be confused with Muscadelle or Muscadet).

- **Madeira:** This subtropical island lies more than 500 miles to the southwest of Portugal. For nearly four centuries, Madeira has produced one of the world's most famous fortified wines. Bual, Malmsey, Sercial, and Verdelho, all white grape varieties, are grown for Madeira wine production, along with Tinta Negra Mole, a red used in simple Madeiras.

In the following table, you'll find a list of Portugal's wines and typical wineries.

PORTUGAL'S WINE REGIONS, WINES, AND TYPICAL WINERIES

REGION	WINE(S)	WINERIES
Douro	Port	Champalimaud, A. A. Ferreira
Dão	Duque de Viseu, Grão Vasco, Tempranillo	Casa de Santar, Sogrape
Alentejo	Periquita, Tempranillo	Periquita, J. M. da Fonesca, J. P. Vinhos
Vinho Verde (Minho)	Vinho Verdes (red and white)	Palácio de Brejoeira, Quinta de Aveleda
Bairrada	Baga, sparkling wines	Luis Pato, Quinta do Carvalhinho
Setúbal	Setúbal (from variations of the Muscat grape)	J. M. da Fonesca
Madeira	Madeira	Blandy's, Leacock's, Miles

Portugal's fresh young white wines are so often upstaged by its heady Ports, Madeiras, and rosés that they lack the international attention they deserve. Portuguese Vinho Verde, or "green wine" (green not in color but in age), is meant to be drunk when very young and goes wonderfully with Portuguese cuisine, grilled fish, and seafood. Vinho Verde may be made from Albariño (which in Portugal is called Alvarinho) and a number of other grapes and is typically light and acidic. Most of the Vinho Verdes produced for export are white, but there are a few red styles as well—some of which are lightly fizzy. Portugal makes a great deal of the popular Spanish Tempranillo, as well as a number of fine reds with international appeal, such as Cabernet Sauvignon.

GERMANY

Until the twentieth century, wine aficionados believed that only two countries produced truly fine wine: France and Germany. (Italy was generally thought of as the place to go for simple but good wines.) Germany could always be counted on to deliver high-quality, focused wines. It continues to do so, although it has much more competition in the fine-wine market today. An increasing number of countries are growing traditional German grape varieties.

> **student experience**
>
> "I have learned that if I look carefully at the labels of German wines and choose one that says it's from the 'Mosel-Saar-Ruwer region,' (the areas near the Saar and Mosel rivers), the wine is likely to be very good."
> —Peggy, professional pianist

Germany is generally considered to be the northernmost of wine-growing climates. Every season, German wine growers struggle to nurse their crops to ripeness in harsh, chilly conditions that frequently are stingy with sunlight. Most German vineyards are set on sunny, stony slopes or near open stretches of water to take advantage of reflected light and capture warmth. A brief ripening time means that German wine grapes keep much of their sour, acidic tang, one of the most typical—and most wonderful—attributes of German wine. Other vineyards are set on steep, slatey soils. These slippery areas are treacherous for vineyard workers but are magnificent for the wine; they impart a classic wet stone flavor.

Somehow, those extreme conditions create wines with extraordinary elegance and character. Classic German wines are low in alcohol, are high in acid, and rarely have their natural flavors muddied by oak. Their sharp, clear flavors are so forthright that German wine is often described as naked, sheer, or transparent.

The vast majority of German wines are white. Germany does produce a few reds—about 18 percent of its total production is red and rosé—but these wines seldom leave the country.

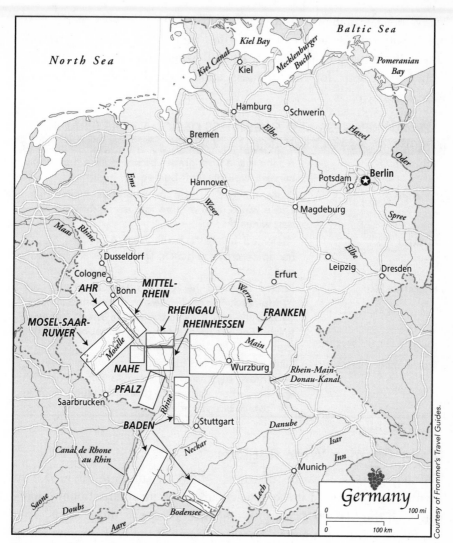

Germany's wine-growing regions.

German Wine Classifications

To an extent, Germany's quality rankings are similar to France's AOCs. *Qualitätswein mit Prädikat* (QMP) wines must conform to specific attributes, areas, yields, and winemaking methods. *Qualitätswein Bestimmter Anbaugebiete* (QbA) is basic, everyday wine from one of 13 regions, and *Landwein* is roughly akin to Vin de Pays. *Deutscher Tafelweins* are usually low-quality blends. Beyond these designations, many fine German wines are classified by their degrees of ripeness: their relative sweetness or acidity. The *Prädikat* indicates how ripe the grapes are at the time of harvest. The following table describes the common designations for the ripeness and sweetness levels of German wines.

GERMAN RIPENESS AND SWEETNESS DESIGNATIONS (PRÄDIKATS)

PRÄDIKAT	DESCRIPTION
Kabinett	A wine made from grapes picked during the normal harvest, typically light bodied.
Spätlese	"Late harvest"; made from grapes picked late. These wines have a more intense flavor than Kabinett wines do.
Auslese	"Selected harvest"; made from super-ripe grapes handpicked by the bunch. These wines are lush with ripe flavors.
Beerenauslese	"Berry selected harvest"; individual grapes are handpicked. The grapes selected are often affected by *botrytis,* which gives the wine a sweet, honeyed finish. (English speakers sometimes abbreviate this term to BA, for "*botrytis* affected".)
Trockenbeerenauslese	"Dry berry selected harvest"; the richest, sweetest, and most expensive of German wines. (English speakers often abbreviate this designation to TBA, for "totally *botrytis* affected.")

Major German Wine Regions

Germany boasts 13 wine districts, which in turn are divided into smaller areas. Nine of these districts are of major international importance. Of the 70,000 grape-growers who operate in these areas, only two-thirds sell to commercial wineries. Some of the best German wines come from small, relatively obscure growers.

- **Ahr:** South of the city of Bonn, near the Ahr and Rhine rivers, Ahr is a small, ancient wine-growing district of breathtaking natural beauty. Its soils hang onto enough heat to enable a few red varieties to grow. Ahr produces a light red wine called Spätburgunder from local Pinot Noir grapes, as well as a number of pale whites.

- **Baden:** Located near Germany's famous Black Forest near the southern border with France and Switzerland (due west of

Stuttgart), Baden is the warmest and southernmost of Germany's wine regions, replete with variety. Some of its best wines grow in volcanic soil near the extinct Kaiserstuhl volcano. Baden grows Müller-Thurgau, Grauburgunder (Pinot Gris), and Spätburgunder grapes.

- **Franken:** Approximately 100 miles northeast of Heidelberg, along the Main River, Franken's brief summers and plentiful frost force vineyards into protected valleys and pockets. Unlike most of Germany's wine regions, Franken grows relatively little Riesling. Its signature wines come from the Silvaner grape, which provides an earthy, honeylike flavor. It also grows a substantial quantity of Müller-Thurgau.

- **Mittelrhein:** This area lies along the Rhine River near Bonn and Koblenz. An area steeped in history and legend, Mittelrhein grows delightful wines with pronounced mineral flavors. Night mists keep temperatures from plummeting. Its steep, slatey slopes grow Riesling and Müller-Thurgau grapes with intense character. Unfortunately, the number of vineyards in this region is shrinking, and many of its wines now cater to the tastes of tourists.

- **Mosel-Saar-Ruwer:** Running along the Mosel River from Koblenz to Germany's border with Luxembourg, this scenic area is probably the greatest of Germany's wine regions. Wine has been growing here for more than 2,000 years. Mosel Rieslings are crystal clear, intensely focused, and almost always sold in Mosel's signature green bottles. Cold, steep vineyards impart a mineral tang to its wines.

- **Nahe:** Located along the Nahe River west of the Rheingau and Rheinhessen (about 50 miles west-southwest of Frankfurt), Nahe is sometimes called "the great tasting room of Germany" because of the broad variety of soil types. Nahe produces finely crafted, intense, elegant German wines. Its style marries the best of the Mosel and Rheingau districts. Nahe produces Riesling and Müller-Thurgau, as well as Silvaner, Grauburgunder, and Weissburgunder (Germany's version of Pinot Blanc).

- **Pfalz:** Southwest of the cities of Mannheim and Heidelberg, near the French border, this area enjoys a warmer, sunnier

climate than much of Germany, as well as a festive atmosphere.
The weather produces classic citrus-flavored wines from Riesling, Grauburgunder, Weissburgunder, and Spätburgunder
grapes, as well as a large number of red wines. Pfalz's winemakers create fruitier wines than most other regions. A large
amount of Germany's popular export, the sweet low-alcohol
Liebfraumilch (mother's milk), comes from this region. Look
for such popular brands as Black Tower and Blue Nun.

- **The Rheingau:** Bordering the Rhine River near the cities of
  Johannisberg, Wiesbaden, and Frankfurt, the Rheingau is considered one of the finest wine regions in the world. Its Rieslings
  are almost unparalleled. The soils impart a rich earthiness to
  these wines, and area winemakers strive to make balanced, elegant, fruited wines. The Rheingau is also known for its Eiswein,
  produced from grapes left to freeze on the vine after the regular
  harvest.

- **The Rheinhessen:** Located due south of the Rheingau, the
  Rheinhessen is the largest of Germany's wine regions and the
  source of much of the nation's casual wines. The Rheinhessen
  is also home to the sweet export Liebfraumilch. Rheinhessen
  wines are typically sold in brown bottles.

In the following table, you'll find popular German wines and wineries listed by region.

NOTEWORTHY GERMAN WINE REGIONS, WINES, AND WINERIES

REGION	WINE(S)	WINERIES
Ahr	Spätburgunder	J. J. Adeneuer, Kreuzberg, Meyer-Näkel
Baden	Gewürztraminer, Grauburgunder, Spätburgunder	Bercher, Dr. Heger, Salwey
Franken	Müller-Thurgau	Burgerspital, Juliusspital, Hans Wirsching
Mittelrhein	Müller-Thurgau, Riesling, Sekt	Toni Jost, August Perll, Adolf Weingart

REGION	WINE(S)	WINERIES
Mosel	Riesling	Fritz Haag, Dr. Loosen, Richter, Zilliken
Nahe	Grauburgunder, Müller-Thurgau, Weissburgunder	August Anheuser, Crosius, Plettenburg
Pfalz	Gewürztraminer, Grauburgunder, Riesling, Sekt, Spätburgunder, Weissburgunder, Liebfraumilch	Becker, Kurt Darting, Lingenfelder
Liebfraumilch		
The Rheingau	Eiswein, Riesling	August Eser, Weingut Grimm, Franz Kunstler
The Rheinhessen	Liebfraumilch	J. B. Becker, Kunstler, Prinz, Robert Weil, Black Tower

Germany's two most popular grape varieties are Riesling (made into sweet and dry wines) and Gewürztraminer (spicy, also made into sweet and dry styles). Germany exports these grapes in great quantities, and numerous winemaking countries around the world now grow them. Aside from the user-friendly Liebfraumilch, Germany's other two widely exported specialties are its popular sparkling wine, Sekt, and its Eiswein, produced from frozen grapes.

AUSTRIA

The wines of Austria share a lot of common ground with Germany's wines but seem to take German wine attributes to an even greater degree. Their wines are spicier, drier, fuller bodied, fruitier, and more intense. And Austria's warmer climate allows vineyards to grow many varieties that chilly Germany can't produce.

Austrian winemakers have embraced modern technology and international winemaking standards. The country has always been concerned with quality and, in light of current international trends, is redoubling its efforts, although it also makes a substantial amount of jug wine. It produces nearly three times as much wine as its neighbor Switzerland.

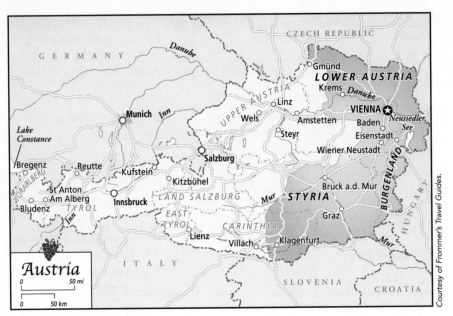

Austria's wine-growing regions.

Austrian Wine Classifications

Austria's wine laws are notoriously strict and are similar in structure to Germany's. Austrian law dictates, among other things, where a grape variety can be grown, the yield per hectare, and the amount of alcohol in the finished product. *Qualitätswein* comes from regions that have been given this designation; *Landwein* ranks next, and then *Tafelwein*, the least-regulated category. Austrian wines are also categorized according to the ripeness of the grapes at harvest.

Austrian Wine Regions

Austria's major wine regions, from north to south, are Lower Austria, Vienna, Burgenland, and Styria.

- **Lower Austria:** This large area in Austria's northeast corner nearly envelops the area of Vienna to the south. Its premier grape varieties are the peppery Grüner Veltliner and the crisp Riesling. It also produces Chardonnay, Weissburgunder (Pinot Blanc), and numerous rare local grapes.

- **Vienna:** This is the region immediately surrounding the city of Vienna. Grapes grow even within the city limits. Riesling is the major grape grown here, but Vienna also grows Weissburgunder, Gewürztraminer, and Cabernet Sauvignon.

- **Burgenland:** Running along Austria's eastern border with Hungary, this area is known for its sweet, botrytized wines, the most famous of which is Ausbruch. Burgenland also grows Weissburgunder, Chardonnay, and Hungary's famous grape, Furmint.

- **Styria:** This small, southernmost region is flanked to the north by the Central Alps and by Austria's border with Slovenia to the south. The city of Graz is located in this region. Styria makes a Chablis-style Chardonnay, as well as Weissburgunder and Sauvignon Blanc.

In the following table, you'll find popular Austrian wines and wineries listed by region.

NOTEWORTHY AUSTRIAN WINE REGIONS, WINES, AND WINERIES

REGION	WINES	WINERIES
Lower Austria	Cabernet Sauvignon, Chardonnay, Riesling, Weissburgunder	Prager, Fritz Salomon, Stadlmann
Vienna	Gewürztraminer, Riesling, Weissburgunder	Fritz Wieninger, Leopold Breyer
Burgenland	Ausbruch, Chardonnay, Furmint, Weissburgunder, Welschriesling	Triebaumer, Schandl, Wenzel
Styria	Chardonnay, Sauvignon Blanc, Weissburgunder	Gross, Sattlerhoff, Winkler-Hermaden

Eighty percent of Austria's wine is white, much of it made from the nation's spicy white Grüner Veltliner grape. This wine has a slight musky quality, with a bite of pepper at the finish. The leading local red grape is the fruity Bläufrankisch, which makes a rich, earthy wine. In addition to local varieties, Austria grows red and white grapes of international distinction. Weissburgunder, grown extensively across all four regions, is Austria's version of Pinot Blanc. Oddly enough, Austria's Welschriesling is not related to Riesling at all. This grape makes a simple white wine with a slightly grassy essence.

HUNGARY

Hungary's ancient vineyards rest on grassy plains, basking in warm summers and crisp winters. A dazzling variety of grapes grow here, and they're made into an array of wine styles. Hungarian culture retains a pronounced Turkish flair, as well as influences from all across Europe. Its wines reflect this diversity; international varieties grow alongside local Hungarian grapes, and numerous winemaking styles are at work.

Much of the wine-drinking world is familiar with Hungary's most famous contribution: the sweet, botrytised Tokay Aszu, widely hailed as one of the world's finest wines. The best Tokay is expensive, although lesser varieties start at about $30. But Hungarian wines in general are finely crafted and of high quality—they just aren't widely known on today's international scene. Until the twentieth century, however, Hungary was considered the third greatest wine-producing country, after France and Germany.

Hungarian wines are typically dry, spicy, and full bodied. Most age well. Their quality is impeccable. Hungary's most famous red is Egri Bikavér ("bull's blood"), a robust, earthy, and dry wine, sometimes with a slight raspberry aroma.

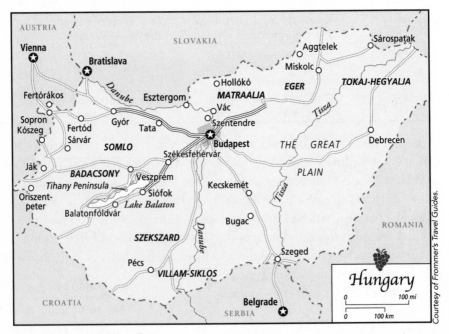

Hungary's wine-growing regions.

Courtesy of Frommer's Travel Guides.

Hungary's major wine-producing regions are Eger, the Matra Foothills, Somló, Badacsony, Great Alfold, Szekszárd, Villany-Siklós, and Tokaj Hegyaljia.

- **Eger:** The home of Egri Bikavér, Eger lies approximately 75 miles northeast of Budapest.

- **The Matra Foothills:** This area, closest to the city of Budapest, is known for fine white wines made from both local and international varieties.

- **Somló:** Approximately 50 miles from the Austrian border, Somló is the farthest west and is home to quaint, old-fashioned–style white wines.

- **Badacsony:** To the south of Somló, Badacsony lies on the shore of Lake Balaton. This region produces a number of French varieties, including Chardonnay and Sauvignon Blanc.

- **Great Alfold:** This region is home to nearly half the country's vineyards, although most of the grapes grown here are made into inexpensive wines for local consumption.

- **Szekszárd:** This area lies nearly due west of Great Alfold.

- **Villany-Siklós:** This is the southernmost region, near Hungary's Croatian border. Szekszárd and Villany-Siklós are leading the way in bringing modern winemaking techniques to Hungary.

- **Tokaj-Hegyaljia:** Home of Tokay Aszu, is in the northeastern corner of the country, farther northeast than Eger.

GREECE

Greece is the original homeland of all European winemaking. Every European grape variety has an ancient Greek ancestor, reflected all the way back to Homer's *Iliad* and *Odyssey*, which speak of the sea as "wine-dark." The ancient Greeks praised wine as an intimate part of their culture. Women in ancient Greece paid homage to Bacchus, the god of wine, mixing their wines with aphrodisiac spices such as mint, cinnamon, and cardamom to make a beverage that inspired carnal passions.

The country that started it all still makes some exquisite wines. Modern Greece grows approximately 300 rare, indigenous grape varieties, most of them thousands of years old, still growing amid olive trees as they have for millennia. The ancient Greeks and Romans enjoyed the grapes Demestike and Limnio, along with the ancestors of today's spicy Nemea and Mantinia wines.

With abundant sunlight reflecting off the sea, warm Mediterranean breezes, and chalky soils, Greece is nearly ideal for wine grapes. As long as strong winds don't damage the vines and the sun doesn't over-ripen the grapes, Greece's idyllic climate can produce wines of astonishing character.

Greece's winemaking regions are basically the same ones that existed 2,000 years ago:

- **Macedonia:** This region is closest to the main body of Europe. Macedonia produces wines from local Assyrtiko, Athiri, Limono, and Xinomauro grapes, as well as classic French varieties like Cabernet Franc and Cabernet Sauvignon.

- **Thessaly:** On the eastern flank of the country's main land mass, this region is made up of a central plain bordered by the Pindus Mountains. Summer rains keep vineyards productive. Thessaly is home to such Greek varieties as Krasato, Mpatiki, and Xinomauro.

- **The Peloponnese:** This large land mass across the Gulf of Corinth from the mainland would be an island unto itself if not for the Isthmus of Corinth. The Peloponnese produces Agiorgitiko, Moschofilero, and Refosco grapes.

- **Aegean Islands:** This smattering of islands is found off the southern tip of Greece, south of Athens, between the Aegean Sea and the Sea of Crete. The climate among these islands is among the warmest in the world for growing grapes, yet grape-growing is possible here because of high-altitude microclimates and cool sea breezes. Also, the ancient varieties grown here have had several millennia to adapt to the harsh conditions. These islands grow such local grape varieties as Aidani, Kostifali, Liatiko, Romeiko, and Vilana.

- **Crete:** This slender island of King Minos and the labyrinth lies due south of the main cluster of the Aegean Islands. Like its neighbors to the north, Crete produces Aidani, Kostifali, Liatiko, Romeiko, and Vilana grapes.

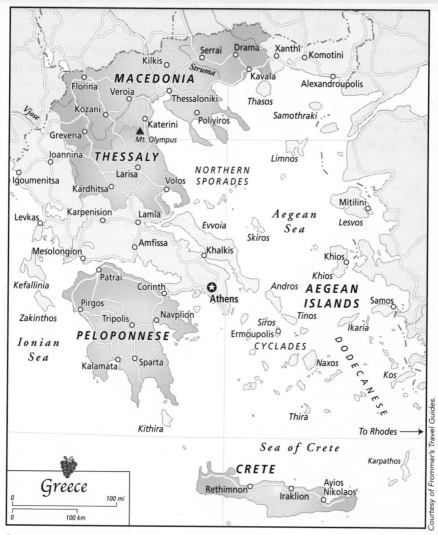

Greece's wine-growing regions.

In the following table, you'll find a few of the typical wines and producers for Greece's major regions.

NOTEWORTHY GREEK WINERIES AND WINES

REGION	WINES	WINERIES
Macedonia	Assyrtiko, French varieties	Domaine Carras, Tsantali
The Peleponnese	Agiorgitiko, Roditis	Gaia Estate, Kourtakis
Aegean Islands	Greek varieties	Boutari
Crete	Greek and French varieties	Manousakis Winery

Although Greece appears to be moving toward producing international favorites, it hasn't lost its fondness for its massive array of ancient, native varieties. Most of these wines are pretty hard to come by outside of Greece. Among the popular truly Greek styles of wine is Nemea, a spicy, heavy wine not unlike Port. Modern Retsina, an oily, pine-scented wine made from a mixture of local grapes, harkens back to the days when wine vessels were coated with pine pitch to protect them from oxidation.

wine regions of australia, new zealand, and south africa

Australian Wines • New Zealand
Wines • South African Wines

If you'd gone into your local wineshop in the 1960s and asked for a nice Australian Shiraz, a South African Pinotage, or a crisp New Zealand Sauvignon Blanc, you'd have gotten a lot of puzzled looks. Only within the past two decades have the fine-wine industries in these countries burst onto the international wine scene. But each of these countries has put itself on the wine map with innovative specialties and bold, modern winemaking techniques. In this lesson, we take a look at the ground-breaking wines of Australia, New Zealand, and South Africa.

AUSTRALIA

Australia's fast-growing wine industry has become internationally famous for cutting-edge technology and bold experimentation. Australian wine-makers scoff at terroir, pruning, and natural corks (many Australian producers prefer synthetic ones) and favor blending varieties for a con-sistent flavor. Australian wine is unpretentious, and easy-going. The country has enjoyed success as an international wine producer largely because it's developed a reputation for making international wines in a user-friendly, laid-back style.

More than 1,000 Australian wineries are busy experimenting with a dazzling array of grapes and styles—most of them big, powerful reds with gamey, berrylike flavors. Australia's biggest claim to fame is its Shiraz, called Syrah by everyone else except South Africans. Australian Shiraz is rustic yet elegant. Australia also grows a nice Sémillon (and, unlike the rest of the world, Australians pronounce the Ls). The nation also grows significant quantities of Cabernet Sauvignon, Chardonnay, and Riesling and produces a number of blended, sparkling, sweet, and fortified styles of wine. Australia produces some blended Rhône-style wines, but, curiously, none of its wines comes from native varieties or hybrids, which don't do well on Australian soil.

Australia's Wine Classification System

An agreement with the European Union has started Australia moving toward a classification system. But for the time being, Australian wine-makers enjoy tremendous freedom to experiment and innovate—and their enthusiasm shows in their vibrant, fun wines. Among our favorites are Kaeseler "Old Bastard" Shiraz, Fifth Leg Sémillon-Sauvignon Blanc, Starve Dog Lane Sauvignon Blanc, and Cockfighter's Ghost Chardonnay.

Australian law does require winemakers to use 85 percent of the grape variety that appears on the wine's label in the wine, and if the label identifies an area, 85 percent of the grapes used must come from that region.

Australia's Wine Regions

Much of Australia is baking, bone-dry desert. With a rim of lush green at its coasts, it is sometimes too wet for grapes. In most vineyards, irrigation is the name of the game. Soil types are almost irrelevant here, though, because Australians pay no attention to terroir. Instead, winemakers

a note from the instructor

AUSTRALIA'S BLENDED WINES

Australia is known for its tasty blends of traditional favorites. Australian winemakers, in the spirit of experimentation, produce such blends as Shiraz-Cabernet, Shiraz-Merlot, Chardonnay-Sémillon, and Grenache-Shiraz. Sometimes more than two varieties are blended, depending on the flavor the winemaker is trying to achieve. These Australian blends are known as combination wines.

grow, vinify, age, and blend according to the particular flavor they're trying to achieve.

The bulk of Australia's wine industry is clustered on the country's western border and southeastern tip, in Western Australia, South Australia, New South Wales, Victoria, and Tasmania.

- **New South Wales:** This Australian state is located on the southeastern horn of the continent, just above Victoria. The cities of Canberra and Sydney are located here. New South Wales's wine regions are Mudgee, Hunter Valley, and Riverina. The Hunter Valley is its most famous region, known for its fine Chardonnays and Sémillons.

- **Victoria:** Due south of New South Wales, on the tip of Australia's southeastern horn, is Victoria, home to the city of Melbourne and 11 wine regions: Murray Darling, Rutherglen, Glenrowan, Goulburn Valley, Bendigo, Pyrenees, Macedon, Grampians, Yarra Valley, Geelong, and Mornington Peninsula. Victoria's hotter inland wine regions grow warm-weather grapes like Cabernet and Shiraz. Those regions close enough to take advantage of the cooler oceanic climate grow Chardonnay and Pinot Noir. Victoria also produces a number of sweet wines (in Australia they're known as "stickies").

- **South Australia:** This state lies along the western border of New South Wales and Victoria, to the east of Western Australia. It's home to the city of Adelaide. More than half of Australia's wine comes from this state. South Australia is known for its

Cabernet Sauvignon, Chardonnay, Riesling, Sémillon, and Shiraz. Its major wine regions are Clare Valley, Barossa Valley, Eden Valley, Adelaide Hills, McClaren Vale, Padthaway, and Coonawara.

- **Tasmania:** This triangular island lies off the coast of Australia's eastern horn. Hobart is its major city. Most of Tasmania's wineries are small, but its cool, lush, maritime climates are excellent for growing wine grapes. Chardonnay and Pinot Noir do well here.

- **Western Australia:** This large state occupies the western third of the Australian continent. The city of Perth is located here. Clustered along the southern portions of the coast are five wine regions: Swan Valley, Perth Hills, Margaret River, Pemberton, and the Great Southern Region. Western Australia's specialties are Cabernet Sauvignon and Shiraz.

In the following table, you'll find Australia's wine regions, along with some of the notable wineries to be found in each region and the typical wines those wineries produce. Each of Australia's regions boasts many more wineries than those listed here, but this table will give you an idea of who's where.

NOTEWORTHY AUSTRALIAN WINERIES AND WINES

REGION	WINERIES	WINES
New South Wales	Allanmere, Arrowfield, Brokenwood	Chardonnay, Sémillon, fortified wines
Victoria	Balgownie, Bannockburn, Dalwhinnie	Cabernet, Shiraz, Chardonnay, stickies
Tasmania	Heemskerk, Moorilla Estate, Pipers Brook	Cabernet, Chardonnay, Pinot Noir, Shiraz sparkling wine
South Australia	Adams, Grossett, Mountadam	Cabernet Sauvignon, Chardonnay, Riesling, Sémillon, Shiraz
Western Australia	Cape Mentelle, Cullens, Leeuwin Estate	Cabernet Sauvignon, Shiraz

Note: Not all the wineries mentioned in this table carry all the wines listed for that particular region.

Australian Wine Characteristics

Australian wines are easy to like. They're unpretentious and fun, but full of personality and often sophistication. They tend to be full bodied, ripe, and fruity, with moderate acidity. Australian Chardonnay is full of

Australia
0   500 mi
0   500 km

Australia's wine-producing regions.

apple and pear flavors, often with a honey or butterscotch finish. Australian Sémillon is full of rich honey tones.

The star of Australia's wine show is Shiraz, the Aussie version of the French grape/wine Syrah. Good Australian Shiraz has many of the qualities that wine lovers adore in a full-bodied red—intense, complex, smoky flavors and aromas—yet it's often lighter and easier to fall in love with than a heavy Burgundy or a serious Bordeaux. Australian Shiraz is both rustic and elegant—a perfect wine for an outdoor barbecue or a crisp fall evening around a fire. Australian Shiraz is generally ready to drink when you buy it, but it can handle a few years of aging.

In the following chart, you'll find common Australian wines and their defining characteristics. Recent good years for Australian wines are 1990, 1994, 1998, 2001, and 2002.

AUSTRALIAN WINE STYLES

WINE	CHARACTERISTICS
Chardonnay	Full-bodied, low in acid; apple, pear, and honey flavors
Sémillon	Medium-bodied; honey flavor
Shiraz	Medium-bodied, low in acid; smoke, plum, berry, spice, and sometimes autumn leaf flavors
"Stickies"	Typically extremely sweet, high in alcohol, and low in acid

NEW ZEALAND

In the 1980s, New Zealand's distinctive, powerful Sauvignon Blanc put the country on the wine lover's map. New Zealand produces a Sauvignon Blanc like none other in the world, with rich, creamy, asparagus-like flavors. When this wine burst onto the scene, it catapulted New Zealand's tiny wine industry to world-class status. On the heels of this initial success, New Zealand has developed a thriving industry of international varieties.

New Zealand started out growing the bland Müller-Thurgau grape but has since enjoyed marked success with Cabernet Sauvignon, Chardonnay, Pinot Gris, Pinot Noir, and Riesling. Many of its vineyards have Maori names in honor of New Zealand's native people. Look for New Zealand to contribute some of the world's best high-end wines in years to come.

New Zealand's Wine Classification System

New Zealand enjoys a great deal of freedom from restrictive wine laws. Unlike their counterparts in France, New Zealand winemakers are not required to limit their wine growing to certain varieties. New Zealand's wine laws primarily dictate the way a wine can be described on its label: If a grape variety is named, 75 percent of the wine must come from that variety, and if a wine is made from two grapes, whichever grape is the majority must be named first. If a place of origin is identified, 75 percent of the wine must come from that region.

New Zealand's Wine Regions

New Zealand's cool, maritime climate is ideal for whites, hearty reds, and German varieties. Its warmer North Island grows most of the reds; the cooler South Island produces the lion's share of the whites.

- **North Island:** With the city of Wellington on its southern tip, New Zealand's North Island is home to the wine regions of Auckland, Gisbourne, Hawke's Bay, Wairarapa, and Martinborough. The North Island is the warmer of the two, and most of its vineyards benefit from cool ocean breezes. Moisture is so abundant that it's sometimes a problem, but it also permits grapes to ripen slowly.

- **South Island:** New Zealand's cooler South Island, with the cities of Nelson and Blenheim on its northern tip and the cities of Queenstown and Dunedin in the south, is home to four wine regions: Nelson, Marlborough, Canterbury, and Central Otago. Because of its long, narrow shape, most of the island enjoys a cool, breezy, maritime climate. Grapes can ripen slowly over a long growing season yet still retain a crisp acidity.

The following table presents a selection of some fine New Zealand wineries and wines.

NOTEWORTHY NEW ZEALAND WINERIES

REGION	WINERIES	WINES
North Island	Collards, Feston, Stony Ridge	Cabernet Sauvignon, Chardonnay, Pinot Noir, Sauvignon Blanc
South Island	Cloudy Bay, Corbans, Hunters, Nautilus	Pinot Noir, Riesling, Sauvignon Blanc

New Zealand Wine Characteristics

New Zealand's produce is famous for its intensity of flavor, and its wines are no exception. New Zealand wines tend to be high in acid and packed with flavor. Sauvignon Blanc is New Zealand's pride and joy and can taste like a virtual salad bar of fruits and vegetables. What often stands out, however, is a creamy, asparaguslike flavor that no other Sauvignon Blanc in the world can match. New Zealand also produces a light Chardonnay with slightly nutty, honeyed fruit flavors; an intense Pinot Noir; and a

student
experience

"You might think that good wine has to come from France, but it doesn't. Australia produces many excellent red blended wines, and New Zealand has some great whites."

—Emma, veterinarian

New Zealand's wine-producing regions.

Riesling that can be either quite dry or sweet enough to serve for dessert.

Good years for New Zealand wines include 1991, 1993, 1994, and 1996. The following chart describes some of the typical wines for each of New Zealand's wine regions.

NEW ZEALAND WINE STYLES

WINE	CHARACTERISTICS
Carbernet Sauvignon	Intense; somewhat Bordeauxlike
Chardonnay	Medium to light body; honey, and tropical fruit flavors
Pinot Noir	Intense; still and sparkling styles
Riesling	Acidic; dry and sweet dessert styles
Sauvignon Blanc	Rich, creamy, intense; citrus and asparagus flavors

SOUTH AFRICA

Seventh in worldwide wine production, South Africa boasts a well-organized winemaking industry that produces wine in enormous co-ops called wine farms. Although half of the country's crop is made into brandy and cheap wine, South Africa produces some world-class Cabernet, Sauvignon Blanc, and Shiraz, as well as Pinotage—a local cross between Cinsault and Pinot Noir—and Steen, its name for Chenin Blanc.

---

abcdefghijklmnopq rstuvwxyzabcdefgh ijklmnopqrstuvwxy

a note from
the instructor

SOUTH AFRICA'S CO-OP SYSTEM

Wine has been produced in South Africa since the mid-1600s, but in modern times, South Africa's wine industry has undergone a radical transformation. Its first few centuries were fraught with political strife, economic instability, and a debilitating attack of the phylloxera mite. To combat these problems, many of South Africa's small wine farms banded together in the twentieth century to form large cooperatives. Today, giant cooperative "wine farms" are the norm in South Africa.

The cooperative system takes the sting out of the otherwise fierce competition among small-scale growers and gives all members access to large-scale expertise and technology. The largest of these conglomerates is KWV, *Kooperatiewe Wijnbouers Vereeniging*, or the Cape Wine-Growers' Cooperative. The KWV regulates production and pricing. Today, the KWV produces more than 50 percent of South Africa's wine. Other noteworthy South African conglomerates are Bergkelder (literally "Mountain Cellar"), which has accelerated the country's move toward quality wines, and the Stellenbosch Farmers' Winery Group, which produces most of the country's brandy.

South Africa's wine industry has taken off since trade sanctions were lifted in 1990 with the release of political prisoner Nelson Mandela. Since then, many South African winemakers have set out to make world-class wines. Unstable politics still wreak havoc on the country's marketing efforts, but many of its wines remain phenomenal. Many of the varietals, though, are not yet mainstream enough to gain international attention.

South Africa's Wine Classification System

South Africa began regulating the labeling of its wines in 1973. Its *Wine of Origin* (WO) regulations offer a voluntary certification program. The WO certifies wine according to vintage and grape variety, as well as estate (the equivalent of France's château), region, and district. A certified wine that identifies a varietal must contain at least 75 percent of the named grape.

South Africa's Wine Regions

Although much of South Africa is too hot for wine (as is much of the African continent—only 8 of Africa's 50 countries grow wine), South African grape-growers plant most of their vines in the country's cooler high-altitude microclimates. South Africa's major wine regions are:

- **Constantia:** Located due south of the city of Cape Town on the Cape of Good Hope, Constantia is the oldest of South Africa's wine regions, dating to the first European settlements from around the 1650s. This area grows noteworthy Sauvignon Blanc.

- **Stellenbosch:** Due east of Cape Town, this region is a bit cooler than the others and benefits from a slight sea breeze, which permits the growing of Pinot Noir and a few hardy white wines. This area and Paarl are considered the two highest-quality wine regions in South Africa.

- **Paarl:** Northeast of Cape Town and due north of Stellenbosch, Paarl is a warm region known for producing fortified wines in the styles of Port and Sherry, as well as Pinotage.

- **Franschoek Valley:** This area, northeast of Stellenbosch, is nicknamed the "French Corner" for the French Huguenots who settled there in the late seventeenth century. The area produces good Chardonnay.

In addition to these major areas, South Africa boasts a number of smaller wine regions, including Durbanville, Swartland, Tulbagh, Worchester, Robertson, Swellandam, Klein Karoo, Elgin, Mossel Bay, Walker Bay, Douglas, and the Lower Orange River. All but the last two are located within 50 miles of the ocean.

In the following chart, you'll find a few of the wines and wineries that are typical of each of South Africa's major wine regions.

NOTEWORTHY SOUTH AFRICAN WINERIES AND WINES

REGION	WINERIES	WINES
Constantia	Groot Constantia Estate, Klein Constantia Estate	Sauvignon Blanc
Franschoek Valley	L'Ormarins	Chardonnay
Paarl	Boschendal, Nederburg	Cabernet Sauvignon, Riesling, Sauvignon Blanc
Stellenbosch	Kononkop, Neethlingshof, Zonnenbloem	Pinotage, Riesling, Shiraz

South African Wine Characteristics

In addition to its unique Cinsault-Pinot Noir cross, Pinotage—a perfumed, spicy, young wine that's great for barbecues—South Africa makes an interesting Chenin Blanc, which it calls Steen. It's also doing well with Cabernet Sauvignon, Riesling, Sauvignon Blanc, Chardonnay, and Australian-style Shiraz. Recent good years for South African wines are 1990, 1991, 1993, 1995, and 1996.

In the following table, you'll find a few of South Africa's popular wines with a description of each wine's flavors and styles.

SOUTH AFRICAN WINE STYLES

WINE	CHARACTERISTICS
Cabernet Sauvignon	Often blended Bordeaux-style; sometimes harsh
Chardonnay	Buttery, fruity; in a variety of weights and styles
Chenin Blanc (Steen)	Fruity; sweet to dry styles, some sparkling
Pinotage	Rustic, spicy, plummy
Riesling	Often sweet
Sauvignon Blanc	Acidic, sometimes with an unusual gooseberry flavor
Shiraz	Smoky, with hints of raspberry

South Africa's wine-producing regions.

south america's wine regions

Chilean Wines • Argentinian Wines

Ask the average wine lover to name countries that produce fine wine, and he or she might get pretty far down the list before mentioning Latin American nations. Yet Chile and Argentina have cultivated notable fine-wine industries in recent years. The wines these countries produce for export are typically high in quality, and at the moment they can still be found at relatively reasonable prices.

CHILE

Ninth in worldwide wine production, Chile has been talked up as a fine-wine producer for a while, but it's only just starting to live up to the hype. Its fine wines have been improving steadily from year to year. Chile boasts secluded, Mediterranean-like conditions, lots of available labor, and, best of all, no phylloxera mites. Its Cabernet Sauvignons are especially good.

As with most wine producers, the bulk of Chile's output is simple, everyday wine for local consumption, made from native grapes like Pais

a note from
the instructor

CHILE'S CABERNET SAUVIGNONS

Cabernet Sauvignon has become Chile's most important wine variety in recent years—which only goes to show that it's smart to find something you do well and stick with it. Chilean wines in general are fruity and soft, and its Cabernet is no exception. Chilean Cabernets also often exhibit a spicy, earthy, mineral quality. They can be enjoyed young or may be put away to age for three or four years.

(similar to California's Mission grape and Argentina's Criolla Chica). But its fine exports blend some of the best Old World styles (Burgundy, Bordeaux, and the Loire, for example) with California attitudes and technologies. Its Cabernet Sauvignon, Chardonnay, Merlot, and Sauvignon Blanc are of such a fine caliber that French, Spanish, and U.S. winemakers have invested in Chilean wineries.

Chile's Classification System

Chile established its wine classification system in 1995 with nine wine-producing appellations. Chilean law states that when a region is identified, 85 percent of the wine must come from that region. The law also sets specific standards for quality ranks: Reserva, Gran Reserva, and Reserva Especial. When these ranks appear on the label, 75 percent of the wine must conform to the rank's legally specified standards.

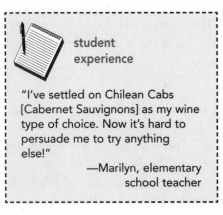

student experience

"I've settled on Chilean Cabs [Cabernet Sauvignons] as my wine type of choice. Now it's hard to persuade me to try anything else!"

—Marilyn, elementary school teacher

Chilean Wine Regions

Most of Chile's vineyards are located in valleys separated by mountain rivers. Several are at high altitudes. Ocean breezes help keep vineyard temperatures cool. Chile's wine regions are:

- **Aconcagua Valley:** The northernmost of Chile's wine regions, this valley is Chile's hottest wine region. Cabernet Sauvignon and Merlot manage here, but the temperatures remain too high in this region for delicate grape varieties.

■ **Casablanca Valley:** South of the Aconcagua Valley and due east of the city of Santiago, this area produces Chile's finest white wines.

■ **Central Valley:** This vast region spreads across Chile's mid-section. Within the Central Valley are the Maipo, Rapel, Curicó, and Maule valleys. Maipo Valley produces a highly acclaimed Cabernet Sauvignon. Chardonnay, Merlot, Malbec, and Sauvignon Blanc are also grown in this region.

■ **Itata Valley:** This valley is sandwiched between the Central Valley to the north and the Bio Bio Valley to the south.

■ **Bio Bio Valley:** The southernmost of Chile's wine regions, the Bio Bio Valley is transected by the Bio Bio River.

NOTEWORTHY CHILEAN WINERIES

REGION	WINERY	WINE(S)
Casablanca Valley	Viña Casablanca	Chardonnay
Maipo Valley	Concha y Toro	Syrah, Cabernet Sauvignon
Maule Valley	Santa Rita	Sauvignon Blanc
Rapel Valley	Los Vascos	Cabernet Sauvignon, Sémillon

*Note: Not all the wineries listed here necessarily make the wines that follow for that region.

Chilean Wine Characteristics

Chilean Cabernet Sauvignon is noteworthy, with a soft, herbal, slightly smoky flavor. Its Sauvignon Blanc is often good but seldom exceptional. Chilean Merlot and Chardonnay are generally good values.

ARGENTINA

Wine enthusiasts may be surprised to learn that Argentina is the fifth largest wine producer in the world until they understand just how much of that wine is consumed by Argentinians themselves. Argentina has one of the highest levels of wine consumption per capita in the world. High wine consumption is usually a recipe for mass production of cheap, coarse wines, and Argentina is no exception. But in the 1980s, much in need of a financial boost, the country began to follow Chile's lead and began to target the international fine-wine market, growing the kinds of varietals that appeal to international wine tastes.

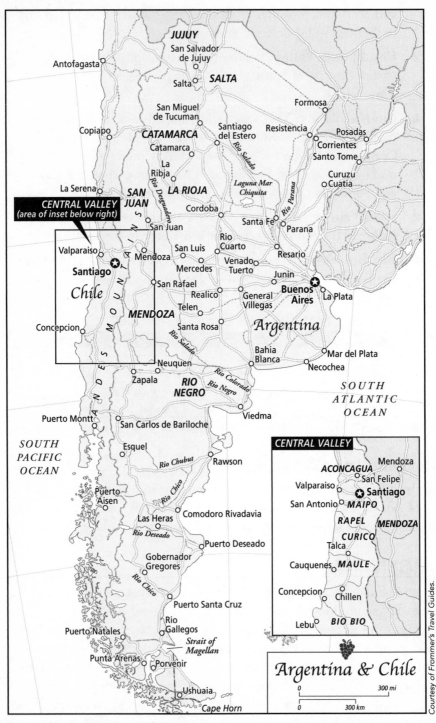

The wine-producing regions of Chile and Argentina.

Courtesy of Frommer's Travel Guides.

---

*abcdefghijklmnopq
rstuvwxyzabcdefgh
ijklmnopqrstuvwxy*

a note from
the instructor

PEÑAFLOR: ARGENTINA'S GALLO?

Argentina's massive Peñaflor winery has been hailed as the second largest family-owned wine-producing operation in the world, after California's Ernest & Julio Gallo Winery. Peñaflor, founded and owned by the Pulenta family, owes a large measure of its success to a brand of wine it calls Trapiche, which it developed specifically for the U.S. market.

Argentina produces a better Malbec—a perfumed, plumlike red from France's Bordeaux region—than those currently grown in the grape's native France. Argentina also grows several popular international varieties and is adapting its local grapes, such as the pink-skinned Criolla, to an international style. Its relaxed wine-growing laws allow for freedom of experimentation.

Argentina's Classification System

In contrast to Chile's legal definitions, Argentina leaves the definition of such terms as "Reserva" up to individual winemakers. On the other hand, it does place restrictions on wines meant for export. All wines destined to be sold abroad must meet the standards for "vino fino"; for example, 85 percent of the wine must come from the region identified on the bottle.

Argentina's Wine Regions

Most Argentinian wine is grown in the river-fed interior, at high altitude, to take advantage of cooler temperatures. About 60 percent of Argentina's wines are red.

From north to south, Argentina's wine regions are:

- **Jujuy:** At the northernmost tip of the country, this area produces fine Cabernet Sauvignon. It also produces a Muscatlike white grape known as Torrontés.

- **Salta:** Due south of Jujuy, this region also produces a noteworthy Cabernet Sauvignon.

- **Catamarca:** Southwest of Salta, on the eastern fringe of the Andes.

- **La Rioja:** Due south of Catamarca, cut through by the Desaguadero River. Argentina's oldest wine region, La Rioja specializes in making wine from the Torrontés grape. It also produces Barbera, Cabernet Sauvignon, Malbec, and Merlot.

- **San Juan:** Southeast of La Rioja, San Juan is Argentina's second largest and second most important wine region after Mendoza. Dolcetto, Sangiovese, Tempranillo, and other southern European grape varieties are grown here.

- **Mendoza:** Due south of San Juan, Mendoza is Argentina's primary wine region and produces 70 percent of the country's wine. Although it also produces Cabernet Sauvignon, Merlot, Syrah, Tempranillo, and others, its claim to fame is the Malbec grape.

- **Rio Negro:** The southernmost Argentine wine region, Rio Negro is somewhat cooler than its neighbors. Much of Argentina's sparkling wine comes from this region.

NOTEWORTHY WINERIES AND WINES OF ARGENTINA

REGION	WINERIES	WINES
La Rioja	Menem	Barbera, Cabernet Sauvignon, Malbec, Merlot, Torrontés
Mendoza	Catena Zapata, Luca, Tikal	Cabernet Sauvignon, Malbec, Merlot, Syrah, Tempranillo
Salta	Echart, Michel Torino	Cabernet Sauvignon, Malbec, Torrontés
San Juan	Santiago Graffigna	Dolcetto, Sangiovese, Tempranillo

Note: Not all the wineries listed here necessarily make the wines that follow for that region.

Argentinian Wine Characteristics

Approximately 60 percent of Argentina's exported wines are red, due to the warmth of the country's climate. In addition to the French reds mentioned in the preceding table, Argentina grows a number of Spanish and Italian grapes, including Barbera, Sangiovese, and Tempranillo. But Malbec is its claim to fame. Argentina's Malbec is intense and well structured.

buying wine

Negotiating the Wine Store • Buying Wine Elsewhere •
Your Wine Collection

Just as ordering and serving wine can cause a novice wine lover to break out in a sweat, selecting and purchasing good wine can fill a beginner with trepidation. Wine shops, Web sites, and catalogs—not to mention wine *labels*—aren't always user-friendly. Often, the only way to know what you're getting is by trial and error, which probably explains why many wine drinkers end up sticking with a short list of tried-and-true favorites. But wine buying isn't entirely a roll of the dice. In this lesson, we offer a number of guidelines to help you accelerate the learning curve—and avoid some of the most common pitfalls.

FEELING YOUR WAY AROUND A WINE STORE

If you've ever stepped into a wine store and felt as though you'd somehow wandered into a foreign country, you're not alone. Wine shops can be daunting. But if you develop a rapport with a knowledgeable staff member and arm yourself with enough basic knowledge that you can distinguish trendy, overpriced wines from solid values, you'll be able to purchase wine with confidence.

Choosing a Good Wine Shop

When you're after serious wine, forget about supermarkets and liquor stores that feature primarily beer and hard liquor; these outlets probably carry only mainstream, commercial wines and they're unlikely to have anyone on staff who's truly knowledgeable about wine. A shop that specializes in fine wines is a much better choice. Even among wine shops, though, there are good and not-so-good options. If you enter a wine shop and you see any of the following signs, don't walk, run to the nearest exit—your odds of finding quality wines are almost zero.

- Most of the wine is standing upright rather than on its side. (See "Two Signs That a Wine Has Been Mishandled" for information about why this is a problem.)

- The wine is stacked randomly, whites and reds together with no discernible sense of order.

- The shop is lit by fluorescent lights (which damage the wine).

- The shop smells funny.

- The shop is so warm that you immediately want to take off your jacket (if you're wearing one).

a note from
the instructor

TWO SIGNS THAT A WINE HAS BEEN MISHANDLED

It's displayed upright on the wine shop's shelves. Usually, you can't tell how long it's been sitting that way. If a wine with a natural cork sits upright long enough, the cork can dry out, allowing air to seep into the bottle and ruin the wine. When bottles are kept on their sides, the wine moistens the cork and maintains a tight seal against the bottleneck. Wines with synthetic corks or screwcaps are fine standing upright, as are Sherries and other fortified wines.

You find sticky residue on the outside of the bottle or stains on the label. These are signs that the cork is faulty and the wine is refermenting in the bottle—and escaping.

Look for a shop that organizes its wines by country, by type, or by some other means. Also note the age of the wines for sale, especially the whites. A good wine shop has no white wines older than four years (except those that age well, like Riesling, Chenin Blanc, White Burgundy, and a handful of others) and has at least one person on staff who knows wine and can answer your questions intelligently.

Understanding What the Numbers Mean

In an attempt to standardize wine quality, winemakers and tasters often assign points to a wine. You may see a card next to the wine rack with a number in a little circle and effusive praise for the wine's attributes. Does this praise guarantee the wine's quality? Are you going to like a 91 better than an 87? The point system can work for you as a rough guideline—after all, wine experts do know what they're talking about at least once in a while. Even so, don't get too wrapped up in the numbers. Just because *they* liked it doesn't necessarily mean that you will, too.

Using Wine Charts

When you're deciding which wines to look for, you may find the information in wine charts helpful. Like wines themselves, wine charts come in a dazzling number of varieties, from those that suggest serving temperatures, age profiles, and foods that pair well with each wine, to those that rate the wine's vintage or assign letter values: E for "early drinking," R for "ready to drink," and so on.

Wine charts can be valuable resources, but translating their information into data you can use may prove tricky. They may give you a clearer idea of what you're looking for, but not tell you how, where, and when to find it—or at what price you should find it. Also, like wine reviews and points, the information they contain can be subjective. As long as you keep that in mind, you'll never become overly dependent on them.

Look for wine charts in fine-wine magazines and current wine books, as well as on the Internet at such sites as wine pro Robert Parker's www.erobertparker.com.

Indicates the vintage of the wine

Regions/Wines		Classic Vintages	91	92	93	94	95	96	97	98	99	0	1
California	Cabernet Sauvignon	78-84-85-86-87	9.5	9.1	9.0	9.7	9.4	9.5	9.8	9.0	9.3	9.1	9.8
	Chardonnay	Do not age	9.2	9.1	9.0	9.5	9.3	9.4	9.6	9.0	9.2	9.0	9.4
	Pinot Noir	86-90	9.1	9.2	9.0	9.6	9.3	9.0	9.1	8.7	9.1	8.2	9.1
	Zinfandel	78-82	9.2	9.1	9.0	9.5	9.4	9.0	9.2	8.5	9.1	8.9	9.1
France	Bordeaux Red	61-82-85-88-89-90	7.5	7.6	8.5	8.1	9.4	9.2	7.5	9.0	9.2	9.2	9.6
	Burgundy Red	78-85-88-89-90	8.6	8.1	9.3	8.2	8.9	9.7	9.0	9.1	9.5	8.6	9.0
	Burgundy White	85-86-89-90	8.2	9.1	8.9	8.8	9.0	9.8	9.2	8.8	9.1	9.2	9.1
	Rhone	89-90	8.0	8.1	8.2	8.9	9.0	8.2	8.5	8.5	9.6	9.2	9.5	9.2
	Champagne	75 -79-82- 85- 88-89- 90	-	8.8	8.9	-	9.5	-	9.5	-	-	-	-
Italy	Piedmont	78-82-85-88- 89-90	6.9	7.1	8.7	6.9	8.8	9.6	9.7	9.5	9.1	9.4	9.1
	Tuscany	82-85-88- 90	8.5	8.0	8.5	8.5	8.9	9.0	9.8	9.2	9.2	9.0	9.2
Portugal/Port		63-70-77-83-85	9.2	9.4	-	9.9	9.3	8.9	9.3	9.1	8.6	9.8	-
Germany		71 -76-83-88-89- 90	8.4	8.5	8.9	8.7	8.9	9.1	8.9	8.8	8.9	8.5	
Australia		62-86-90	9.9	8.9	9.0	9.1	8.5	9.5	9.2	8.9	9.1	9.4	9.1

Color Code:
- Still Improving - Superior
- Ready and waiting
- No vintage wine produced
- Could be past its prime

Learn About Wine   Vintage Chart

www.LearnAboutWine.com   310-451-7600 Classes/Reservations

Chart courtesy of LearnAboutWine.com.

Key indicates the current readiness of the wine

This number is the score the wine received out of 10 points, as rated by the vintage chart creator

Once you have chosen which type of wine you wish to buy, wine charts can help you hone in on a particular wine. For example, if you already know you want to get a Zinfandel, the wine chart can help you locate a good vintage and region.

What's So Important about Vintage?

Wine enthusiasts often use vintage to identify a banner year for a given wine. But vintage isn't as cut and dried as it may sound, because any given year could be a good, bad, or mediocre year for the country, the region, the variety, or the specific winemaker. Don't reject a wine simply because it was made in an unpopular year. Let vintage serve only as a guideline.

If you're buying wine to put away for a few years, remember this general rule: The finer the vintage, the longer the wine may take to reach maturity. Wines from a so-so year generally don't require as long to reach their full potential because they don't have as much potential to reach.

Pricey Wines Aren't Necessarily Better

Although there's some truth to the saying "You get what you pay for," don't use it as a hard-and-fast rule when buying wines for immediate drinking. Yes, collectible wines are typically expensive to begin with and increase in value; quality is always worth something. But good wines aren't always "lay me down in the cellar" wines. Currently, amazing wine values can be found in Spain, Italy, Australia, and the south of France. Pay a buck or two more for a wine shop to guide you to a great find. If the shop deserves your trust, you have an instant inside contact to buying great wines of value. Once you're adept at choosing wines, you'll find wonderful buys all the time. Value is in the eye of the consumer.

Wines are frequently overpriced for a variety of reasons, and good wines come in nearly all price ranges. In general, wines from famous places come at famous prices. Take, for instance, California's Napa Valley: Although you can still find great values from this region, many Napa Valley wines command top dollar because they're trendy and demand outstrips supply. Many of Napa Valley's wines are expensive not just because they're good but also because they're popular.

As long as you don't become a raging wine snob, you'll still be able to find easy joy in a cheapie, like the Charles Shaw wines that the Trader Joe's grocery chain made famous. These wines became known as "Two Buck Chuck" for their rock-bottom price, due to California overplanting in the 1990s and the fact that Trader Joe's business practice is to buy directly from a supplier, thus eliminating the middleman. Another way to find cheap wines is to check the bargain rack for varieties you haven't tried before. Just remember that these low-price closeouts are probably on sale because nobody's buying them, and there's probably a reason for that. Plus, they may be approaching retirement age, particularly if they're white. Be careful.

---

abcdefghijklmnopq rstuvwxyzabcdefgh ijklmnopqrstuvwxy

a note from
the instructor

"PETIT CHATEAU" AND "GARAGE" WINES

"Petit chateau" and "garage" wines refer to wines produced in tiny quantities by obscure winemakers. All of them are rare; some of them are excellent.

Petit chateau—literally, "little estate"—wines are often grown on tiny plots of land in the same famous wine regions that legendary wine giants inhabit. When the region has a good year and the famous makers are getting outrageous prices for their wines, these smaller-batch wines sometimes can be had for a fraction of the cost. An example of a successful petit chateau is Chateau Pierrail in Bordeaux.

When you want a wine of any real quality, expect to spend at least $8, and more like $12 or $14. Reserve wines for "laying down" are probably going to run you close to $20 or more—from here on up we're talking special-occasion wines unless money is no object. Don't freak out if a special, hard-to-make wine, like Sauternes, has a $30 price tag. The more labor-intensive the wine, the higher its cost.

Your best ally against wine rip-offs is experience. The better you know your wines, your local wine stores, and your own tastes, the easier wine shopping will become. So experiment now while your enthusiasm is high. Set the goal of trying a new wine each week or each month. Compare several varieties, several styles, or several winemakers. Keep notes. You'll be astonished at how quickly your wine-buying confidence will grow.

> **student experience**
>
> "Serving wine at home used to make me very nervous because I wasn't comfortable buying and serving wines I didn't know well. Now I have two or three stand-bys that I always have stocked at home; when I'm not up for trying out a new wine on my guests, I can pull out a predictable, familiar bottle. Having favorite wines on hand has made me a much more relaxed host."
>
> —Max, linguist

Bordeaux   Burgundy   Alsace & Mosel   Champagne   Fortified Wine   Ice Wine

The shape of the bottle can give you a clue as to the kind of wine in the bottle, even before you look at the label.

What Bottle Shape Tells You

Traditionally, winemakers have used bottle shape to indicate their wine's region of origin. Bordeaux bottles, for example, have high, round shoulders, and Cabernet Sauvignon typically comes in a high, round-shouldered Bordeaux bottle even if it was grown in California (although no law governs bottle shape there). A Burgundy bottle has softer shoulders and tapers into a pyramid; Alsace bottles are slender.

HOW TO READ A WINE LABEL

Any bottle of wine that you purchase commercially has at least a front label, and likely a back label as well. The front lists, at a minimum, the name of the producer and the name of the wine, plus it gives some indication of where the wine was produced. How specific or clear this information is depends on the producer and on the wine laws for that area. The wine's name may be a grape variety, as in Cabernet Sauvignon; a wine style, as in Châteauneuf-du-Pape; the name of the wine's production area, as in Rioja; or a propietary name, like Cordon Rouge. On the back or the front of the bottle, you usually find an indicator of alcohol level, a fluid measurement, and various mandatory warnings.

For wines produced in the United States, this information is generally easy to access. But the labels of imports often leave even experienced wine lovers scratching their heads. In this section, we decipher some of the common label conundrums you're likely to run across. For simplicity's sake, we start with the labels of U.S. wines and then move on to the more befuddling issue of import labels.

U.S. Wine Labels

All wines sold in the United States must contain the following information on their labels:

- A brand name
- The name and address of the producer or bottler and the relationship between the bottler and the source
- A geographical reference (at least the country if the wine is imported; usually also the region)
- A type (table, sparkling, or dessert) or the grape from which the wine came
- The percentage of alcohol

- The volume in milliliters
- The warning "Contains Sulfites" (see Lesson 3 for details)
- A "General Warning" that cautions against driving or operating machinery while drinking and cautions pregnant women against drinking alcohol

Most American-made wines tell you everything you need to know in plain English: the grape variety, where the wine was made and in what style, the vintage, and so forth. If a vintage is identified, 95 percent of the wine must come from that year. If the wine is blended from grapes of different years, it's called *nonvintage,* or NV. The bottler or producer is

Name of the varietal — PINOT GRIGIO

Name of the winery — CASTELLO BANFI
MONTALCINO

Name of vineyard

Vintage of the wine

Name of town where wine is produced

Appellation

Description of the wine (not present on all labels)

Producer information

Importer information

Country of origin

US mandated sulfite and health warning

Percentage of alcohol

Label courtesy of Banfi Vintners.

This example shows that some wines will carry two labels, a larger one on the front of the bottle and a smaller one on the back. The front label provides some basic information about the wine and is often fairly decorative. The back label is usually smaller and provides the remainder of the required information.

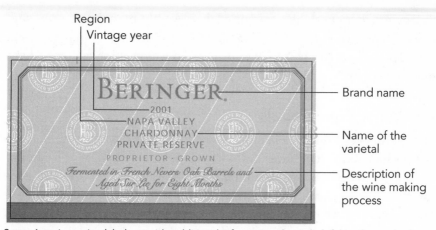

Region

Vintage year

BERINGER.

2001

NAPA VALLEY

CHARDONNAY

PRIVATE RESERVE

PROPRIETOR · GROWN

Fermented in French Nevers Oak Barrels and
Aged Sur Lie for Eight Months

Brand name

Name of the
varietal

Description of
the wine making
process

Some American wine labels provide additional information that is helpful to the reader. In this case they have offered a description of the wine making process used to create this Chardonnay.

always mentioned, although the bottler and the vintner may not be the same company. If the bottler is not the producer, the label normally states something to the effect of "Bottled for (the producer) by (the bottler)." The producer's address or location appears somewhere on the label.

VARIETAL WINES

If you spend much time around wine lovers, sooner or later someone's bound to start talking about varietals. This term is often bandied about by wine experts but is seldom explained to the satisfaction of those who are new to wine.

In a nutshell, a *varietal wine* is made primarily from a single type of grape, like Cabernet Sauvignon or Gewürztraminer. Each varietal has a distinctive flavor. Wine experts generally can identify a varietal by its taste. It's implied, but not imperative, that a varietal wine was crafted to be a typical example of its grape. When a wine tastes strongly of its varietal grape, wine lovers say that it has "varietal character." The attributes that identify a varietal are its "varietal characteristics."

Basically, if the wine is named after a grape, it's a varietal. If it's not a varietal, the wine may be called whatever the producer chooses. For instance, when Maryland's Elk Run Winery produces a Riesling, the wine is simply called Riesling. But the winery's blend of 75 percent Cabernet Sauvignon and 25 percent Cabernet Franc is called Sweet Katherine.

If the label identifies a varietal, does it mean that the wine comes from only one type of grape? Not necessarily. Nearly every country has laws dictating the percentage of wine that must come from that grape if a variety is named—normally somewhere between 75 and 85 percent. In the U.S., it's 75 percent; in Australia and the European Union, it's 85 percent.

Some American labels go out of their way to be helpful, even suggesting what foods to serve with the wine and the best temperature at which to serve it. Many New World-inspired winemaking countries have followed America's easy-access label style.

European Wine Labels

Many European wine labels are baffling at best. Unfortunately, because most winemaking countries follow Europe's model, they also follow Europe's wine-labeling style (often with their own local variety of confusion thrown in—which is why the merchant handed you something labeled "Steen" when you asked for a South African Chenin Blanc). But if you stick strictly to U.S. wines to avoid the boggling labels on international wines, you're going to miss a lot of joy.

The European Union has a naming classification system for wine that each EU nation must follow. Each country's local laws conform to this system. The EU recognizes three classes of wine:

- **Quality:** Quality is indicated by the wine's appellation of origin, which includes not only where the grapes were grown but also the grape variety, the method of production, and other

Beaujolais Villages

APPELLATION CONTRÔLÉE

Louis Latour

MIS EN BOUTEILLE PAR LOUIS LATOUR NÉGOCIANT-ÉLEVEUR
A BEAUNE - CÔTE-D'OR - FRANCE

This wine is made from the Beaujolais grape, but Villages indicates that this wine is from one or more of 39 villages in the northern part of the Beaujolais region.

Label courtesy of Louis Latour, Inc.

factors (see the figure that follows this list). In English, this EU category is called QWPSR (Quality Wine Produced in a Specific Region). Other EU countries call it VQPRD.

- **Table:** Wines in the EU that don't have an official appellation of origin receive this designation. There are two kinds of table wine: those that state their geographic origin on their labels (like France's Vins de Pays) and those that don't.

- **Wine:** This class includes wines from countries outside the EU.

    A number of major wine-producing countries have specific abbreviations or phrases for their quality designations. When you buy wine from the countries listed in the following table, look for these designations on the label. Most—but not all—are similar to France's AOC (Appellation d'Origine Controllée) system, which regulates the production of each designated wine-growing area (although most countries don't control wine production as strictly as France does). If a country has more than one quality rank, we list them here from highest to lowest. See the individual lessons on these countries for details.

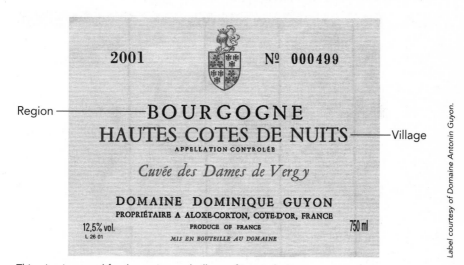

This wine is named for the region and village of its production.

All Champagnes labeled with a capital 'C' in Champagne, come from the Champagne region of France

Town of origin

Indicates the degree of sweetness

The Champagne house, cooperative, or grower that produced the wine

Date of vintage

Indicates the type of Champagne

Label courtesy of Kobrand Corp.

The label on a bottle of Champagne can tell you quite a bit. In this case, the use of a capital C in Champagne is the first indication that this sparkling wine is from the French region Champagne. Under the name of the producer, we find "à Reíms, France": The Montagne de Reíms is one of four broad areas that make up the Champagne region. Brut indicates that this wine is very dry, the presence of a date indicates that this is a vintage Champagne, and "blanc de blancs" means that this wine is made only from the Chardonnay grape.

WINE QUALITY DESIGNATIONS

COUNTRY	DESIGNATION(S)
Austria	Qualitätswein, Landwein, Tefelwein
Canada	VQA
France	AOC, VDQS, Vin de Pays, Vin de Table
Germany	QMP, QBA, Tafelwein
Greece	OPAP, OPE
Hungary	Minoségi Bor
Italy	DOCG, DOC, Vino di Tavolo
New Zealand	Certified Origin
Portugal	DOC, IPR, VR, Vinho de Mesa
South Africa	Wine of Origin
Spain	DOC, DO
United States	AVA, Table Wine

France's, Italy's, and Spain's local laws governing wine production are far more rigid than those of the U.S. But in these countries, producers typically print only the name of the region—or even simply the name of the village—on the label. This name tells the highly educated a lot, but the rest of us are left to figure out by trial and error what kind of wine a Côte-Rôtie, Asti, or Rioja is.

The only effective weapon against this kind of confusion is to recognize that European wines are more commonly named for their place of origin (as in Bordeaux) or their style (as with Sherry). Once you know your grapes from your place names and you get a handle on some of the most common European wine styles, you won't suffer from label shock nearly as often.

Words That Sometimes Show Up on Labels

Wine lovers can easily become confused by such cryptic label terms as "sur lie," "Reserve," and "estate bottled." Here's a quick rundown on some common terms you see on wine labels:

- **Estate bottled:** The wine's grapes came from the winery's own vineyard, and the wine was bottled on the premises. This term normally indicates a higher-quality wine. On a French wine label, it may be stated as "château bottled"; on a German label, "gutsabfüllung."

- **Reserve:** The wine is meant to be aged. Grand Reserve wines are usually of higher quality and can age for longer than a simple Reserve wine can. In the U.S., this term has no legal definition. The term Private Reserve is normally meant to indicate top quality, but there's no legally regulated standard in the U.S. to back it up.

The name of the producer

The vintage year — 1997

NOVAL
FINE PORTS SINCE 1715

1997

UNFILTERED
LATE BOTTLED VINTAGE — Indicates the style of Port
PORTO

The year it was bottled — BOTTLED IN 2002 BY
QUINTA DO NOVAL
VINHOS S.A. PINHÃO

ALC. 20% BY VOL. PRODUCE OF PORTUGAL   750 ML

All vintage port must be bottled in Portugal

Label courtesy of Quinta do Noval.

Note the use of the name Porto on the label above. Calling this wine a Porto, rather than Port, signals that it is from Portugal.

- **Sur lie:** On a white wine label, this term indicates that the wine was aged in contact with its *lees,* or spent yeast cells, which usually results in a richer wine. In the U.S. and other English-speaking countries, it might be stated simply as, "aged on its lees."

MAKING YOUR PURCHASE

Decide before you buy what purpose you're buying for. Is this wine going to be a casual sipper, or is it going to be a major part of an important dinner? Are you going for a sure thing, or are you buying to experiment? Will you be drinking this wine in a month, a year, or a decade?

- If you're buying for a meal, make sure you know what foods are going to be served (see Lesson 13 for more information about pairing wines with food).

- If you're buying wine for "laying down," choose wines that will age well: the high-tannin ones or the finer whites.

---

abcdefghijklmnopq rstuvwxyzabcdefgh ijklmnopqrstuvwxy

a note from
the instructor

WINE AS A HOST OR HOSTESS GIFT

Wine makes an excellent gift to give to people who have invited you to their home for some reason: a meal, the weekend, or a party. Here are some tips for bringing wine:

- Find out what your host—and other guests—like and don't like.
- Don't insist or assume that the wine you bring will be served at the meal, or that you'll get to have any. Remember, you're bringing a *gift:* The recipient has every right to decide how, when, and on whom he or she will use it. Nothing is more obnoxious than guests who force their wine opinions on the host and demand that what they brought be served instead of the host's selection.
- Consider bringing a dessert or aperitif wine: The host probably already has a selection in mind for dinner.
- Drink what you're offered with grace. Don't make faces or comments—even if you are served a jug wine. Enjoy the company and be a good guest.

■ If you're buying for experimentation, or if you're stocking up on some of the favorites you've discovered, see if your wine store will give you a case discount (a case is 12 bottles). Then mix and match your case according to your tastes.

BUYING WINE THROUGH AUCTIONS, CATALOGS, WINE-OF-THE-MONTH CLUBS, AND THE INTERNET

Today, you have more means at your disposal than ever before to ferret out great values and discover immense pleasures. In this section, we take a look at buying wine through auctions, catalogs, clubs, and the Internet.

Auctions

Wine auctions are great places to find rare, hard-to-come-by wines. They're also the place some wine collectors go to sell the "investment" wines they've had aging quietly in their cellars for years. So if you're looking for mature fine wine, auctions can be a terrific source.

They can also be dumping grounds for bad wines, such as a particular vintage that didn't live up to its makers' promises. Collectors who find that a couple of cases have passed their prime occasionally try to dispose of their geriatric wines. Sometimes the truly dishonest pass off bottles of spoiled or mishandled wine. So watch out.

Wine magazines, newsletters, and Web sites can be sources of information about wine auctions in your area. Some auction organizations furnish ahead of time a catalog of the wines they plan to auction. If you're interested enough in a particular wine that you're considering bidding, do your homework in advance: Find out as much as you can about that particular wine. Develop a working knowledge of recent prices for the wine, and decide beforehand what your maximum bid will be. That way, you won't get swept up in the excitement and end up bidding more than the wine's really worth. Remember, too, that most serious wine auctions charge a premium for the winning bid, often 10 to 20 percent of your bid amount. Factor that cost into your bid ceiling as well.

abcdefghijklmnopq
rstuvwxyzabcdefgh
ijklmnopqrstuvwxy

**a note from
the instructor**

WINE SHIPPING WOES

Each state makes its own laws governing the shipment of wine. In the District of Columbia, for example, each individual can receive a shipment of only one bottle per person per month. California, Idaho, Iowa, New Mexico, Oregon, and West Virginia permit two cases of wine per month to be delivered to the same address, but in Idaho and Oregon, a buyer can't have both cases delivered to the same address simultaneously. In Illinois, Minnesota, Missouri, and Washington, residents can receive only two cases per year. Shipping *any* wine to Florida, Kentucky, Maryland, Oklahoma, Tennessee, or Utah is a felony.

Fortunately, one notable exception to wine shipment laws exists: If you purchase wine while visiting a winery, you can ship it home to yourself, even if you live in a state that considers wine shipping a felony.

When you arrive at the auction, examine the bottles for mishandling: sticky residues on the bottle or stained labels. Pay particular attention to the cork—is it sitting higher in the bottleneck than normal? Is it wine colored? These are signs of seepage and air entry. How low is the liquid level in the bottle? If it seems lower that normal, the wine may have been exposed to air. If you're not sure about any aspect of the wine, ask the seller before you bid.

If the quantity of wine for auction is large, the seller might open a bottle for tasting. If you have the opportunity, by all means taste before bidding. Look at the color of the wine: Reds past their prime turn brownish; whites sometimes turn an almost urinary yellow. Inhale the wine's aroma: Is it musty, caramelized, or corked? Finally, taste. (See Lesson 2 for details on wine tasting.) Is it worth the money you're considering investing?

Catalogs

A number of wine sellers offer wine shopping via catalog: You select and order the wines you want, and the company ships them directly to you. Wine Enthusiast, Wine.com, and 800wine.com, among many others, publish wine catalogs. Numerous other wine catalogs are advertised in the pages of *Wine Spectator* magazine.

Catalog wine shopping can be a terrific time-saver, since you don't have to travel all over town looking for the best price on a particular wine. It may also offer you more variety and more information about the wines you're interested in purchasing. But catalog shopping comes with two built-in drawbacks:

- You can't sample before buying. (What, scratch-and-sniff wouldn't work? We thought bouquet was everything!)
- Having wine shipped to you can be a pain, depending on the alcohol laws in your area (see "Wine Shipping Woes"). Your best bet is to buy from catalogs those wines you've already tasted and deemed to be winners, and to verify that the company can ship to your area before placing an order.

Wine-of-the-Month Clubs

Wine-of-the-month clubs can be a lot of fun. Looking forward to a new arrival of wine each month is pretty neat. Just keep in mind that they are not true clubs. They don't exist to share your enthusiasm for wine, as the name "club" might imply. They're businesses. They exist to make money by selling you wine on a prearranged basis instead of waiting for you to find a reason to mosey into a wine store. Still, as long as the club lets you choose which wines you'll get, it may be worthwhile.

Online

Still in its infancy, buying wine online may prove in the near future to be as convenient as buying from catalogs and clubs—maybe more so. But it's sure to have all the same drawbacks as the first two options (particularly in regard to shipping wines across state lines), plus an additional one: Although several reputable, well-established online wine retailers exist, not everyone in cyberspace is honest. The best way to avoid getting cyber-scammed is to deal only with reputable online wine sellers, such as www.wineaccess.com, www.tableandvine.com, and www.sams-wine.com.

COLLECTING WINE

Plenty of wine lovers content themselves with buying a few bottles here and there, maybe a case now and then if they happen upon a wine they really like. But if you've truly fallen in love with wine and you crave the pleasure of collecting fine, rare, and unusual wines—and aging many of them yourself—you've entered the realm of the wine collector.

In your zeal, you may be tempted to buy gallons of a newfound favorite. But resist the temptation to buy too much of one kind—your tastes will probably change over time, and you may find that you've outgrown the wine that you bought by the case. Or you may not be able to drink it before it gets too old.

Buy a balance of different wines for your collection. Have several ready-to-drink selections available in addition to those you plan to age awhile. Buy both whites and reds, and don't shun rosés just because they're a little bit unfashionable. Keep a few Champagnes and sparkling wines on hand for celebrations, and a dessert wine or two in case that decadent sweet tooth strikes. And if you, or your guests, enjoy them, stock one or two fine Ports, Sherries, or other fortified wines. But for the most part, buy what you know you'll drink.

Aging

Laying down your wines to age can be fun and rewarding, particularly if you look at it more as a grand experiment than as an investment. Just to clarify, when we talked about aging in Lesson 1, we referred to the aging process the wine goes through before it leaves the winemaker's hands, whether in a tank, barrel, bottle, or some combination of the three. Now, we're talking about the aging that takes place after the bottle has been sold.

Many wine experts freely admit that aged wine is an acquired taste. Aging changes the character of a wine in many of the same ways that it changes the character of human beings: They become deeper, more mellow, and more complex. It's not so much that what was there when they were young changes into something else; it's that their essential character develops a certain polish. See the following chart for examples of how aging can affect certain wines.

HOW AGING AFFECTS A WINE'S FLAVOR

WINE	YOUNG FLAVOR	MATURE FLAVOR
Chardonnay	Green apple	Apple cobbler
Sauvignon Blanc	Freshly cut hay	Hay barn
Sémillon	Honeysuckle	Caramel
Cabernet Sauvignon	Blackberries	Black currants
Syrah	Green pepper	Black pepper
Fino Sherry	Raw almonds	Toasted almonds

To be a candidate for aging, a wine must be relatively high quality to begin with, both in its lineage and in its upbringing—in other words, it has to be well made from good grapes. But in general, if it's going to sit there quietly maturing for years on end and not simply fall apart, it must contain lots of acid, lots of tannin, or both.

Only a few white wines age well. Most white wines are created to be drunk when they're young, and they don't gain anything by aging. They come to the wine store ready to drink and have a meaningful lifespan of only one to two years. A few fine, complex whites—some of the better Chardonnays, Chenin Blancs, Rieslings, and Sémillons, for instance—may stand up to a few years of aging, but they're the exception. Of course, some of this depends on the wine's style: A Sauternes (from Sémillon or Sauvignon Blanc grapes) or a fine white Champagne (from Chardonnay grapes) can handle a decade or more of aging. Most sparkling wines are created for drinking young, but Champagne is the extreme exception to this rule. If you're not sure which whites you should buy for aging, ask your contact at the wine store for recommendations.

Rosés are hardly ever a good choice for aging, with the exception of rosé Champagne. The nature of rosés is to be fresh, young, and sprightly, so they're naturally at their best when they're only a year or two old. They generally have neither the acid nor the tannin to withstand much aging.

Not all reds are meant for aging, either. Most of the light red styles, the majority of what's available, don't gain much by aging. Most of these wines are ready to drink when you buy them. More than a few years of aging will cause them to lose their delicate magic. But high-tannin reds can handle the passage of years. The more tannin a wine has, the longer it can go. Fine, tannic reds do best; the better the vintage, the longer they may need to age to reach their true potential. For example, Bordeaux wines from 1988, 1989, and 1990 are just now coming into their prime, whereas wines from lesser, more recent years are ready for drinking already.

For the long term, buy full-bodied red wines like Cabernet Sauvignon, Cabernet Franc, Barolo, Barbaresco, and the finer fortified Ports and Sherries. Rioja, Shiraz/Syrah, and Pinot Noir also develop nicely with aging, although they're not quite as long-lived as their higher-tannin colleagues. The better the wine and the higher the tannin, the longer the wine will take to mature. Some excellent, well-made reds from exceptional vintages may take 15 or 20 years to reach their zenith—and the finest of all can go nearly a century.

Determining if Your Aged Wine is Ready to Drink

How do you know when a given wine is ready to drink? Sadly, there's no way to tell for sure except to open it and drink it, an all-or-nothing proposition. The best you can do is to arm yourself with information. Find out, if you can, how long the winemaker recommends that the wine be aged. The following chart may proved a few general rules:

HOW LONG TO AGE YOUR WINES

WINE	RECOMMENDED AGING TIME
Reds	
Pinot Noir, Rioja, Shiraz, Zinfandel	About 3 years
Barolo, Cabernet Sauvignon, Merlot	5 to 10 years
The finest Bordeaux, Burgundy, Champagne	10 to 20 years
Whites	
Fine Chardonnay, Chenin Blanc, Riesling, Sauvignon Blanc, Sémillon	About 3 years
Sauternes/Barsac/Tokay Aszu, Champagne	10 to 20 years

See Lesson 13 for more information.

 a note from
the instructor

DO I NEED TO HAVE A CELLAR TO COLLECT WINE?

Say you're crazy about wine and you've decided you want to collect it. You envision yourself strolling blissfully along the rows of wine racks in your impressive underground cellar, admiring your fine acquisitions. There's only one problem: You live in a condo, and you hardly have room for a corkscrew, let alone a wine cellar.

If space is at a premium in your home, you don't have to give up your dream of collecting wine. If you can find a dark, quiet shelf in a closet and your home stays relatively cool throughout the year, you can create a space where fine wine will be happy. If you have a basement that's relatively quiet and free of strong odors, you can earmark a portion of it for your wine collection. Even a well house, shed, or garage can be remodeled into a wine cellar, as long as it provides a cool, quiet environment. (See Lesson 13 for details on storage conditions.)

lesson 13

getting started with wine

How to Select Wineglasses and Equipment • Wine Storage and Handling • How to Open and Serve Wine • Enjoying Wine While Dining Out

Many wine beginners meet with frustration from the moment they begin to wrestle with the cork; others live with a nagging sense that they're not serving their wine the "right" way. They worry that, at best, they're not getting as much out of the experience as they could and, at worst, that they'll look like fools in front of their guests for not knowing the "proper" procedures. Not to worry. By the time you finish this lesson, you'll know how to chill, open, and serve your wine; which glasses, corkscrews, and decanters to use; what to do with leftover wine; and how to order wine with confidence in a restaurant.

CHOOSING WINEGLASSES AND EQUIPMENT

If you plan to serve wine on a regular basis (even if you serve it only to yourself!), it makes sense to invest in a few pieces of equipment that will minimize the frustration and maximize the joy. You don't need to spend a huge amount of money on silver-plated corkscrews, mono-grammed ice buckets, and crystal decanters, but you do want your wine paraphernalia to be well made and highly functional. And, as you're about to discover, a good set of wineglasses really can make your wine taste better.

Wineglasses

The right wineglass heightens the wine-drinking experience. In general, for still wines (especially for reds), choose glasses with big bowls and thin rims. The large bowl enables the aroma to accumulate and unfold. Bordeaux glasses are shaped like plump tulips; large-bowled Burgundy glasses flare slightly at the top. Flutes—long, tall glasses, often with a slight taper—are for Champagnes and sparkling wines; they hang onto the bubbles. If you serve still wine in these glasses, you'll lose some of the aromatic magic of the experience because you won't be able to swirl the wine or stick your nose in the glass. Conversely, if you serve a sparkler in a wide-rimmed glass, you might have a sparkling wine for about a minute, and then it will go flat.

Basic Wineglass Shapes

Curved rim traps bubbles

Narrow opening traps bubbles

Flared rim

Large bowl

Long stem

Tulip

For Champagnes or sparkling wines

Flute

Burgundy glass

Designed specifically for Burgundies

Bordeaux glass

Good all-purpose wineglass

Wineglass shapes for specific wines.

Old-fashioned trumpet-shaped wineglasses (shaped like martini glasses, only longer), which you still may find in some shops, aren't the best choice for sparkling *or* still wines, because they neither permit a wine's aroma to accumulate nor hold in the bubbles of a sparkling wine.

Other Considerations When Buying Stemware

All wineglasses should be clear and thin rimmed, since wine is also enjoyed with the eyes. The stem of the glass should be long enough for you to hold without touching the bowl—if you have to hold your glass by the bowl, heat from your hand can affect the wine. The best way to hold a wineglass is to curl your three smallest fingers under the base and pinch the bottom of the stem between your thumb and forefinger.

Is crystal better than glass? Experts voice no clear preference in terms of the way glass or crystal affects the flavor and aroma of wine. But many people seem to agree that crystal adds an extra facet of elegance to the experience.

How about plastic? If you're having a party, is it gauche to serve wine in plastic glasses? It depends on the party. If you're serving up a casual blush among close friends, who's going to care? When you're at the beach, by the pool, or on a picnic, you're probably better off without breakables. But if you're opening a fabulous, mature Bordeaux on a formal occasion, plastic throwaways will seem out of place. Match the glassware to the wine and the wine to the occasion.

---

a note from the instructor

RIEDEL: THE WINEGLASS KING

Numerous wine experts and wine lovers the world over are convinced that no finer wineglass exists on Earth than that made by Austrian manufacturer Riedel (pronounced "ree-del"). Over several generations, Riedel has perfected the science of wineglass design, discovering in the process the best shapes for bringing out the magic of various types of wine, from Bordeaux to Champagne. Riedel's glasses aren't cheap, but if you're after the ultimate wine-drinking experience, you owe it to yourself to try one sometime.

How Many Glasses Do You Need?

How many glasses of each type do you need to own? Unless you're a wine fanatic, you'll get by just fine with one set of basic large-bowl glasses for still whites and reds, and perhaps another set of flutes or tulips if you frequently serve Champagne and sparkling wine. A number of wine experts recommend against smaller glasses for dessert and fortified wines, claiming that the tiny glasses rob the drinker of the full aromatic experience. Instead, use the same wide-bowled thin-rimmed glasses you use for tables wines.

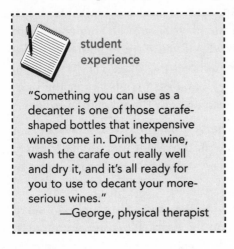

student experience

"Something you can use as a decanter is one of those carafe-shaped bottles that inexpensive wines come in. Drink the wine, wash the carafe out really well and dry it, and it's all ready for you to use to decant your more-serious wines."
—George, physical therapist

The number of glasses in each set depends on the number of guests you typically serve. If 90 percent of your entertaining consists of modest dinner parties for three or four couples, why do you need to own more than a dozen multipurpose wineglasses? Here's a good general rule: Buy the number of wineglasses that will match the number of china place settings you own. If you need several dozen wineglasses two or three times a year, by all means purchase them if you wish, but don't forget that party rental stores routinely carry them.

Decanters

Any container works as a decanter as long as it is made of an inert material and can hold an entire bottle's worth of wine and still allow it plenty

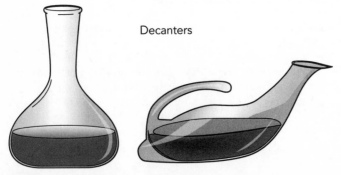

Decanters

Here are two common styles of decanters.

of room to breathe. In general, a vessel that's broad at the bottom is best. As with wineglasses, feel free to get as fancy or as simple in your choice of decanters as you wish.

Corkscrews

Your choice of corkscrew can make the task of opening a bottle of wine a joy or a frustration. Choose the one you're most comfortable with:

- **Screwpull:** The best cork remover by far, this device fits over the top of the bottle and lifts the cork out as you twist in the screw. Screwpull brand cork removers retail for $85 and up; Rabbit, the alternate brand, uses a similar cogged system to extract the cork.

- **Wing type:** This corkscrew features a pair of arms that ratchet upward as you turn the screw into the cork. When the screw is all the way in, you simply push the arms back down and draw the cork up the bottleneck and out. Many people find this type of corkscrew frustrating because the screw is shorter than other types of corkscrews and can break off the cork in midpull.

- **"Waiters' friend":** Many of these quick-and-easy corkscrews fold like pocketknives and include a bottle opener on one end for guests who prefer beer. You insert the screw slightly off-center and twist in as far as it will go, and then lever the cork out. Some of these corkscrews are uncomfortable to grip—if you end up with one that bites your fingers as you twist and pull, wrap a cloth around it for padding. The best corkscrews have long, Teflon-coated screws and a comfortable grip.

- **Two-pronged "ah-so":** This type of cork remover slides two prongs alongside the cork and lifts it out. The name, so the legend goes, comes from the common remark one makes upon seeing it in action: "Ah—so *that's* how it works!" It may prove difficult to use on very tight corks. It's also nicknamed "the butler's friend" because, in theory, a thirsty butler could pull the cork on his employer's wine and sample it, and then reinsert the cork without leaving behind a telltale bore hole.

- **Cork extractor:** This elaborate device fits over the bottle and levers the cork out with a handle. Cork extractors are expensive but relieve stress.

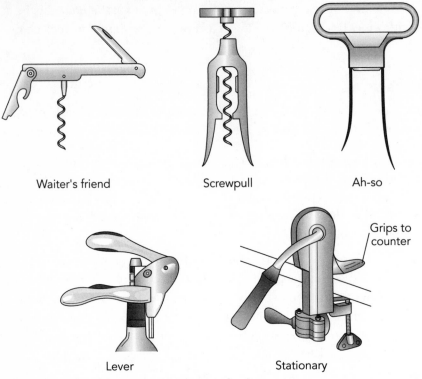

Waiter's friend   Screwpull   Ah-so

Lever   Stationary

Grips to counter

Here are examples of the most common types of corkscrews.

Ice Buckets and Wine Chillers

Whether you buy a bucket specifically designed for wine or you make do with whatever container you happen to have, make sure that your ice bucket is deep enough that the wine can sit in icy water up to its neck.

A trendy development on the ice bucket front is a wine cooler made of terra cotta. This device looks like a long, tall flowerpot, often painted or otherwise decorated. The beauty of such a device is that it maintains a cool temperature without the need for ice or water around the bottle. You simply chill the container in the fridge or in ice water for several hours beforehand, dump out the water, and then place the prechilled wine bottle inside the empty container.

ice bucket   terra cotta

You can use an ice bucket or a terra cotta wine chiller to chill your wine.

Champagne Gadgets

If you serve Champagne regularly, you may want to consider purchasing a few of the gizmos available to make opening a bottle easier. We know plenty of Champagne lovers who make do just fine without these devices, but they're available if you feel the need:

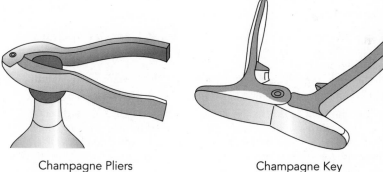

Champagne Pliers   Champagne Key

Two ways to open Champagne are to use Champagne pliers or a Champagne key.

- **Champagne keys,** shaped like the symbol for *pi*, grip the cork and make it easier to remove.

- **Champagne pliers** are shaped like regular pliers, but have teeth for gripping the cork.

- **Champagne stars,** another gadget that follows the same principle, are designed to help you overcome the obstacle that stands between you and your bubbly.

---

a note from the instructor

WHEN THE INEVITABLE HAPPENS

You're opening that long-anticipated bottle, the one you've been saving for a special occasion. You can almost taste the wine already as you start to tug on the cork, when suddenly—snap!—the cork breaks, leaving a ridiculous-looking half-cork on the tip of your corkscrew and the other half still stuck fast in the bottleneck. You try to dig the remaining half out with a pocketknife, only to have it plop into the bottle, leaving a trail of little cork bits floating in your wine. Now what?

Don't panic. For every cork disaster, a remedy exists. Wine shops occasionally sell devices that can assist you in the event of just such a crisis, but you really don't need special rescue equipment. You can probably get the job done with items you have on hand:

- **When the cork breaks off in the bottleneck:** Carefully reinsert the corkscrew—or, if necessary, find another one with a longer screw. It may help to bore in at a different angle. If you can't get enough of a hold on the remaining cork, try pushing it all the way into the bottle. Then follow the next procedure.

- **When the cork falls into the wine:** Some wine shops sell a device called a cork retriever or a corkfish, designed to help you recapture the bobbing piece(s). But you can accomplish the same task with a clean shish kebab skewer or chopstick: Just use the chopstick to trap the cork against the side of the bottle while you pour the wine into a decanter.

- **When the wine has crumbled cork bits floating in it:** Pour the wine into a decanter through a clean coffee filter or a piece of cheesecloth.

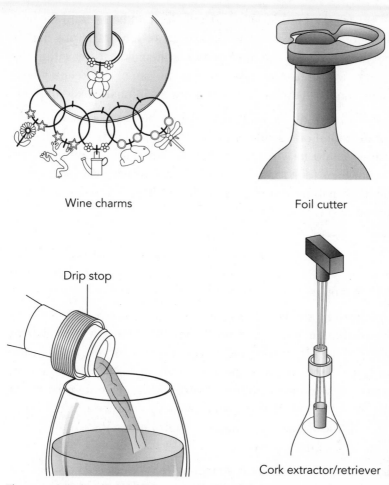

Wine charms

Foil cutter

Drip stop

Cork extractor/retriever

There are many handy gadgets you can use as well. Wine charms will help your guests keep from mixing up their glasses so that they don't know whose is whose. A foil cutter can help you easily remove foil wrappers from the tops of bottles. Drip stops help you pour wine cleanly without dripping all over tablecloths, etc. And, as mentioned earlier in this lesson, a cork extractor/retriever is extremely handy for getting wayward corks out of bottles.

STORING AND HANDLING WINE

If you're like a lot of wine drinkers, most of the bottles you purchase are going to be empty within 48 hours. Many people tend to be occasion wine buyers, ducking into a wine store for a last-minute bottle to accompany a special get-together. For these wines, storage is mostly a matter of keeping the bottles out of extreme heat and cold until it's time to chill them for drinking. If you've picked up several intriguing bottles at the wine store with the intent of drinking them sometime within the next few weeks or months, the procedure is the same. But keeping your wine on hand longer than that requires a few additional considerations.

If you won't be drinking your wine within the next several months, you'll want to store it on its side or upside down so that the cork doesn't dry out, which could let air into the bottle. Any bottles with synthetic corks or screw caps (don't laugh—some decent wines come with screw caps these days) can be stored upright. Keep them relatively cool, dry, quiet, and out of direct sunlight.

Suppose you've *really* caught the wine bug and you want to purchase a bunch of fine wines and age them yourself for several years. If this idea appeals to you, you'll want to do a bit of advanced planning to make sure that you can give your wines a fitting place to mature.

The practice of "laying up" a good wine is a more recent development than you might think. Not until the widespread use of airtight corks in the eighteenth century was it even possible to store a good wine long term. Until then, wine was mixed with brandy as a preservative or, in Mediterranean regions, was often covered with a layer of olive oil to separate it from the air. Modern wine owes its longevity to the cork. Without it, our fine wines would spoil in their bottles instead of slowly transforming into liquid poetry.

The best thing you can do for your long-term wine is to protect the cork by keeping the bottle on its side or upside down so that the cork stays in contact with the liquid and remains swelled and sealed tight against the bottle. Almost as important are cool temperatures, darkness, and quiet. The following list takes a closer look at the ideal conditions for aging wine:

- **Temperature:** 55 degrees Fahrenheit is optimal for wine storage, but make sure that the temperature is less than 70. Keeping wines too warm can age them too quickly, and they'll lose some of their richness and complexity. Even one degree of difference can have a profound effect on the wine's flavor. If you've just bought wine on a hot summer day, don't leave it in the trunk of your car while you run other errands—not even for a few hours. Cooking seems to work beautifully for Madeira, but it makes most other wines taste of burnt sugar and boiled cabbage.

- **Bottle position:** When you bought your wine, hopefully it was shelved on its side (see Lesson 12) unless it was one of the exceptions—such as a Sherry or fortified wine—to that rule. Likewise, you will want to store your wine on its side or upside down to keep its cork moist so that it won't shrink. Wines stored upright long term can oxidize when their corks pull away from the sides of the bottle and let in air.

- **Light:** Keep your wine away from direct sunlight, which can cause oxidation. Avoid fluorescent lights as well. Wines prefer very low light or darkness while they're aging. Look at pictures of famous wine cellars: They're always in the kinds of places a vampire would feel at home. That's what wine likes.

- **Humidity:** A healthy bit of moisture in the air is good for your wine; it keeps the cork full and supple so that excess air can't get into the bottle. Sixty percent humidity or more will help keep your corks from drying out. Don't worry if the bottle gets moldy on the outside—it won't hurt the wine. The fungus that may grow on the cork itself (which results in the wine becoming "corked") *might* be a problem, although it's a rare one. Corked wine isn't toxic; it's just unpleasant—like drinking fermented wet cardboard.

- **Vibrations:** Vibrations are another enemy of wines that are quietly aging to perfection. They can prevent the components from blending fully. Don't keep your wine too near a washing machine, power generator, treadmill, subwoofer, commuter train, or other vibrating machinery.

- **Odors:** Be careful where you store your wine collection—corks are porous and can allow odors to pass into the wine. Store your fine wines too near laundry detergents, motor oils, or household cleansers, and in a few years you may end up with wines that have a pronounced bouquet of Clorox, Quaker State, or Ty-D-Bowl!

- **Consistency:** Keep your wine's environment consistent— temperature fluctuations and too much handling can wreck its subtlety.

When you're buying wine specifically for aging, your best bets are high-quality reds with lots of tannin—for instance, wines made with Cabernet Sauvignon or Nebbiolo grapes. The tannin acts as a preservative and provides a "scaffolding" to support the subtle flavors as they evolve. Every wine is different, and it's impossible to know exactly when a given wine will reach its peak, but in general, age your finest reds for at least five years, if not ten. Keep your nice-but-not-primo red wines for about three years. Cheap to medium red wines are usually ready to drink as soon as you find them in stores. (See Lesson 12).

You can also age some fine white wines, although generally for considerably less than ten years. High-acid wines like Riesling age well because the acidity preserves them. Extremely sweet wines like Sauternes can also be aged because the sugar acts as a preservative.

PREPARING AND SERVING WINE

Many hosts quiver with trepidation at the thought of serving wine to their guests. They worry that they'll do something so glaringly wrong that they'll be branded rubes forevermore. Their fear of looking stupid may even prevent them from serving wine at all. Think of all the joy they and their guests are missing!

First of all, if your guests are going to judge you that harshly for something as minor as a slight etiquette gaffe, maybe you need to get some new friends. Second, serving wine is nowhere near the mystical high science that some wine snobs make it out to be. This section covers the basics of choosing, preparing, opening, and pouring wine so that you can put those wine-serving jitters behind you forever.

abcdefghijklmnopq rstuvwxyzabcdefgh ijklmnopqrstuvwxy   a note from the instructor

DON'T MIX WINE AND HARD LIQUOR

When serving wine to your guests at home, don't offer them hard liquor beforehand—the liquor will dull their palates. If you're planning to serve both wine and hard liquor at the same event, save the hard stuff for after-dinner drinking.

What Kinds of and How Much Wine Do You Need?

The wine you choose to serve at a given event depends largely on the occasion. Obviously, if you're offering wine with a meal, you want to choose wines that go well with the foods you're serving (see Lesson 14 for suggestions on pairing wine with food—but, as always, let your own experience and preferences be your ultimate guide). For nonmeal occasions, let the mood decide: Celebrations (birthdays, graduations, retirement parties, and the like) naturally lend themselves to festive Champagnes and sparkling wines. An evening of deep discussion with close friends might suggest a Port or a Sherry, or perhaps a fine aged wine. A summer lounging session on the patio goes well with a light blush, a crisp white, or a sparkler.

Specific events aside, what types of wine should you keep on hand for spontaneous get-togethers, casual at-home dinners, or those awkward times when a guest doesn't like the wine you're serving? Obviously, you want to stock up on the wines that you and your frequent guests (best friends, family members, and so on) prefer, and keep a few common crowd-pleasers on hand as well: easy Chardonnays, Zinfandels, and light sparkling wines. Champagne is a perennial favorite. If your spouse comes home with news of a surprise promotion, wouldn't it be fun to have a few bottles of bubbly on hand for a spontaneous celebration? It's also fun to have a few unusual wines on hand in case an adventurous mood strikes: a Gewürztraminer (just pronouncing this word before your guests will introduce a certain levity to the moment) or a South African Pinotage can serve as both a beverage and a conversation piece.

How do you determine how much wine to prepare for your dinner guests? First, count the number of guests. Assume that each guest will want at least three glasses of wine. (Some wine experts recommend that you estimate an entire *bottle* per person if the event going to be a long one with lots of drinking.) Each standard-sized bottle contains about five glasses of wine, assuming that you fill an average-sized wineglass only halfway.

What if your event is a wedding or bar/bat mitzvah—a special event rather than a dinner? Because people frequently do more drinking at such events than they do at a meal, you might choose to have one or two more glasses' worth of wine on hand per person than you would for a dinner. But keep in mind that many of your guests may be driving home after the event. Serve responsibly. Consider offering a few elegant non-alcoholic alternatives, like sparkling water or festive juices.

a note from
the instructor

BEST-BET WINES FOR NOVICE WINE DRINKERS

Chardonnay: Mild, soft, and flexible, Chardonnay may well be the world's most popular wine. A light California Chardonnay is an excellent choice for a first-time wine drinker.

Light, sweet German wines: For those guests who want to partake but are sensitive to alcohol, many German wines are low-alcohol choices. Gravitate toward the drier, low-acid wines like Gewürztraminer and Spätlese; avoid Rieslings, which can have a nasty, sour bite when young.

Zinfandel: If the occasion calls for red wine, Zinfandel's cheerful, berry-like personality is about as unintimidating as red wine gets.

Light sparkling wines: Spumante, Cava, and other sparklers are fun and easy to drink. Most have a low alcohol content.

If you'll be serving both red and white wine, serve the white first, but have both bottles open and available on the table. Let your guests' wishes, not a hard-nosed notion of etiquette, rule your wine service.

Knowing Which Wines to Serve When

Let's assume for a moment that you're planning to serve more than one kind of wine at your next event. How do you determine which wine should come when? By now, you know how skeptical we are of so-called wine rules, so if you find that these suggestions don't work for you, you have our blessing to toss them out and never look back. But if you're looking for some kind of structure to get you started, consider the following:

- **White before red:** If you serve the red first, you may find that the tannin in the red dulls your ability to enjoy some of the nuances in the white. For instance, if you have a Sauvignon Blanc and a Cabernet, serve the white as an aperitif and the red with the main course.

- **Light before heavy:** Likewise, you'll probably get better results if you build up from lighter wines to heavier ones, because if you do it backward, the lighter wines may seem weak by comparison. Serve Beaujolais before Malbec, Muscat before heavy Chardonnay, for example.

- **Young before old:** In general, serve your wines in chronological order, from youngest to oldest. Serve a young Cava as the opening act; save the Rioja Gran Reserva for the finale.

- **Simple before complex:** Serving a complex wine first might wreck your guest's palates for the simpler drink. Give them that monochromatic Zinfandel or Chardonnay first, and then the fine Cabernet.

- **Chilled before room temperature:** Start off with the well-chilled, refreshing appetite chargers, like a crisp, cold Pinot Grigio or a light sparkler, and then segue to the warmer wines (lightly chilled whites or reds and room-temperature fine reds) that may blunt the appetite.

Chilling Wines

Chilling a white wine, sparkling wine, or Champagne makes its alcohol less noticeable and can enhance and sharpen its flavors. Don't chill a wine until you're about to drink it: Long exposure to cold will alter the wine's flavor. Although reds are generally served at room temperature, chilling a red slightly can enhance its taste, particularly if it's light and fruity. Don't chill a really wonderful, complex old red at all—you'll lose some of the subtle flavors.

Wine can be chilled effectively in the refrigerator (or even quick-chilled in the freezer for ten minutes—just don't forget to take it out!), but the ice bucket remains the faster method. Submerge the wine up to its neck in a mixture of half water, half ice for 15 minutes if it's a white wine. Give Champagnes and sparkling wines a full 30 minutes to chill. (See the following table for recommended chilling times for various types of wine.)

Although traditionalists may look askance, some wine drinkers prefer even their red wines slightly chilled. No law says that you can't lightly chill a red wine for five minutes. Light, fruity, sweet, or sparkling reds like Sangiovese, Beaujolais, sweet styles of Zinfandel, and Cava seem to benefit from a modicum of chilling. But, as a general rule, the colder the wine, the less you'll be able to taste the alcohol, as well as the subtler flavors. Most red wines are at their best at around 65 degrees Fahrenheit.

SERVING TEMPERATURES

WINE	IDEAL TEMPERATURE	FRIDGE TIME
Champagne	38-40F	30 minutes
Sparklers, simple whites	41-45F	20-25 minutes
Complex whites, rosés	41-45F	15-20 minutes
Fine whites	43-50F	10-15 minutes
Simple young reds	50-55F	5-10 minutes
Aged reds, Sherry, Port	55-60F	5 minutes
Really old reds, 8+ years	Room temperature	None

Aerating and Decanting Wines

There are two reasons to pour wine from the bottle into a decanter: to aerate it and to decant it. Unless you never drink anything but old wine, you won't need to take this intermediate step very often. Most everyday wines can go straight from the bottle to your glass. Generally, only age-worthy wines need aerating and decanting.

What's the difference between aerating and decanting? *Aerating* is the process of exposing the wine to oxygen; *decanting* is the means of separating an aged wine from accumulated sediments.

Aerating enables the wine's flavors and aromas to unfold. Remember, though, that once wine and oxygen meet, the wine is doomed. You'll have to drink it within a few hours to get the full effect, because its flavor will soon begin to fade. Pouring a wine into a decanter or carafe is an effective way to aerate it. You can aerate reds and whites alike this way (both reds and whites that have aged for several years may benefit from aeration), but beware of letting whites sit for too long in the unchilled container—as they warm, they lose some of their delicate flavors.

Don't aerate truly delicate wines like old Pinot Noir, Rioja, or Chianti. They'll lose some of the magical subtlety they gained by aging.

> **student experience**
>
> "I don't think I have a very discerning tongue with wine, but I was amazed at the extra flavor and boldness decanting can add to a glass of red wine. Now I almost always decant a bottle a bit before we're ready to drink it."
> —Cindy, writer

a note from the instructor

SERVING VINTAGE PORT

Because of its advanced age, fine Vintage Port requires a bit of special care and handling. Vintage Port, as well as Crusted Port and Single Quinta Port (the label should tell you which kind the Port is), carries a lot of sediment and needs to be decanted carefully. Tawny Ports and other styles don't require decanting. Stand the bottle of Vintage Port upright for a while before you open it—if possible, stand it up the day before to allow the sediment plenty of time to settle to the bottom. If your Port is really old (ten years or more), open the bottle and decant the wine about 12 hours before you plan to drink it. Decant it carefully and let it aerate fully.

As for decanting, you'll need to do it only to wines that have a visible accumulation of sediment in their bottles. When wines reach the bountiful age of eight years or more, they begin to require decanting. Few whites, and only the greatest of reds, make it this far—and those that do are bound to produce a certain amount of sediment. The sediment isn't harmful to drink; it's unpleasant. For this reason, you should stand an old wine upright for three or four hours before opening it to allow the sediments to settle to the bottom of the bottle.

As you move, open, and pour from the bottle, try to jostle it as little as possible. Decant the wine carefully, pouring until you see the sediment rising into the bottle's neck. If you can't see into a dark-tinted bottle well enough to recognize the sediment, pour with a light behind it. Hold a candle (okay, you can use a flashlight, too, but how romantic is that?) behind the bottle so that the sediment appears in silhouette.

Pouring

Pour each glass half full or less to enable the air inside the glass to capture the wine's bouquet. Wine etiquette dictates that if you're pouring in front of your guests, you should never cover the bottle with a towel as you pour. You're supposed to keep the label visible, lest they suspect that you're serving them inferior stuff. If the bottle is wet, dry it gently before you pour.

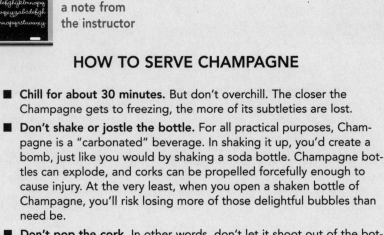

a note from
the instructor

HOW TO SERVE CHAMPAGNE

- **Chill for about 30 minutes.** But don't overchill. The closer the Champagne gets to freezing, the more of its subtleties are lost.

- **Don't shake or jostle the bottle.** For all practical purposes, Champagne is a "carbonated" beverage. In shaking it up, you'd create a bomb, just like you would by shaking a soda bottle. Champagne bottles can explode, and corks can be propelled forcefully enough to cause injury. At the very least, when you open a shaken bottle of Champagne, you'll risk losing more of those delightful bubbles than need be.

- **Don't pop the cork.** In other words, don't let it shoot out of the bottleneck on its own. You'll lose too many bubbles, as well as create a potential safety hazard. Loosen it, and then ease it out inside a towel. It will come out with a lively hiss instead of a percussive pop. Hold the open bottle at 45 degrees to keep it from foaming over.

- **Serve Champagne in tall flutes.** This style of glass holds in more bubbles.

- **Serve Champagne in glasses that are approximately as cold as the Champagne itself.** But don't frost or wet the glasses—doing so will cause them to fog over, and your guests won't be able to observe the merry dance of bubbles inside.

- **Pour correctly.** Hold the bottle at the bottom. This isn't absolutely necessary, but if you want to add a little panache to your Champagne service, grip the bottle near the bottom with your thumb in the punt (the deep indentation in the bottle's bottom) and place your fingers up the side. Turn the label to face forward so that it's visible as you pour.

- **Don't tip the glass unless you or your guests really don't like the foam.** Champagne lovers claim that the creamy foam or "mousse" is the best part—it carries much of the wine's flavors and aromas. Pour the first inch or two into each glass, and then, when the foam has calmed down a bit, return to top them off.

- **Don't top off half-finished glasses.** Champagne is at its best when chilled. If you keep mixing lukewarm wine in the glass with chilled wine in the bottle, your guests will never get a properly chilled drink after their first glass.

WHAT TO DO WITH LEFTOVER WINE

Wines will keep overnight if you recork them tightly. Some hardy wines may last as long as 48 hours, but, like fresh-cut flowers, nearly all wines begin to lose their luster after three days. If you have a great quantity of leftover wine and you don't anticipate using it up within three days, try the following:

- **Create a vapor barrier.** Some wine shops carry canisters of inert gas that you can spray into the bottle. The odorless, flavorless gas settles on the surface of the wine and seals it off from the air.

- **Pour the leftover wine into a smaller bottle.** Save, wash, and reuse half-bottles and single-serving bottles for storing leftover wines. You'll get the best results if you leave as little air at the top as possible.

- **Seal the bottle with an airtight plastic top.** If you're worried that your cork is too mangled to keep air out, your favorite wine shop probably carries these little plastic wine resealers that may do the trick.

Don't refrigerate your leftover wine. Unlike leftover food, wine doesn't benefit from long-term refrigeration. Exposure to cold can wreck the wine's delicate structure and can render certain white wines almost flavorless.

ORDERING WINE AT A RESTAURANT

In terms of sheer terror, ordering wine in front of friends seems to rank a close second to serving it to guests at home. Once again, the specter of looking gauche when everybody else is in the know creeps up to spoil your pleasure. But ordering wine is considerably less complicated than serving it—and as you've just seen, that's no big deal. If you've come this far in the book, you're already armed with the basic knowledge you need to order wine well. The following sections give just a few additional pointers.

Reading the Wine List

Restaurants don't always make it easy on would-be wine buyers. They often don't give you the information you need to make an informed selection. Most good restaurants have various tiers of pricing available; they typically list house, standard, premium, and sometimes reserve wines. House selections almost always feature a Chardonnay (often with a brand name you'll recognize) and a Merlot, often a Zinfandel as well, and perhaps a few other popular types. These are the cheapest wines on the menu. On the next level up, you'll probably find a greater variety, perhaps a Pinot Grigio or a Cabernet Sauvignon, plus a few additional Chardonnay choices. The promium list features a more expensive selection, which usually translations into higher quality wines. The reserve list, if the restaurant has one, holds the most expensive options—and—as we've mentioned, expensive doesn't necessarily mean better.

Most of the time, you'll be safe with the house wine; this is usually an easygoing selection, if not exactly a thrilling one. Many restaurants carry a house wine not because it's great, but because they can get a large quantity of it for a low price. It's probably not the thing to order if you're after an extraordinary wine to accompany your meal.

If the restaurant offers a choice of glass, carafe, or bottle, you'll usually find that buying by the bottle or carafe is more cost effective than buying by the glass, because the restaurant charges proportionately more per glass than per carafe or bottle to cover the cost of opening an entire bottle for the sake of a single glass.

Beyond the house selections, a good wine list will offer several wines by the glass: half a dozen reds, half a dozen whites, and at least one sparkler. The restaurant will likely have several bottles available for $25 or less. A rotten wine list will have nothing but mass-market brand-name wines, mostly Chardonnays and Merlots, and they'll often charge you for these wines as though they were something better.

When all else fails, choose a few likely candidates and ask the waiter for a recommendation, or ask to see the bottle so that you can read the label (see Lesson 12 for information to be gained by reading the label).

Handling the Presentation Ritual

When the waiter presents the bottle, make sure that it's what you ordered. Never accept a bottle that has already been opened. Insist that any bottle you order be opened in your presence.

Tradition has it that when a waiter opens the wine at your table and hands you the cork, you're supposed to smell it. While no rule says that you *can't* smell the cork, doing so won't tell you much about the quality of the wine, except in rare cases when the wine is "corked"—tainted by a moldy cork. The cork of a corked wine has a distinctly musty, wet cardboard aroma. But you'd discover this problem just as quickly by taking your first sniff of the corked wine. If you don't wish to smell the cork, you can simply look at it; make sure that it's moist, firm, and in good condition, an indication that the wine has been stored properly.

When the server pours you a small amount of wine, smell it carefully. You may taste it, too, of course, but the aroma is all you need to verify whether the wine is spoiled, corked, or stale—and this is why you're sampling. The initial inspection pour is not to see whether you like the wine, but only to verify that nothing is wrong with it. If you suspect that something is wrong, say so immediately—you probably won't be able to return it later. If it smells like cardboard, chemicals, caramel, vinegar, or sulfur, send it back (see the following table for these and other undesirable aromas). If it smells okay, take a sip—again, this taste is to verify what your nose has already told you: whether the wine is spoiled or is in any way defective, not whether it tastes good. If all's well, allow the wine to be served. (For details on how to taste a wine, see Lesson 14.)

UNDESIRABLE WINE AROMAS

AROMA	IS A SIGN OF
Beer, cheese, cider, milk, sauerkraut, yogurt	Poor fermentation
Acetate, bananas, nail polish	Chemical imbalance
Cow manure, mold, swamp	Poor quality
Caramel, burnt, prune	Oxidation; hasty maturation
Cat urine, green pepper	Underripe grapes
Dirt, dust, mushrooms	Wine needs aeration

pairing wine with foods

Why Certain Wines and Foods Match • How to Pair Food and Wine • How to Cook with Wine

Although wine all by itself can be a glorious pleasure, there's nothing quite like an elegant glass of wine to complement a good meal. Over the centuries, a certain folk wisdom has developed concerning which wines to drink with which foods. Unfortunately, because wine lovers tend to be passionate people, these recommendations sometimes get expressed as rules, as though there's something inherently wrong with you if you enjoy a glass of white wine with your steak.

Now, if a classic food-and-wine combination has stood the test of time, there's probably a reason for it. But bear in mind that all so-called "rules" of food and wine pairing are simply guidelines. In this lesson, we offer up some of the conventional wisdom concerning the marriage of food with wine, but we hope that you'll use it in the spirit in which it's intended: as suggestions only. As with all things related to wine, your own tastes and preferences should be the ultimate authority.

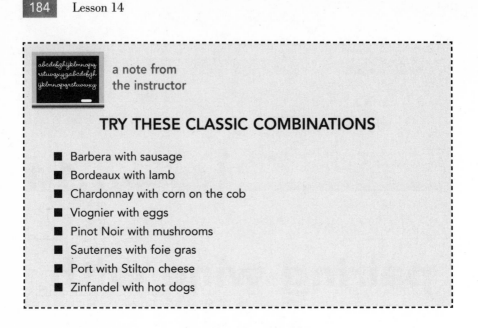

a note from
the instructor

TRY THESE CLASSIC COMBINATIONS

- Barbera with sausage
- Bordeaux with lamb
- Chardonnay with corn on the cob
- Viognier with eggs
- Pinot Noir with mushrooms
- Sauternes with foie gras
- Port with Stilton cheese
- Zinfandel with hot dogs

WHY CERTAIN WINES AND FOODS GET ALONG

Although today's devil-may-care attitude is to choose whatever wine you think is best with whatever food (rather than the traditional idea of pairing only reds with red meats, whites with white meats, and so on), some wines naturally go well with certain foods. What makes a wine a good match for a particular food? Most of it has to do with the chemistry of their interaction.

Sometimes it works best to match wines with foods that have contrasting qualities (see the instructor sidebar on the next page for details). High-tannin wines go well with heavy meats and cheeses because the tannin balances the proteins and fats in the meat or cheese. Some experts say acidic wines work with spicy dishes because the wine's acids help neutralize the spice's fire. Others recommend sweet wines to quell the heat of the spice. Put sweet dessert wines with tart desserts so that the wine still tastes sweet in comparison.

Other times, it works better to choose wines that are similar and complementary to the food, like a fruity wine to go with a fruity sauce.

The following table lays out some basic rules for pairing food with wine.

TASTES AND TEXTURES: PAIRING FOOD AND WINE

IF THE FOOD IS	CHOOSE A WINE THAT'S	SUCH AS
Salty	Fruity, low oak	Cabernet Sauvignon, Zinfandel
Sweet	As sweet or acidic	Sauternes, Riesling
Spicy	Fruity, sweet, low in alcohol	Muscat/Moscato, Beaujolais, Spätlese, rosé
Fatty or oily	Acidic	Riesling, Sauvignon Blanc
Acidic	Acidic and fruity	Pinot Grigio

FOOD-MATCHING BASICS

One of the best methods for matching wine to food is to identify the dominant flavor and texture in the dish and match it with the dominant flavor and texture of the wine's principal grape. Match light with light, hearty with hearty, sweet with sweet, and so on.

Be forewarned: The meal's dominant characteristic may not be its primary ingredient. Light pasta might call for a light, sheer wine—until you heap on a heavy cream sauce. Now that pasta needs something with a little more presence. The richer and heartier the dominant ingredient, the more acidic or tannic the wine must be.

---

*a note from
the instructor*

WINE AND FOOD CHEAT SHEET

Sometimes you need a simple way to remember the guidelines of food and wine pairing. One of the simplest is this: "Simple wine with complex food; complex wine with simple food."

Say you're having a beef stew that contains lots of different vegetables and fresh herbs. It has a complex flavor and many textures. Nothing goes better with this type of meal than a simple wine. Try a juicy young Merlot.

But what if you're having barbecued leg of lamb? The flavor of the lamb is simple: Every bite tastes pretty much like the next. This simple flavor calls for a complex-flavored wine—maybe a rich Cabernet Sauvignon full of flavors like ripe berries, chocolate, black currants, and plums.

Butter, cream, oil, and eggs can add substantial weight to otherwise light foods. Strong spices can add dimension and complexity, as can high-acid sauces. For acidic sauces like tomato and lemon, choose a wine that's high in acid, but with a fruity-enough presence to counteract some of the tang.

Cooking methods also affect a food's compatibility with wine. The way you cook your food can radically alter its texture—compare fried chicken to boiled, for example. It may affect its flavor as well, particularly in the case of frying, which adds a flavorful food substance (fat). The following table shows you how cooking methods affect foods and suggests wines to pair with each method.

WINES WITH COOKING METHODS

COOKING METHOD	EFFECT ON FOOD	COMPATIBLE WINES
Boiling	Suppresses flavor	Medium/full reds, fruity whites: Burgundy, Bordeaux, Pinot Grigio, Sauvignon Blanc
Frying	Enhances flavor/texture	Light, fruity, acidic: Zinfandel, Pinot Gris, rosé
Grilling	Sears and accentuates	Full reds: Shiraz, Cabernet Sauvignon
Roasting	Caramelizes, accentuates	Mature reds: Barolo, Barbaresco
Steaming	Enhances delicate flavors	Light, fruity, primarily white: Viognier, Pinot Grigio, Riesling
Stewing	Mixes flavors	Full whites and reds: Chardonnay, Bordeaux, Chiantí Classico, Rioja

Just as wine enhances the flavor of food, food amplifies the flavors of wine. That's why many otherwise ho-hum wines like Pinot Blanc find their true selves when paired with food.

Matching Compatible Personalities and Weights

Beyond the basic chemistry of sweet with sweet, fruity with spicy, and so on, choose wines that have the same "personality" as the food. In general, you want to serve big-flavored, big-presence wines with heavy, flavorful foods; delicate wines with delicate foods; and elegant wines with elegant foods. Don't serve white Zinfandel with beef Wellington, and don't break out that 20-year-old Bordeaux for pizza night unless it's really stellar pizza!

abcdefghijklmnopq
rstuvwxyzabcdefgh
ijklmnopqrstuvwxy

a note from
the instructor

BUYING WINE FOR A DINNER PARTY

- Find out what your guests like and don't like. If they aren't familiar with wines by grape or name, ask them what flavors they prefer.
- Of the wines your guests like, choose the best fit with the foods you'll be serving—including sauces and spices.
- Buy both red and white, and offer your guests both at dinner. Also be prepared to offer a nonalcoholic selection (sparkling water and so forth)—not everybody drinks.
- Consider offering both a "tame" wine (Zinfandel or Spumante) and a more adventurous selection.

Remember that you want to identify the food's dominant characteristic. If the main course is savory and full of herbs and spices, your best bet may be a wine that has a personality that's compatible to the dominant herb or spice. In the following table, you'll find a list of wines that go well with particular herbs and spices.

WINES WITH HERBS AND SPICES

HERB/SPICE	WINE
Basil	Chianti, Tempranillo, Orvieto
Bay	Sangiovese, Barbera
Capers	Sauvignon Blanc, Riesling
Cinnamon	Pinot Noir, Gewürztraminer, Syrah
Dill	Sauvignon Blanc
Garlic	Côtes-du-Rhône
Ginger	Gewürztraminer, Muscat/Moscato
Mint	Gamay, Muscat/Moscato
Mustard	Riesling, Barolo
Nutmeg	Pinot Noir, Chardonnay
Oregano	Sauvignon Blanc
Pepper	Cabernet Sauvignon, Gewürztraminer, Syrah
Rosemary	Barolo, Shiraz, Syrah
Sage	Merlot, Zinfandel

Your chicken in dill sauce, then, will probably be content alongside a crisp Sauvignon Blanc; if you're serving chicken with a tangy mustard sauce, you may be better off pairing it with a Riesling. Your ginger chicken will harmonize well with a Gewürztraminer, but those ginger cookies you're serving for dessert may sing a sweeter tune when accompanied by a Moscato.

You're on solid ground whenever the wine that matches the herb or spice is the same one you'd pick anyway, like Sauvignon Blanc with chicken. But you'd probably never think of serving Merlot with turkey if it weren't for the strong flavor of sage in the dressing. Don't lose sleep over pairing white meat with red wine. Just keep the dominant flavor in mind. If you just can't stand the idea of serving a lesser-known combination to dinner guests, give it a test-drive first: Serve the wine and food to your family or friends one night and see what they think.

Match the food's weight with the wine's body: Pair lightweight foods with light-bodied wines (Dover sole with Pinot Blanc), medium foods with medium-bodied wines (burgers with Zinfandel), and heavy foods with full-bodied wines (sausage with Barolo). What do we mean by weight? We mean the actual physical weight of the food—compare a serving of quiche to a serving of T-bone steak, for example. But weight also takes into account the food's flavor. A tiny samosa, with enough spice, can pack as much of a wallop as a much heartier food.

This is a good place to segue into a discussion about meats. Most of the time, when you talk about pairing wine with a meal, you're talking about matching it up with the meat that will be served as the main course. Particularly in Western culture, the main-course meat is the hub around which the rest of the meal revolves. Nine times out of ten, you'll probably pick your wine by this factor alone.

The following table offers a few suggestions of wines that pair well with certain meats. As with all the tables you'll find in this book, we don't want you to become a slave to what's written here. Your journey might begin with a cold Chablis served alongside crab cakes, but where it ends is limited only by your imagination.

WINES WITH MEATS, POULTRY, AND SEAFOOD

MEAT	WINE
Beef	Cabernet Sauvignon, St.-Emilion, Merlot, Syrah
Chicken	Sauvignon Blanc (white meat), Côtes-du-Rhône (dark meat)
Cold cured meats	Barolo, Chianti, Moscato, D'Asti
Crab	Muscadet, Chablis
Duck	Pomerol, Châteauneuf-du-Pape, Graves
Fish	Pinot Grigio, Verdicchio, Riesling
Game (wild)	Barolo, Syrah, Côtie Rotie; Châteauneuf du Pape; Côtes-du-Rhone
Goose	Chianti, Châteauneuf-du-Pape, Spätlese Riesling
Ham	Pinot Noir, Beaujolais, Gewürztraminer (depending on how the ham is seasoned)
Lamb	Bordeaux, Rioja, Cabernet Sauvignon
Liver	Médoc, Champagne (if foie gras, serve Sauternes)
Lobster	Mersault, Chardonnay, Viognier, Prosecco
Pork	Pinot Noir, Pinot Gris, Tempranillo
Shrimp	Muscadet, Sauvignon Blanc

In these examples, the meat's "personality" echoes something in the wine's. For instance, the strong, musky flavor of game such as venison or pheasant (or even buffalo) needs a strong presence, like Syrah's or Barolo's. Because the meat's flavor is so strong, the sauce or the preparation method can't do much to alter its imposing character. But tamer meats don't behave the same way: Orange chicken exudes a vastly different personality than barbecued chicken does. In this case, you'd probably want a lightly spicy wine like Gewürztraminer for the former and a heartier wine like Côtes-du-Rhône for the latter.

Similarly, fish varies not only by preparation method and sauce but also, most widely of all, by fish type. The delicate flavor of flounder wants a delicate wine like Pinot Blanc or Orvieto, but shark steak is like red meat; it requires a wine bold enough to hold up to its power. For a white meat that behaves like red meat, your favorite wines may turn out to be reds, such as Merlot or Pinot Noir.

Finding Wines to Go with International and Regional Cuisines

Usually a safe bet in food pairing is to match the cuisine with a wine from the area. Nearly every country with a special food makes a wine that's designed to go with it. The nuances in the region's air, soil, and plant life will be the same in both the food and the wine since they were grown in the same place. But don't feel that you're obligated to do it this way every time. Mixing and matching can be fun: German food with Spanish wine, Mexican food with Australian wine, French wine with California cuisine. Why not?

Then there are the cuisines that have no "typical" wine to pair with because their countries aren't major (grape) wine producers: Chinese, Japanese (who frequently drink rice-based sake), Thai, Indian, and others. These cuisines often frustrate wine lovers, not only because they have no "natural" match but also because many of their specialties are spicy mélanges of many different foods, resulting in complex layers of texture and flavor. The following table offers a few suggestions for pairing wine with hard-to-match cuisines.

WINES WITH INTERNATIONAL AND REGIONAL CUISINES

CUISINE	WINE
Cajun	Beaujolais, Riesling
Caribbean	Riesling, Rioja
Chinese	Cabernet Franc, Pinot Grigio, Gewürztraminer
Indian	Vouvray, Merlot
Japanese	Muscadet, Champagne, Pinot Grigio
Mexican	Zinfandel, Shiraz [rosé]
Middle Eastern	Cinsault, Pinot Noir
Thai	Gewürztraminer, Sauvignon Blanc, Pinot Grigio

The slightly sweet spiciness of Gewürztraminer can stand up to a great deal of the spiciness in Thai and Chinese food. And Zinfandel's berrylike fruitiness can put out the fire in hot Mexican dishes. Choose low-tannin wines with spicy foods.

Pairing Wines with Hard-to-Match Foods

Most dishes pair decently with any number of wines, but a handful of notorious foods can leave even the most knowledgeable wine expert baffled. Asparagus, artichokes, caramel, and chocolate are among the most difficult to match. But even some of these confirmed wine bachelors will settle down when they meet the right wine. Asparagus (and another similarly flavored wine nemesis, artichoke) has a formidable partner in New Zealand Sauvignon Blanc because of its distinctive,

abcdefghijklmnopq rstuvwxyzabcdefgh ijklmnopqrstuvwxy

a note from
the instructor

Suppose you want to serve just one wine with an entire meal. Is there any type of wine that's versatile enough to go from appetizer to dessert? Some of the best sparkling wines can do just that—particularly the sweeter ones with decent acidity. A semisweet Riesling also works with most foods. And when all else fails, stick with a good Champagne—it goes with just about everything.

creamy, asparaguslike flavor. The intense, bittersweet creaminess of chocolate seems like a tough call until you try it with a fine, ruby Port—and some people swear by Cabernet and chocolate, because of the chocolate influences in Cabernet.

Whenever a particular food has you stumped, go with a mild, neutral wine like Pinot Blanc or a lightweight sparkler like Prosecco.

Not All Wines Go Well with Food

Watch out for wines whose flavors are so overwhelming that they drown out the subtle flavors in your food. Oaky Chardonnays may do so, as will tannin bombs like Cabernet Sauvignon and Barolo. In general, invite only low-oak wines to dinner, and if the tannic reds are coming, you'd better be serving something like a roast or grilled red meat, because these are the only foods bold enough to stand up to a lot of tannin.

Watch out, too, for high-alcohol wines, such as some Chardonnays and nearly all fortified wines—too much alcohol can numb your palate and mask that good food flavor. This is probably why fortified wines, with their added alcoholic kick, are classed separately from table wines; the implication is that they're not meant for the dinner table—although there are exceptions to this rule. If you've ever had a glass of Sherry with split pea and ham soup (or poured some Sherry *in* the soup!), you know what we mean.

Wines seem to need a certain amount of acid to go well with food. Acid makes you salivate and helps break down both the food and the wine, releasing their flavors. But acidity alone may cause the wine to get lost

a note from the instructor

HOLD THE VINEGAR!

If you're serving wine with dinner, don't serve foods prepared with vinegar—not even sweet pickles or vinaigrette on the salad. The sour flavors in the vinegar will affect your guests' palates, and that wonderful wine you've lovingly chosen will taste as though it, too, has turned to vinegar! Substitute lemon juice for the vinegar in salad dressing when wine is on the menu. Or, if you simply can't do without a dinner of sauerkraut and pickled pigs' feet, serve an aperitif wine before and/or a dessert wine after the vinegar-laden meal.

if the food itself is acidic and intense. A wine needs a certain amount of sweetness, fruitiness, or both to keep its balance against such fare.

WINES FOR SPECIFIC MEALS AND APPETITES

Now that you have a handle on the basics and you know which wines tend to get along with which foods, we'll look at specific events that call for wine and explore some of the choices that complement them.

Wines for Appetizers and Parties

When you're serving wine before a meal or with snacks at a party, keep it light and fun. The best aperitif wines are light enough, and low enough in alcohol, that they don't wreck your guests' palates or appetites for the food that's to come. Consider choosing fruity, slightly sweet wines like Pinot Blanc, Muscat/Moscato, and Champagne. Or match your wine to the appetizers and party foods you're serving: Try serving Bardolino with raw veggies and dips (or Pinot Grigio if the veggies are fried). Oysters on the half shell? Try Sancerre. Sauvignon Blanc works with shrimp cocktail; Sherry is wonderful with olives and nuts. If you get stuck, refer to the tables in this chapter that deal with the qualities of different foods and some of their more amiable wine matches.

Hardly anyone can get through a party, let alone the appetizer portion of a meal, without putting some cheese on the table. The following table lists popular cheeses served at parties and a few suggestions for matching them with wine.

WINES WITH CHEESES

CHEESE	WINE
Brie	Pomerol, Chardonnay
Camembert	Côtes-du-Rhône, Médoc
Cheddar	Perequita
Chevre	Riesling, Sancerre
Colby	Zinfandel
Cream cheese	Muscat/Moscato
Feta	Chablis
Gorgonzola	Red Burgundy
Havarti	Cava
Monterey Jack	Chardonnay
Mozzarella	Pinot Grigio, Orvieto
Roquefort	Sauternes
Stilton	Port

Of course, not all these cheeses have mass party appeal. Some crowds might look at you funny if you gave them nothing but Stilton, Feta, and Chevre (goat cheese); but by all means serve the stronger cheeses (and their wine companions) if you and your guests are into them. With cheeses that just about everybody recognizes—Mozzarella, Monterey Jack, and Cheddar—serve the easygoing wines that they pal around with (Chardonnay, Pinot Grigio, and Zinfandel); you can hardly go wrong.

And don't forget that a number of cheeses make scrumptious after-dessert courses. A light, sweet Havarti with Cava or bleu cheese with Sauternes can bring down the curtain nicely on a wonderful meal.

Wines for Vegetarian Meals

When we were talking about the way Westerners tend to think of meat as the heart of a meal, we were neglecting a small but often health-conscious portion of the population: vegetarians. To pair wine with a vegetarian meal, you use the same principles, only you match to the bean, grain, vegetable, or other dish that serves as the focal point.

Beans and grains often replace meat as a vegetarian meal's primary source of protein. The following table takes a look at some of the likely combinations.

WINES WITH BEANS AND GRAINS

BEAN OR GRAIN	WINE
Couscous	Cinsault, Shiraz
Lentil soup	Merlot
Macaroni and cheese	Graves, Sémillon
Polenta	White Burgundy
Rice with beans	Burgundy, Chablis
Rice with vegetables	Chablis

The hearty flavor of baked beans calls for a fairly muscular wine like a fruity Zinfandel. Similarly, a fruity Chardonnay can alleviate some of the blandness of rice. But keep in mind that if you're serving bean/grain items in any kind of sauce, the sauce, rather than the main ingredient, is likely to dominate, and you should make your wine selection accordingly.

The following table offers popular combinations of wine and vegetables. Because few people sit down to a meal of a single vegetable, once again you'd choose your wine according to the dominant flavors and textures of the meal.

WINES WITH VEGETABLES

VEGETABLE	WINE
Artichoke	Viognier, New Zealand Sauvignon Blanc
Asparagus	Muscat/Moscato, New Zealand Sauvignon Blanc
Avocado	Sancerre
Brussels sprouts	Pinot Noir
Cabbage	Pinot Noir
Carrots	Gewürztraminer
Eggplant	Zinfandel, Chianti
Green beans	Sauvignon Blanc
Mushrooms	Pinot Noir
Olives	Sherry
Onions	Pinot Grigio
Peas	Sherry
Spinach	Pinot Noir
Raw vegetables	Bardolino

If you've ever uncorked and sniffed an aged Pinot Noir, you know why it goes well with cabbage. It often has something approaching a cabbagelike aroma, which logically makes it complement the vegetable when served alongside it. Similarly, Pinot Noir can have a rich, mushroomlike flavor and aroma, and New Zealand Sauvignon Blanc is famous for its asparaguslike quality.

Vegetable dishes don't have to be meatless for these combinations to work. A main dish of green beans with ham cubes still pairs well with Sauvignon Blanc—unless it contains five cubes of ham for every green bean. As long as the vegetables are dominant, they'll work with the wines listed.

Wines for Holiday Meals

There are those traditional meals that come around year after year, the menu little changed from the year before. Imagine what a hit you'd be with your friends and family if you showed up with a great new wine to match these holiday favorites.

WINES FOR HOLIDAY MEALS

HOLIDAY	WINE
Passover: salmon, chicken, turkey, asparagus—no flour	Sauvignon Blanc (kosher for Passover*)
Easter: ham	Pinot Noir, Beaujolais
Easter: lamb	Pauillac, Rioja, Bordeaux
Thanksgiving: turkey and sweet side dishes	Sémillon, Hermitage, Gamay Beaujolais, Gewürztraminer, Zinfandel
Christmas: duck or goose	Pinot Noir, Shiraz, Châteauneuf-du-Pape, Côte Rôtie
Christmas: roast beef	Cabernet Sauvignon, Burgundy

See the section on kosher wines in Lesson 5 for details.

But what happens if you serve a sage dressing with your turkey, as many people do, and the flavor of the sage is stronger than the flavor of the bird? Do you serve a Sémillon, as recommended in the preceding table, or a Merlot, as we suggest for sage in the earlier spice table? And how is your decision affected if you know that some of the folks coming to dinner prefer dark meat over white?

The answer is simple: Serve both. It's not at all uncommon to offer a choice of white or red wine with a meal, just as you would offer a choice of light or dark meat from the turkey. Place both open bottles on the table and let your dinner guests' own preferences guide them.

Wines for Dessert

When it comes to desserts, you really have to worry about only one issue: Don't serve a dessert that's sweeter than the wine, which would make the wine taste bland. If you're serving wine with dessert, serve a mild or tart food with a sweet, rich dessert wine—for example, fruit tarts with Sauternes.

Serve a Port or Sherry with semi-sweet chocolate and/or nuts. If you're serving a dessert with walnuts in it, you simply *have* to try serving it with an oloroso Sherry. Some people even pour sweet Sherry on their ice cream. Sweet sparkling wines are also great dessert choices because they're so versatile—and they generally go well with light, fruity desserts.

Don't forget that many of the cheeses we mentioned back in the wine-with-cheese table make great desserts as well. Then, if you're really feeling adventurous, you might try the following recipe.

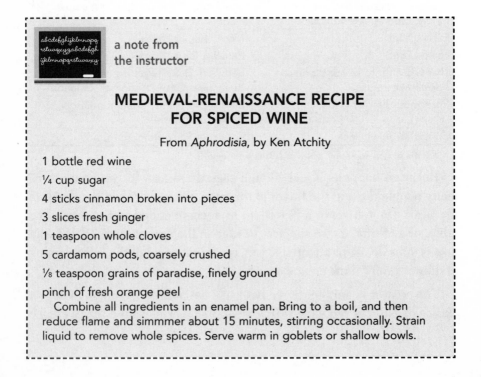

a note from
the instructor

MEDIEVAL-RENAISSANCE RECIPE FOR SPICED WINE

From *Aphrodisia*, by Ken Atchity

1 bottle red wine

¼ cup sugar

4 sticks cinnamon broken into pieces

3 slices fresh ginger

1 teaspoon whole cloves

5 cardamom pods, coarsely crushed

⅛ teaspoon grains of paradise, finely ground

pinch of fresh orange peel

   Combine all ingredients in an enamel pan. Bring to a boil, and then reduce flame and simmmer about 15 minutes, stirring occasionally. Strain liquid to remove whole spices. Serve warm in goblets or shallow bowls.

COOKING WITH WINE

As a cooking ingredient, wine adds a wonderful dimension to foods, particularly when it's a rich, flavorful wine like a nutty Sherry or a tawny Port. But table wines work well in cooking, too. In general, follow the same rules that apply when choosing wines for drinking: match compatible personalities, textures, and chemistry.

The following list offers a few guidelines for cooking with wine:

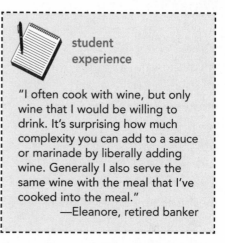

student experience

"I often cook with wine, but only wine that I would be willing to drink. It's surprising how much complexity you can add to a sauce or marinade by liberally adding wine. Generally I also serve the same wine with the meal that I've cooked into the meal."
—Eleanore, retired banker

- **Cook with quality wines:** If you wouldn't drink it, don't put it in your food. Most cooking wines available at grocery stores are of poor quality and have undesirable additives—use table wine instead. Cook with leftover wine only if it's still drinkable. Never cook with stale or spoiled wine.

- **When a recipe calls for red:** The heavier the food, the more full-bodied the wine should be. For the most part, choose reds with earthy flavors, like Pinot Noir. If you're making a tomato-based sauce, use a high-acid red wine like Barbera or Gamay.

- **Alcohol content in cooking:** The longer you cook a dish to which you've added wine, the more alcohol will evaporate. If you want the alcohol to be prominent, add it near the end of the cooking process. Once you remove the food from direct heat, you'll be able to retain most of the alcohol, even if the dish stays very warm.

- **When the recipe calls for white:** Cook with white wines that are high in acid, with little or no oakiness—as Chardonnay often has—the oak flavor can overwhelm delicate foods. Most of the time, you can't go wrong with Sauvignon Blanc because of its complementary herbal flavor.

- **When the dish is hot and spicy:** Strong, fruity whites can hold their own against spice. Try Muscat or Viognier.

fun things to do with wine

Exploring Vineyards and Wineries • Going to and Hosting Wine Tastings

After learning the basics, many novices are ready to find fun ways to incorporate wine into their lives. Now that you've grasped the nuts and bolts on wine, your path is clear to really start enjoying it. Start at home and in your local area and go from there. Once you're through with this lesson you'll have the confidence to host a wine-tasting party, drop in on a local winery, or even book a trip to a famous wine-producing region.

TOURING VINEYARDS AND WINERIES

Nothing deepens your appreciation of wine like going to the source. When you visit wineries and vineyards, talk to the people who nurture the wine from bud to bottle, smell the air, and feel the same sunlight and wind on your skin that the growing grapes feel on theirs, you'll find that the experience comes alive for you in a vivid new way. Plus, it's a natural fact that wine-growing regions tend to be some of the most beautiful spots on Earth.

Starting in Your Own Backyard

Don't feel as though you have to book an expensive trip just to become a wine tourist. Your wine adventures can start right in your own neighborhood. There's no need to run straight off to Napa Valley—unless you happen to live in San Francisco!

If you start out touring local wineries, you can pace yourself: Make a day or a weekend of it rather than committing to several weeks. It's cheaper this way, too, and a great way to support local commerce. And you never know what treasures might be lurking in your own backyard!

After you've explored local vineyards, you can expand to those that are near places you travel to frequently: Visit the wine hotspots near your friends and family when you're in the area, and see the ones that are close to your favorite vacation destinations and the places you routinely travel to on business.

> **student experience**
>
> "I'd read a few articles on wine and tried to pick up a different type of wine every week or two, but just couldn't discern the various types. That all changed when I visited a local winery. There, I was able to taste several varieties of wine at one time and began to learn to compare and contrast. Since the tastings were free, I didn't break the bank either."
> –Roxane, law enforcement officer

Most wineries understand the benefits of meeting customers face to face and will welcome your visit. The grand-scale wineries, like many in California, open their doors to the public on a daily basis and often run cafes and souvenir shops that cater to a regular flow of tourists. Napa's Sterling Winery even boasts an aerial tram. Most smaller wineries will also welcome your visit if you schedule an appointment ahead of time by phone, fax, or letter. Many wineries stay open longer in tourist-heavy summer months but may be open only on weekends during the winter. Again, call ahead to be sure.

You can find information about local wineries at tourism information offices and local chambers of commerce. If you're interested in the wineries of a particular region, try doing an online search using the name of the region and the word *wine*. As you're driving, be on the lookout for road signs with pictures of grapes: Many countries, the U.S. included, use this symbol to direct tourists to wineries.

For Web sites, books, and other information about tourism-friendly wineries, see the Resources and Recommended Reading section at the back of this book.

What You'll Encounter When Visiting a Winery

Wine tours range from a simple walk through the facility followed by an informal tasting to a lavish affair complete wih a gourmet meal and a stop at the gift shop. How involved you want to get is up to you. Many wineries give extensive step-by-step tours, where you can see the fermenting must, the equipment, and the aging process. At the very least, you'll have access to someone who is knowledgeable about the wine and how it's produced. You'll be able to taste a variety of wines without having to buy each one separately, and you'll learn much more about the winery's products than if you bought them in a store. When you're done, you can select wines to take with you, or possibly to drink immediately—many wineries have picnic facilities where you can drink a bottle on site.

Taking a Wine Trip

Most countries that are serious about their wine actively encourage wine tourism and make the job of finding, scheduling, and experiencing a winery tour as convenient as possible. You'll find nearly all wineries receptive to a visit if you approach them politely beforehand—with one exception: A few large commercial wineries in other countries make cheap jug wine exclusively for already-established local markets. They have no need, or desire, to invite the wine-touring public inside their facilities. And when it comes down to it, there probably isn't all that much to see in these operations anyway. Stick to the wineries that welcome visitors.

If you're serious about taking an all-out wine trip of several days or more, a travel agent can help you plan it or can put you in touch with travel companies that specialize in wine tour packages. In tourist-friendly regions such as Napa Valley and Australia, you can make your way from winery to winery by just about any means imaginable: horse and buggy, antique limousine, Harley Davidson, hot-air balloon, or a self-guided walking or cycling tour. Napa Valley even offers a wine train in which you can luxuriate over a gourmet meal on your way to the vineyards (see www.ilovenapa.com for details).

a note from
the instructor

VISITING FOREIGN VINEYARDS

Plan ahead as much as possible when touring vineyards in other countries. Unless you're part of a prearranged package tour, you'll need to call, write, or fax to make the arrangements yourself. If you're visiting a country in which English isn't widely spoken, make arrangements for how you'll communicate with the winery staff—don't assume that someone there will understand you. It goes without saying that you should respect the customs of the place you're visiting: When you're on their turf and in their place of business, do it their way.

ATTENDING AND HOSTING WINE TASTINGS

Wine tastings are a great way to add an exciting new facet to your enjoyment of wine. They're also terrific opportunities to socialize with other wine lovers, whether you attend a tasting at a wine shop, winery, or club event or host one of your own.

Attending a Wine Tasting

Wine tastings are held for all sorts of reasons, some directly related to the wine, some not. Wine lovers typically gather for tastings to further educate their palates, to taste new wines without having to purchase them all, to benefit from the wine experience of others, and for the sheer fun of it. Wine tastings are also a great way to get acquainted with other wine lovers.

Some tastings are like lectures, and others are like informal social gatherings. Tastings are held at restaurants, convention centers, wine stores, vineyards, and festivals, among other places. Check with your local wine store, in your favorite wine publication, or online for tastings in your area.

Common Types of Tastings

How do the people organizing a tasting decide which wines to serve? Tastings are generally organized around a particular theme, whether it's vintage, style, region, or some other factor. Here are a few common types of tastings:

- **Vertical:** Tasting several vintages of the same wine (for example, Bartoli 1985, 1987, and 1989)
- **Horizontal:** Tasting wines of the same vintage from various wineries (Sonoma Valley Chardonnays from 1999, for instance)
- **Comparative:** Tasting various examples of the same style or type of wine: varietals, appelations, etc. (such as Cabernet Sauvignons from Chile, Argentina, and Mexico)

student experience

"Some restaurants offer 'wine flights'—a fun way to try new wines. It's like getting a sampler. There is usually a theme to the flight, like Zinfandels from various places or Spanish wines of various types. Anyway, you get to try several, then you can choose which one you want more of—another glass or even a bottle. If you really like it, be sure to write down the name of the vintner, the name of the wine, and the year it was produced. That way, you can pick up a bottle at your local wine retailer, or ask them to order you a case."
—Ben, mechanical engineer

To Spit or Not to Spit

At professional and formal wine tastings, wine tasters don't swallow the wines they're sampling. They spit each mouthful of wine into a spittoon. Here are some of the reasons for doing so:

- **To stay sober.** How many people could drink the equivalent of a dozen glasses of wine and still drive home?
- **To keep the palate fresh.** Because the wine is in contact with a smaller portion of the mouth, and probably for less time, the palate doesn't get fatigued as quickly.
- **To save calories.** Each glass of wine contains about 75 calories. If you drank the equivalent of ten or more glasses at a tasting, that would mean a lot of extra time at the gym.

Normally, there are one or more communal spittoons for tasters' use. These spittoons may or may not contain sawdust or sand to absorb what gets spat into them. Don't worry about looking gross: Everyone else will be doing it, too. And don't worry about your aim—you spit into the sink every night after brushing your teeth; how often do you miss?

Other Tips for Proper Wine-Tasting Behavior

On the day you're planning to attend a tasting, don't smoke or wear heavy perfume. Wine is about subtleties of aroma and flavor, and any heavy odors lingering about you may disrupt your and your fellow tasters' ability to appreciate them.

Don't eat spicy, strong foods before a tasting, either: The lingering flavors and aromas of the food can numb your palate and skew your perception of the wine. For the same reason, don't drink hard liquor before a tasting.

When you're tasting wines, wait until the people around you begin voicing their opinions before you offer yours. If you start talking right away about your impressions, you may rob others of the chance to form unbiased opinions. This is a good opportunity to spend time in listening mode—you'll be able to learn from the more experienced-tasters around you.

Hosting a Wine Tasting

Hosting an informal wine tasting of your own can be a lot of fun. It's a nice excuse to get friends together, and you'll be amazed at how many more people will show up to a party when they know that wine will be involved! It's also a great way for wine lovers to educate themselves and each other on the wines that are available in their area.

Try to invite guests who enjoy wine enough to spend an evening focusing on it and talking about it. If you invite people who strongly prefer hard liquor to wine, they may not get much out of the experience: Because hard liquor dulls the palate (it has a numbing effect on the taste buds and other senses), they probably won't be able to enjoy the wine's nuances. Discourage your guests from smoking at the tasting, as the tobacco smoke can blot out much of the wine's subtleties.

a note from
the instructor

ORDER OF SERVING

If you're serving more than one type of wine at a tasting (white and red, light and full, table and fortified, and so on), try to arrange the wines in a sequence that doesn't dull your guests' palates too quickly. A high-tannin wine can leave your guests' mouths too numb to appreciate the subtleties of a delicate wine. The more body, alcohol, tannin, and sweetness a wine has, the later it should come on the serving list. In general, serve:

- White before red
- Light-bodied before full-bodied
- Low tannin before high tannin
- Sparkling before still
- Nonfortified before fortified

Arranging Your Setting

If you're hosting an informal tasting, you don't need any special equipment beyond glasses and a corkscrew. But if you wish, you may provide your guests with additional paraphernalia. You might offer pitchers of water so your guests can cleanse their palates. A few bland, dry crackers help, too. Provide a spittoon for guests who choose to spit. You may want to make sure that there's a clean white surface somewhere in the room (such as a wall or a tablecloth) for your guests to use as a background when they examine the wine's color. Pens and pads of paper also come in handy if your guests wish to jot down their impressions.

Deciding on a Type of Tasting

It's your event—feel free to organize it in whatever way appeals to you. You can borrow from one or more of the professional types of tastings we discussed earlier, try the following ones, or come up with an idea of your own. You're limited only by your imagination.

- **Blind tastings** (in which the bottles are covered by bags so that the labels and shapes can't be seen) create a sense of adventure as guests voyage into the unknown. You can approach blind tastings in a variety of ways: Serve several wines of one type (Ports, Champagnes, and so forth), one vintage, or several types from one region, country, or vineyard. You can serve wines one at a time or open a variety of bottles and let guests choose for themselves.

- **Practical tastings:** You and your friends can help each other discover good wine values in your area by having everyone bring their own bottle of wine, in a range of prices, for everyone to taste. Let each person rank all the selections. The favorite wine may not be the most expensive choice—in which case you've uncovered a bargain.

---

student experience

"My friends and I make a game of seeing who can find the best bottle of wine for $10 or less. Once a month we all gather at someone's house, and we each bring one bottle and a couple wineglasses. We pop the corks and everyone tastes the same wine at the same time. We write down the names of all the wines and rate them from A to F. At the end of the evening everybody gives a dollar to the person who brought the wine that got the best grade. It's nothing fancy, but it's a lot of fun and we all get to try seven or eight different wines for the price of one bottle!"

—Jennifer, sales manager

How many wines should you serve at your tasting? It largely depends on the level of expertise of the people you're inviting. Experienced tasters will happily go through a dozen wines or more and will be able to keep track of them all. Novices may have trouble processing more than five or six wines. For your first event, your best bet is to keep the selection limited to half a dozen or fewer so that you don't overwhelm your guests or yourself. The main objective is to focus on—and enjoy— the wine.

Appendix A

wine pronunciation guide

Albariño (Alvarinho): al-ba-REEN-yo (al-va-REEN-ho)

Asti: AH-stee

Barbaresco: bar-ba-RES-co

Barbera: bar-BEAR-a

Barolo: ba-RO-lo

Beaujolais: bo-jzho-LAY

Cabernet Franc: ca-ber-NAY FRONK

Cabernet Sauvignon: ca-ber-NAY so-veen-YON

Chardonnay: shar-do-NAY

Châteauneuf-du-Pape: sha-to-NOOF doo POP

Chenin Blanc: she-NEEN blonk

Chianti: kee-AN-tee

Côtes-du-Rhône: COAT-dew-ROAN

Côte-Rôtie: COAT-ro-TEE

Dolcetto: dol-CHET-to

Fumé Blanc: FOO-may blonk

Gamay: ga-MAY

Gewürztraminer: ge-VOORTZ-tra-mee-ner

Graves: grahv

Merlot: mer-LOW

Muscat: mus-CAT

Petite Sirah: pe-TEE sir-AH

Petit Verdot: pe-TEE vair-DO

Pinotage: pee-no-TAZH

Pinot Blanc (Bianco): pee-no BLONK (bee-AN-co)

Pinot Gris (Grigio): pee-no GREE (GREE-zhee-oh)

Pinot Noir: pee-no NWAR

Pouilly Fuissé: poo-WEE FWEE-say

Riesling: REEZ-ling

Rioja: re-OH-ha

Sauvignon Blanc: SAW-veen-yon BLONK

Sémillon: SAY-mee-yon

Shiraz: shi-RAZ

Syrah: sih-RAH

Tokay Aszu: to-KAY a-ZOO

Verdicchio: ver-DIK-ki-oh

Vinho Verde: VIN-ho VAIR-day

Viognier: vee-YON-yay

Zinfandel: ZIN-fan-del

Appendix B

resources and recommended reading

BOOKS

General Knowledge

Brenner, Leslie. *Fear of Wine: An Introductory Guide to the Grape*. New York: Bantam Books, 1995.

Clarke, Oz. *The Essential Wine Book*. New York: Simon & Schuster, 1996.

Eyres, Harry. *The Bluffer's Guide to Wine*. London: Oval Books, 2002.

Gabler, James M. *How to Be a Wine Expert*. Baltimore: Bacchus Press Limited, 1987.

Gluckstern, Willie. *The Wine Avenger*. New York: Fireside Books, 1998.

MacNeil, Karen. *The Wine Bible*. New York: Workman Publishing Co. 2001.

McCarthy, Ed, and Mary Ewing-Mulligan. *Wine for Dummies*. Indianapolis, IN, Wiley Publishing, Inc., 1995.

McCarthy, Ed, and Mary Ewing-Mulligan. *Wine Buying Companion for Dummies*. Indianapolis, IN, Wiley Publishing, Inc., 1997.

Robards, Terry. *The New York Times Book of Wine*. New York: Quadrangle/The New York Times Book Co., 1976.

Robinson, Jancis, ed., and A. Dinsmore Webb, ed, and Richard E. Smart, ed. *The Oxford Companion to Wine*. Los Angeles: Getty Center for Education in the Arts, 1999.

Zraly, Kevin. *Windows on the World Complete Wine Course*. New York: Sterling Publishing Co., 1998.

Pairing Wine with Food

Breitstein, Ron, and Hendrik Van Leuven. *Wine & Dine: California Fine Wines Matched with Gourmet Recipes*. Santa Barbara CA: Capra Press, 1996.

Johnson-Bell, Linda. *Pairing Wine with Food: A Handbook for All Cuisines*. Short Hills, NJ: Burford Books, 1999.

Wine-Growing Regions

Casas, Penelope. *The Foods & Wines of Spain*. New York: Alfred A. Knopf, 1982.

Doerper, John. *Wine Country: California's Napa & Sonoma Valleys*. Oakland CA: Fodor's Travel Publications, 1998.

Ewing-Mulligan, Mary, and Ed McCarthy. *Italian Wine for Dummies*. Indianapolis, IN, Wiley Publishing, Inc., 2001.

Fielden, Christopher. *A Traveler's Wine Guide to France*. New York: Interlink Books, 1997.

Hobley, Stephen. *A Traveler's Wine Guide to Italy*. New York: Interlink Books, 1997.

McCarthy, Ed, and Mary Ewing-Mulligan. *French Wine for Dummies*. Indianapolis, IN, Wiley Publishing, Inc., 2001.

Stewart, Kerry Brady. *A Traveler's Wine Guide to Germany*. New York: Interlink Books, 1998.

MAGAZINES AND JOURNALS

Wine Spectator: a highly authoritative and well-respected wine magazine; www.winespectator.com.

The Wine Advocate: Wine expert Robert Parker's newsletter; www.erobertparker.com.

International Wine Cellar: Wine expert Stephen Tanzer's newsletter; www.wineaccess.com.

Liquid Assets: a wine investment newsletter by Orley Ashenfelter; www.liquidasset.com.

Decanter: Britain's popular wine magazine; www.decanter.com.

WEB SITES

www.americanwinesociety.com: the official Web site of the American Wine Society.

www.aboutwines.com: a searchable source of wine information, particularly helpful for regional information.

www.ilovenapa.com: the official Web site of wine experts Jim White and Jeremy Benson.

www.learnaboutwine.com: the offical Web site of wine authors Ian Blackburn and Allison Levine.

www.winedirectories.com: another good source of regional wine information.

www.erobertparker.com: the official Web site of wine expert Robert Parker.

glossary of wine terms

Acid, acetic: acid present in all wines. An excess of acetic acid produces a soured, vinegary wine.

Acid, ascorbic: acid frequently added to wines at bottling, to prevent *oxidation*.

Acid, citric: acid present in grapes, particularly in white varieties, responsible for "fruity" and "citrus" aromas and flavors.

Acidity: one of the primary qualities affecting a wine's flavor. Too much or too little can cause a wine to lose its *balance*.

Aftertaste: see *finish*.

Appellation: the region in which a wine's grapes were grown. See also *terroir*.

Aroma: the individual smell of a wine. In a fine aged wine, any given aroma is one of many. Wines have primary, secondary, and tertiary aromas, which collectively are called its *bouquet*.

Aromatic esters: compounds developed during the wine's *fermentation* process.

Auslese: a white German wine made from sweet, late-harvested grapes.

Balance: the quality that exists when all of a wine's characteristics (sweetness, alcohol, acidity, etc.) are equally present and none is stronger than another.

Barrel fermented: wine that ferments not in steel tanks but in oak barrels.

Bianco: Italian for white.

Blanc de noirs: white wine made with black or red grapes.

Blanco: Spanish for white.

Bleeding: pouring off a quantity of the wine during *fermentation*. The wine that is bled is often used to make lightweight wines.

Blending: a process of creating wines mixing varieties.

Blind tasting: tasting wine without knowing anything about its type or origin.

Body: the perceived "weight" of the wine in the mouth, described as light, medium, or full. Red wines, high-alcohol wines, and wines from hot climates tend to be fuller bodied. Typically, a wine with a pronounced *tannin* structure is full-bodied. Full-bodied wines age best.

Botrytis cinerea: also known as "noble rot," a fungus that may form on grapes, causing their juices to become more concentrated, allowing for the creation of such sweet dessert wines as Sauternes and Barsac.

Bottle sickness: an absence or imbalance of flavors that occurs in certain young wines or when a wine has been mishandled. Bottle sickness normally passes with aging and quiet conditions.

Bouquet: the total combination of *aromas* in a wine—the wine's most distinguishing characteristic. A wine's bouquet develops during the time it spends aging in the bottle.

Brut: a French term to describe extremely dry sparkling wine.

Burnt: see *Madeirized*.

Caramel: a flavor associated with such long-aging fortified wines as Madeira.

Cedar: a desirable flavor characteristic typical of fine Bordeaux.

Château: an estate that produces wine.

Claret: a British term for red Bordeaux wines.

Classico: Italian term for wines from the heart of their region. These are expected to be of higher quality.

Cold stabilization: a technique for clarifying wine that involves briefly lowering its temperature to 32 degrees Fahrenheit.

Complex: a term describing a wine with multiple characteristics and layers of *aromas,* flavors, and textures.

Corked: wine that smells musty or like "wet cardboard" as a result of mold on the cork.

Cru: a rank ascribed to France's finest vineyards. Since 1855, high-quality vineyards have been assigned one of five crus.

Cuvée: a batch from a particular blend. From the French *cuve,* meaning container or vat.

Decanting: pouring the wine from the bottle to a separate container, both to rid it of *sediment* and to aerate it.

Demi-sec: French term for semi-sweet. See *sec.*

Doughnut: a wine is said to have a "doughnut" if its flavors drop out momentarily midway through the taste experience.

Dry: the relative absence of *sweet*ness. Wines may be described as dry, or semi-dry. The French term for this is *sec;* in German, *trocken.*

Earthy: wine containing *aromas* and flavors reminiscent of soil, moss, or mushrooms.

Estate bottled: wine that is crushed, fermented, and bottled in the same place its grapes are grown.

Fermentation: the process, which occurs in the presence of yeasts, that turns the sugars in the grape must into alcohol and carbon dioxide.

Flint: a slightly smoky metallic flavor desirable in small quantities, also called "gunflint."

Floral: a desirable flowerlike aroma that can occur in both white and red wines, also called *perfume.*

Fining: clearing the wine of particles before bottling.

Finish: the flavors that linger in your mouth after you've swallowed the wine.

Fortification: adding additional alcohol to a wine.

Foxy: a musky, unpleasant smell. Foxiness commonly afflicts wines made from Concord grapes.

Fruity: a wine with distinct fruitlike aromas. This can be said of any fruitlike flavor except grape. See *grapey*.

Grapey: a normally undesirable flavor that suggests an immature wine. Grapiness is more acceptable in Concord and Muscat, two naturally grapey varieties.

Grass: a flavor characteristic, also described as hay or *herb*, which is desirable in small quantities.

Green: a flavor in wine associated with grass, moss, or vegetables. Often used negatively to describe a wine whose grapes were picked before they were fully ripe.

Halbtrocken: German term for half-*dry*. See *trocken*.

Herb: see *grass*.

Hybrid: a cross between two species of grape. Seldom produces excellent wine.

Jammy: sweet, berrylike wines with a quality similar to jam.

Kabinett: superior dry white German wine.

Lees: spent yeast cells that collect in white wine during fermentation. These are eventually racked off *(racking)*, but may be left in contact with the wine to deepen its character. See *sur lie*.

Legs: the long globs of wine that remain on the inside of a glass when the wine is swirled, caused by the glycerol in the wine—not an indicator of quality.

Madeirized: an undesirable characteristic describing severely *oxidized* wine that has spoiled and turned brown from poor handling or age. Named for Madeira, which is intentionally produced this way.

Malic: acid with an applelike flavor.

Mature: a wine that has been aged for an appropriate amount of time and is ready to drink.

Minty: a taste characteristic of California Cabernet Sauvignon.

Must: the juice of crushed grapes.

Native yeast: the yeast naturally present on the grape. Once the sole source of yeast in wine production, now the native yeasts generally receive a boost from added commercial yeasts.

Nose: see *bouquet*.

Oaky: a flavor characteristic of California Chardonnay and white Burgundy.

Oxidation: the chemical reaction caused by allowing wine to come in contact with air. Oxidation affects the wine's flavor, *aroma* and appearance.

Palate: the sense of smell and the ability to discern nuances of aroma and flavor.

Pasteurization: heat-sterilization, typically performed on low-quality wines, to kill harmful microorganisms.

Peppery: a taste characteristic reminiscent of pepper, or which prickles the nose and palate as pepper does.

Perfume: see *floral*.

Phylloxera: a plant louse native to the United States that destroys the roots of grape vines. In the mid-1800s, phylloxera nearly destroyed Europe's vineyards.

Principal grape: in wines that are a blend of varieties, the grape that makes up the greatest percentage. For example, in a wine that is 80% Tempranillo and 20% Cabernet Sauvignon, Tempranillo is the principal grape.

Racking: separating the wine from *sediment* and *lees* by transferring it from one container to another.

Reserve: wines intended for aging, typically higher quality.

Rim: the color of the wine at its edge as it sits in the glass.

Riserva: Italian for *reserve*.

Sec: French term describing slighty sweet champagne. See *demi-sec*.

Sediment: the deposits in the bottle of red wine, made up of *tannins*, minerals, and other solids.

Sommelier: at a fine restaurant, the person who manages the wine list, makes recommendations, and serves the wine.

Sparkling: effervescent wine.

Spätlese: German wines made from late-harvest grapes.

Spumante: Italian for *sparkling*.

Stemming: separating grapes from stems and other nongrape material.

Stemmy: a wine that tastes unpleasantly of matter other than grapes.

Sulfur dioxide: this chemical is added to wine to slow *fermentation,* kill harmful microorganisms, and prevent oxidation.

Superiore: an Italian designation for wines typically higher in alcohol and able to age longer.

Sur lie: literally, "on its lees." A term describing white wine that is left in contact with its spent yeast cells (*lees*) for a period of time, to enhance its character.

Sweet: a relatively high concentration of sugars, as contrasted to *dry.*

Tannin: the chemical compounds found in grape skins responsible for the bitter flavors and the "structure" that enables a wine to age.

Tastevins: the shallow silver wine tasting cup traditionally carried by sommeliers and wine stewards.

Terroir: a term of French origin describing the character imparted to a wine by its natural environment: climate, soil, geography, weather, and surrounding vegetation. Each vineyard has a unique combination of elements that make up its terroir.

Trocken: German term for *dry.* See *halbtrocken.*

Ullage: the empty space between the surface of the wine and the inside of its container, whether barrel or bottle. The ullage increases as the wine evaporates, and is especially pronounced in older wines.

Varietal: a wine made from a single type of grape. A wine described as varietal is named for its *principal grape.*

Vin gris: French for "gray wine." White wine made from red grapes.

Vintage: the year a given wine's grapes were harvested. Each year's harvest varies in subtle ways as a result of climate, cultivation techniques, and other variables.

Viticulture: the science, study, and cultivation of grapes.

Index

GREAT NEW BOOKS FROM

The Learning Annex Presents Feng Shui
By Meihwa Lin

Whether it's analyzing your house or apartment's energy flow, improving a particular aspect of your life, or just learning for fun, *The Learning Annex Presents Feng Shui* will give you the basic tools and knowledge you need to improve your feng shui and improve your life, all in just an evening.

ISBN 0-7645-4144-7 $14.99   216 pages

The Learning Annex Presents Uncluttering Your Space
By Ann T. Sullivan

From identifying your clutter patterns and taking stock of your home, to annihilating clutter room by room or even redesigning your space and your storage to keep clutter from coming back, *The Learning Annex Presents Uncluttering Your Space* helps you get your house and your life back in order.

ISBN 0-7645-4145-5 $14.99   216 pages

The Learning Annex Presents the Pleasure of Wine
By Ian Blackburn and Allison Levine

Navigating the local wine store, planning a dinner party, visiting wineries, or just ordering in a restaurant can all be intimidating. In one evening, *The Learning Annex Presents the Pleasure of Wine* demystifies wine and gives you the basic tools and knowledge you need to confidently navigate each discussion and situation.

ISBN 0-7645-4146-3 $14.99   240 pages